STORRINGTON
IN LIVING MEMORY

STORRINGTON
in Living Memory

Joan Ham

PHILLIMORE

1982

Published by
PHILLIMORE & CO. LTD.
London and Chichester

Head Office: Shopwyke Hall,
Chichester, Sussex, England

ISBN 0 85033 453 3

Typeset in the United Kingdom by:
Fidelity Processes - Selsey - Sussex

Printed and bound in Great Britain by
BILLINGS BOOK PLAN
Worcester

CONTENTS

LIST OF PLATES

(between pages 18 and 19)

LIST OF TEXT FIGURES

You have done so much to further this book,
that it owes you a great deal
—so with my love
this book is dedicated to my dear husband

ACKNOWLEDGEMENTS

So many people have helped me with this book, that I can only list them below with my thanks.

Mr. Frank Adsett; Mr. Harold Adsett; Mrs. Bacon; Mrs. Banfield; Mr. D. Banks; Det. Con. M. Barratt; Mrs. Barrow; Mr. Bob Bashford; Mrs. Alice Batchelor; Sister Beckenham; Mr. Bevis; Mr. George Blunden; Mrs. Bourn; Mr. C. A. Brace; Miss Brazier; Mr. and Mrs. Broadbridge; Mr. and Mrs. D. Carn; Mr. G. Carter; Fr. K. P. Cassidy; Mr. A. Charman; Mr. and Mrs. Charman; Miss E. Clark-Williams; Mrs. Connell; Miss J. and K. Connor; Mrs. Cooper; Mr. Richard Cothard; Mr. Cowdry; Mrs. A. Cripps; Mr. G. Cripps; Mrs. R. Cripps; Mr. S. Dean; Mr. B. Dibble; Mrs. Dodds; Mrs. Dubreil; Mr. G. W. Elliott; Mrs. Ewins; Mr. B. Farhall; Mrs. Featherstone; Mrs. Foulton; Mr. Francis; Mrs. Francis; Mr. Frewer; Mr. Michael Frostick; Mrs. Gatley; Mrs. E. M. Gatley; Mrs. A. de S. Georgano; Mr. G. N. Georgano; Mrs. Goldsack; Mr. R. Gowland; Miss F. Greenfield; Mr. and Mrs. R. Greenfield; Mr. John Gregg; Mrs. Hamilton; Mr. Haycroft; Mr. Fred Hearn; Miss E. Howard; Mr. D. Howey; Mr. and Mrs. E. Hues; Mr. Huffer; Mrs. Jelpke; Mr. Johnson; Miss M. Kent; Mr. A. L. King; Mrs. Kirkby; Mr. and Mrs. H. Knight; Mr. S. Knight; Miss Langhorne; Mr. Lidstone; Mr. J. Linfield; Sister Lutgardis; Rev. G. Mackenzie; Mr. Maurice; Mrs. A. Miller; Mrs. Mitchell; Mr. E. Mitchell; Mrs. Mortimer; Rev. J. Norman; Mr. K. Palmer; Miss I. Parsons; Mr. J. Parsons; Mr. R. Perrin; Mrs. P. Pickworth; Mr. Piper; Mrs. Pledger; Mr. E. Post; Miss J. Post; Miss B. and L. Puttick; Miss P. Rankin; Mrs. Rapley; Miss A. Rapley; Mr. B. Reeves; Mrs. Richardson; Mr. S. Ridge; Miss G. Rogers; Mr. D. Rudram; Mrs. A. Sager; Mrs. Pat Saw; Mr. F. Scutt; Mrs. L. Scutt; Mr. L. Selden; Mr. J. Skinner; Miss M. Skinner; Mr. Small; P.C. T. Smart; P.C. E. Sweeney; Mr. Sweet; Mr. Sutherland; Mrs. P. Tritton; Mr. and Mrs. J. Turner; Mrs. Virgo; Mr. D. Walker; Mr. C. R. Waller; Mrs. Whitbourn; Mr. D. White; Mr. G. Whitehead; Mr. I. Williams; Mr. M. Williams; Mr. J. Woolgar; Mrs. J. Woolgar; Mr. H. Woolgar; Mrs. Young.

INTRODUCTION

Storrington in Living Memory is the story of the last 100 years. Nonagenarians in the village have celebrated the Relief of Mafeking, seen the Diamond Jubilee of Queen Victoria, the five subsequent coronations, and lived through the horrors of two World Wars. They have travelled at the leisurely pace of the horse in carriages, traps and carts, been transported by the splutters and bangs of early motor cars, and aeroplanes from as close as the parish of Cootham, and in the clear night sky above the village have seen the moving stars that tell them that man can now travel outside his own world. When the carrier's cart brought news, parcels and passengers from distant Worthing and Pulborough, it was an event to be able to leave the village for a day! They have worked by the flickering light of candles, the soft glow of paraffin lamps, and seen these replaced by hissing gas and then the clean convenience of electricity. During their lifetime, water has been delivered to every home at the turn of a tap, clean and fit to drink, but they will remember drawing it from wells, complete with aquatic life and pollution.

Storrington has grown from a small market town with cattle-pens in the street on Fair days, to a sprawling town with supermarkets, housing and industrial estates, and with the natural resources developed that provide the work once supplied by great houses.

This book is a tribute to the people of Storrington, who have given their time to talk to me, and lend me pictures of Storrington's vanished past. My thanks to them all.

I would also like to acknowledge the help and courtesy from official sources — the Southern Water Authority, the Post Office, the Telephone service, the Sussex Police, the West Sussex County Library Service, local schools, R.A.F.A. Sussexdown and the West Sussex Record Office. I would also like to thank those who have written to me from all parts, adding to the information in *Storrington in Pictures* and telling me of their memories. One of these, the Head Librarian of the National Motor Museum, Beaulieu and grandson of George Trotter, has rendered much advice and help.

I started this book with a list of people I needed to see for information, and as with *Storrington in Pictures*, one person gave me several other names, so that although I have spent a year visiting people and places, the list has never grown shorter; indeed, there are still many people I would like to see. A book, however, must have an end, although I am still interested in talking to people and in collecting old pictures and memories to add to my Storrington archive.

A village archive is continuous, and I hope I shall never stop the fascinating task of compiling it, both from records and people.

JOAN HAM

1. RECTORS OF STORRINGTON

'The Faithfulls'

IN 1870, REV. JOHN SCOTT-WHITING, rector since 1857, exchanged livings with Rev. George Faithfull who had a parish in Wales. The new Education Act provided Mr Faithfull with an opportunity to start an Army Cramming Establishment, and once settled here, he soon had about 40 wealthy pupils boarded out all over the village, complete with horses, dogs and a pack of beagles. He found his rectory, south of the present Abbey, in such a bad state of repair, that he used the stone to build what is now the centre and northern part of 'the Abbey'. In 1890, he was living in Chanctonbury House, which became the second rectory.

In the time of Rev. George Faithfull, the restoration of the church was undertaken, and the wall and steps to the south and west were added. He also donated land for the Village Hall to be built, and it was during his time as rector that Cootham Hall was built on land given by Lord Zouche, who was concerned at 'dissenting practices' in Cootham (*see* pages 114–117).

Rev. George Faithfull died with the old century, and his son, Rev. Arthur Faithfull was inducted, who, although he did not enjoy good health, farmed the meadow and glebe fields in Greyfriars, and hunted with the Crawley and Horsham. In 1913, Mrs Faithfull bought Orchard Way in Church Street, where they lived, alternating with Chanctonbury House. One interesting discovery made by Mr Faithfull was the clapper of the great bell in the churchyard. Dated 1275, it was thought to have lain there ever since the steeple collapsed in 1745, bringing down the bells and part of the roof. Around the turn of the century, the immemorial custom of ringing the curfew-bell every evening was stopped.

In 1926, the third generation Faithfull became rector of Storrington. Richard Faithfull and his wife, Violet, moved into the rectory, but this was now too large, so the new (and present) one was built in the church meadow in 1934. Rev. Richard Faithfull set about improving the church. The walls, decorated with Tudor roses and fleurs-de-lis during the 1876 restorations, were painted white and the old pews arranged with a centre aisle and two more against the north and south walls; some interrupted with the bases of pillars were cut so that the centre rows could be entered from either end. The pews behind the choir were removed altogether to make the space into a side chapel. In 1942, Rev. Richard Faithfull retired, leaving the advowson to Keble College, Oxford. He died suddenly in the new year, whilst moving to a new house in Sompting.

Rev. W. Frostick

Mr Frostick imbued the church with fresh new life. His congregations soon included men who had not been regular churchgoers. Under his management, the Sunday School and choir improved, and in this he was aided by his wife who was very musical. Concerts were held in the music room of the Abbey to raise money for repairs to the church. Mrs Frostick also worked with the Guides.

Perhaps one of Mr Frostick's best remembered introductions was the Rogation Procession, which, however, did not survive his incumbency. An old photograph shows Bishop Bell leading the Guides, Brownies, and a large choir in procession from the church. Rev. W. Frostick retired to Brighton after leaving Storrington in 1952.

Rev. George Mackenzie

Rev. George Mackenzie was rector of West Grinstead. One day when taking his family out, he stopped to buy ice-cream in Storrington. Mrs Mackenzie said how much she liked the village, and that she wouldn't mind being the wife of the rector of Storrington. The living happened to be vacant, and soon after they arrived back home, the telephone rang. It was Bishop Bell, asking George Mackenzie to go to Storrington. His wife thought he was joking!

In 1952, when the Mackenzies came to Storrington, the parishes of Sullington and Storrington were separate. Rev. W. R. Bassett-Smith of Sullington and Rev. W. Frostick of Storrington both retired at the same time and it was suggested that Rev. G. Mackenzie should be rector of both parishes. The Bishop was patron of Sullington and Keble College of Storrington, but they agreed on the double post with alternate rights of appointment. A strange position then obtained, because the Queen had to sign an Order in Council agreeing to the plurality, and she was then touring Australia: until she returned, Storrington had no rector. Mr Mackenzie had a dispensation to live at the rectory, the churchwardens paying him every week, but although he was rector of Sullington, he was during the interim priest-in-charge of Storrington. It was not until 1953 that he became rector of both parishes after two services of institution, and a curate was installed in Sullington Rectory.

In 1964, Rev. G. Mackenzie became Rural Dean of the parishes in the Storrington Deanery. He instituted the Christian Stewardship Campaign. Another of his ideas was the Parish Club, started in 1962, so that parishioners could meet socially. It still flourishes.

Mr Mackenzie is very fond of music and plays the organ. He held a really good Carol Service on the Sunday after Christmas each year, with the existing choir as a basis, augmented by people of any denomination who would come in for this special occasion. It was known as the 'Rector's Choir'. Prominent villagers read the lessons and the organ was played by Mr R. D. Marten; Mr Mackenzie used to conduct.

He is particularly interested in young people, and started the present Scout Troop with 20 boys. The leader of the Sullington Troop had recently left, so the new troop was registered as the 1st Sullington and Storrington Troop with colours of gold and royal-blue. Mrs Mackenzie ran the Cubs. Mr Mackenzie had been County Chaplain for the Scouts in Sussex since 1947, and until his retirement, was Assistant District Commissioner for Leader Training in Worthing District and a member of the County Training team. He holds the Silver Wolf, the highest personal decoration, given only by the Chief Scout.

Another interest is the Territorial Army. He joined it in 1928 as a subaltern in the Black Watch, and transferred upon his ordination to the Royal Army Chaplain's Department, with which he served until his retirement in 1960. He was awarded the M.B.E. in 1945 for his war-service and holds the Territorial Decoration with two bars. He was with the 42nd Division at Dunkirk and later became Staff Chaplain, First Army. In North Africa, he was senior Chaplain with the 6th Armoured Division, where he once recalled hearing the King's College, Cambridge, service of lessons and carols on an Army Wireless Set No. 19, in a vehicle driven to a high point specially for him, so that the distant signals from England could be received. Then he became Staff Chaplain at Eastern and South-Eastern Commands, which brought him to Sussex and a first meeting with Bishop Bell. His last years as a T.A. chaplain were spent with the Sussex Yeomanry.

George Mackenzie is no longer an active priest, but fills in where needed. In addition, much voluntary work keeps him busy — he is a member of the Diocesan Council for Family Social Work, chairman of Storrington Deanery Committee for Family Social Work and local chairman of the Committee for Knowles Tooth. China, glass and book sales, coffee mornings and other fund-raising events are held in aid of the project. Being chairman of a house committee in Worthing for one-parent families and doing pensions and confidential work for the British Legion, of which he was chaplain during his time in Storrington, fill his time. With so much going on in his life, perhaps it is as well that Rev. George Mackenzie is 'retired'.

Rev. John Norman

Rev. John Norman came from Ticehurst in December 1974. He was presented to the living by his old college, Keble College, Oxford, but became known to many parishioners in a most unorthodox manner. In 1975, Chichester Cathedral celebrated its 900th anniversary, and all Sussex villages joined in a pageant. Storrington sent along a 1929 Leyland Titan bus full of passengers in Edwardian costume to commemorate our no. 1 service. Rev. John Norman travelled on the bus as rector of Storrington, wearing stove hat, tight suit, curly whiskers specially grown, and carrying an old leatherbound volume. The Press were unsure whether he was a real priest or they were having their legs pulled!

In March 1976, Rev. John Norman was appointed Rural Dean. The church faced a shortage of manpower in 1977, and the benefices of Storrington, Sullington, Thakeham with Warminghurst were united with Ashington, Buncton, Wiston and Washington to form a group ministry, the Chanctonbury Group of Parishes, chaired by Rev. John Norman, and comprising three full-time parish priests with retired clerical and lay assistants. The application was put before the Queen in January of that year and came into effect at an Inaugural Eucharist held on 18 February 1977.

The Queen's Silver Jubilee was celebrated in 1977 and all organisations and societies were planning celebrations in their own way. Rev. John Norman brought a lovely idea from his Derbyshire livings — a floral tribute based on well-dressing techniques. Another idea was to stage a Village Heritage exhibition in the church, where old church registers, pictures, postcards, church vestments, matching flower arrangements and the church plate were displayed. For many people, it was a unique opportunity to see their local history in objects and pictures not often accessible to them. Mr Norman fully appreciates the fascination of archive material, as one of his spare-time interests is the study of education and old school log-books of Sussex.

Rev. John Norman introduced the Tiny Tots service for mothers with children at home — a half-hour service on the first Wednesday afternoon of each month. Very small children are introduced to their parish church by a rector who becomes a favourite uncle, telling them stories, familiarising them with church surroundings and encouraging them to join in hymns and clap their hands to the music.

Another feature introduced in 1975 was Parish Communion, followed by a social gathering over cups of coffee, every first Sunday of the month. Mrs Norman took over the Sunday School, and it has now four times as many children attending as when she began. Another of her undertakings is as enrolling member of the Mothers' Union.

In 1975, it became obvious that all was not well with the church bells, Storrington's 'cracked buckets'. The Whitechapel Bell Foundry was contacted, the bells were inspected, and found to be cracked. £3,000–£4,000 was needed to recast and rehang them. A committee was formed and fund-raising began. In a year, £2,360 was raised and by 1977 the fund stood at £3,500. Meanwhile, costs had risen, and another expert was called in to examine the bells. Fund-raising continued, not only by the Parish Church; the Convent held garden fêtes with many organisations taking part and contributing their profits, the Methodist Church organised a Dog Show. In April 1978, the great moment arrived, when the bells were carefully lowered, the task taking two days. They were recast, and in October, reinstalled. The final cost was around £7,000.

The new bells rang out a quarter peal of Bob Minors on 13 June 1979, to celebrate the Silver Jubilee of John Norman's ordination to the priesthood. It was a happy occasion, marked by the presentation of a festal cope, dedicated by Bishop Warren Hunt during Sung Eucharist, which was attended by friends and clergy from other Storrington churches. A reception at the Rectory rounded off the happy occasion. May John Norman long continue to be part of Storrington's living history.

2 HOOVES, WHEELS AND WAYS

Roads – Carriers and Posts – Community Minibus – Blacksmiths,
Wheelwrights, Harnessmakers and Saddlers – Garages and Motor Cars

Roads

STORRINGTON AT THE beginning of the 19th century was reached by winding tracks
and unsurfaced roads that were thick with mud or dust and animal droppings, or by
cross-country paths.

In March 1871, the Vestry Meeting elected Mr Albert Lee and Mr Rowland James
as Surveyors of the Highway. These, and the waywardens were responsible for roads.
At this same meeting, letters were read from Mr Edward Emery of Hurston and Mr
Edmonds of Worthing, which were the first rumbles of a storm to end in the action
Regina v. *Storrington* at the Spring Assizes of 1875, calling upon the ratepayers or
surveyors of Storrington, 'Forthwith to repair with metal and put in good order the
High Road leading from Hurston Mill to Old House, Monk-mead gate and Roundabouts,
also Hurston Hill in the parish of Storrington . . . unless the said roads are put into good
repair *legal proceedings will be taken*'. This was a long-standing bone of contention
whereby the tenants of the mill wanted the road hardened for the purposes of their
business, but the Meeting, claiming that 'no additional traffic is on these roads to what
has been for years past' asserted that under no circumstances should any of those roads
be hardened. They went even further, and informed Mr Edmonds that, in the interests
of the parish, 'should any hostile proceedings be taken' they would take such steps
'as shall for ever put an end to the litigious feeling which has existed for many years . . .'.
A case of 'Let battle commence!'

The first round was lost at Quarter Sessions at Petworth, April 1874. A show of hands
at a subsequent meeting, supported Mr Dalbiac's proposition that the waywardens seek
Counsel's advice on whether to try again at the Sessions or Assizes, and a Parish Poll too
resulted in overwhelming support, 131 for and 42 against Mr Dalbiac's resolution. Meanwhile, the waywardens had been advised to move for trial at the Assize.

A board was put up on the turnpike road, informing travellers that there was 'no road
for Carts and Carriages . . .' but only a track for foot passengers and a bridle way, this
despite Mr Emery's protest.

On 11 February 1875, Mr Mant was instructed to take the necessary steps in the
action *Regina* v. *Storrington*.

The verdict was 'Not Guilty' — the records showed that the road from the foot of
Hurston to the turnpike road at Wiggonholt was *not* a highway.

In March 1876, a select committee of the House of Commons directed the trustees
of the Storrington and Wiston Turnpike to do no repairs after 1 November 1876. The
parish would thereafter be required to repair that part of the turnpike which fell within
their boundaries. Roads became the responsibility of the new County Councils in 1889.

Road surfaces were made of flint, which was freely available and very durable. The
Storrington population in the 1890s was only 900, so traffic was not excessive. Farmers
with land on the Downs, like Tom Gatley of Springhead, used to employ 'rough men'
who did the hoeing on the farms to pick up flints on the hills (locals always assert that
they 'grow' in the fields). This abundant material was piled at the top of the hill and

5

farmers bringing down carts would attach a full sledge of flints to the back to act as a brake. At the bottom, the flints would be heaped at the roadside, thus serving a double purpose. Heaps of flints were a familiar sight in places like the green outside Peacock Tree, where Mr Ayling used to sit on a sack wearing special wire mesh spectacles to protect his eyes from flying chips as he broke up flints with a large hammer. They were spread on the roads and ground into the surface by the broad iron tyres of farm vehicles, carts and carriages. Times do not seem to change in some things. Loose chippings are still rolled into new tar by road traffic!

There were also iron rollers pulled by one or two horses, and in about 1893 the steam roller made its appearance, rolling flints which had first been thoroughly drenched with water. It made a dirty mess at the time, but was a successful roadmaking system. The water carts were pulled by a horse, and one of these made in Arundel can be seen at the Chalk Pits Museum. Mr Rewell and Fred Hearn did this work for the Thakeham R.D.C. and Mr Broadbridge drove the steam roller which was kept at the Council Depot at the site of Rydon School.

In winter, the roads became very muddy. They were 'cleaned' for churchgoers by two men pulling a scraper, which left a 3 ft–4 ft clear path with the mud piled on either side, making an obstacle in the unlit roads. People used to carry lanterns or candles in jars to light them to church. Horses were liable to rake flints out of the roads with their hooves, and people in those days needed much thicker boots and shoes. One resident described the Amberley road in his time as '. . . two ruts and a central mound of grass and horse droppings'! Mr Parsons, who lived at 'The Geddings' in 1910 came a terrible cropper by riding his penny-farthing into some loose flints.

The Bog, or Buck Common road between the park and cottages, had to be built on faggots because of the marshy conditions. The steam roller with an attachment would tear up the road and then scrub from Stopham wood was put down. This was thoroughly drenched with water and then 'slubbed' in. Water Lane was built on railway sleepers in 1917, when the Sandgate timber was being carted away. Charles Mant recalled School Hill being repaired, when 3–4 in. of flints were spread on the surface and took several weeks to be ground in by vehicles using it. The road from Rydon School to Rock and Hampers Lane was just a dirt track which was made up with flints during World War I. This road, too, took a fearful battering from the big Foden engines carting away timber, and the accounts of the Thakeham R.D.C. for 1919 mention the problem: '. . . during the period of the War the roads adjoining Sandgate and Parham Estates were badly damaged by the timber traffic, and the making of an aviation ground to the north of Thakeham was responsible for considerable damage to the roads in that district. The cost of repairing the damage to the Sandgate Roads was estimated at £690 16s. 5d. over and above the normal expenditure, and £176 4s. 11d. for the previous year. These two amounts the Government have promised to repay'.

The Council had anticipated that a large post-war outlay on the roads would be necessary. Expenditure had dropped yearly from £4,561 in 1915 to £2,153 in 1918, and a reserve fund drawn from the surplus money collected was set aside. Since the Armistice, traffic had greatly increased, and it was doubted whether the roads could be raised to pre-war standards before the traffic did serious damage. By 1930, expenditure on highways increased to £11,627 10s. 1d.

Mr S. Dean of Cootham recalled the little wooden bridge at Wickford which was washed away in the wet summer of 1887. A new one was built (the present bridge) and his grandfather, John Dean, working on this bridge, caught pneumonia. Mr Sowter, who lived in Crown Cottages, helped to dig out the road to let the mail through after enormous snowdrifts had blocked it in the hard winter that followed.

In 1920–24, tarmac was first used on the roads. The roadmen had a tar barrel on wheels over a furnace, which had to be pulled along and the tar was hand-pumped. 'Punch' Edwards was a tar-sprayer, working with sacks tied around his legs. This was essential, as bystanders found out when spattered with tar!

'Old Punch' and 'Young Punch' Edwards were familiar figures on the roads; between them, father and son put in over 100 years' service. Mr Edward Edwards began his working life with Thakeham R.D.C., taking a horse and cart up on the Downs from Chantry to Amberley to collect broken flints. His work could take him to Wiggonholt, West Chiltington, and Adversane. The Council at that time had two horses stabled at the old workhouse at Thakeham, where they also kept the tar barrels and other road equipment.

After 1928, the road authorities became the W.S.C.C. and 'Punch' Edwards was to be seen with his dog, keeping the roads and village clean.

Carriers and Posts

The carriers and posts were vital services in the days before motor transport. At the turn of the century, Egbert Townley advertised 'First Class open and close carriages for hire by the Day, month, Year' and 'Pair and Four-horse Brakes for parties'. His waggonette went to Worthing on Monday and Wednesday in the summer. T. Grantham, job and postmaster, was official carrier to the London, Brighton and South Coast Railway Co., based in the White Horse Yard, where he also advertised 'superior Close and Open Carriages by the day or hour', and offered 'lock up coach houses' and horses. This interesting old service continues today in the modern equivalent of lock-up garages, continuing to house Storrington's transport nearly 100 years later.

Newspapers came from Pulborough Station by 'the paper cart', a waggonette which also carried passengers. The papers were sold at a stall in the White Horse Yard, where people could hire a fly and pay 'baits' (board and lodging for horses) and 'livery' (keeping someone's horse and cart). The Worthing carrier was Raymond Cooper from Furze Common.

Many folk remember Charles Reeves from Cootham. His business was based where Cootham Petrol Station now stands. He went to Worthing three times a week, and announced his approach by violently blowing his horn so that people could avail themselves of his services. His Worthing trips would include a call to Potter & Bailey to collect goods for Greenfields, ice for the fish shops and butchers, and the picking up of passengers. Every day, Reeves went from Pulborough to Storrington, and on Saturdays the horn announced his departure from Cootham at 8 a.m. He took a shopping list from local people, fetching their requirements from the chemist and other shops. The Crown at Cootham often had visitors from London, and Reeves' landau would be hired to fetch them from the station at Pulborough. His carrier's vehicle was a closed cart with a tilt, drawn by two horses. He also carted flints from Parham Lane for use on the roads, and had a coal business, collecting his coal from Pulborough station and storing it in a large shed which belonged to Edwin Hammond at the corner of Monastery Lane. After Charles Reeves retired, his son Jim carried on until motor transport finished the carrier's trade.

Les Peto was a carrier who kept up with the times, modernised his transport and extended his business. He built premises in West Street, workshops with flats above. The business card (fig. 1) shows how the radius of the carrier's deliveries extended with the advent of motorised transport. Mr Peto increased his fleet by buying a van with windows in 1935–36, which could be hired to carry parties to dances, cricket matches and other outings. The family also remember one hard winter when they tied a line of sledges behind the van and were pulled along West Street. Another expedition with the van was up to the Downs for a picnic.

The *White Horse* hotel seems to have been a transport centre for many years, and buses used to stop there. Their forerunner was Lee's omnibus (fig. 2) which ran three times a week, timed to meet the Brighton trains. This was in the 1860s and was a horse-bus, which took nearly two hours to cover eleven miles.

Drivers of the early motor-buses used to be out in the open with no windscreen, and just a tarpaulin to cover their legs in bad weather. Wind and rain streamed in on them, and by the time they reached the *Gun* in Findon they would be soaked. Crew and passengers used to disembark and go into the inn for a pint or two, and then when they reached the *Frankland Arms* at Washington they repeated the process. The *White Horse* also enjoyed their patronage, and by driving as fast

L. PETO,

Carrier.

RADIUS OF DELIVERIES.

AMBERLEY	LANCING
BROADWATER	PORTSLADE
BURY	PULBOROUGH
BRIGHTON	ROUNDABOUTS
COOTHAM	SOUTHWICK
COLDWALTHAM	SHOREHAM
FINDON	STORRINGTON
HOVE	W. CHILTINGTON
HEATH COMMON	WORTHING
HARDHAM	WASHINGTON

Brighton Depot:	Worthing Depots:
DRUIDS HEAD.	**29 PORTLAND ROAD.**
Tel. Brighton 349011.	**46 HIGH STREET.**

Figure 1

NOTICE!

ON AND AFTER MONDAY, JUNE 3rd,

LEE'S OMNIBUS

WILL LEAVE THE

White Horse Inn, Storrington,

EVERY

MONDAY, THURSDAY, AND SATURDAY,

At 8h. 45m., a. m.

Arriving at Worthing in time for the 10h. 42m. Train for Brighton; returning on the arrival of the 5h. 20m. Train from Brighton.

Until further Notice.

May 15th. 1861.

Horses and Flys may be had on application to Mr. LEE, White Horse Inn, Storrington.

Walker & Fowling Printers

Figure 2

as possible between these essential stops they managed to keep to the timetable!

A platform for milk churns stood at the *Frankland Arms*, where full churns were taken aboard the bus and empty ones left. Parcels were also carried. During a heavy fog, hardly dispelled by the old acetylene lamps, the conductor would walk all the way from Worthing to Storrington in front of the bus, carrying a lantern. Mr Carn remembers his father driving the bus to Worthing during the General Strike, and keeping a pick handle beside his seat to make sure he got through the pickets.

In 1949, the *Worthing Herald* published a sketch described by Mr E. H. Brockway, Surveyor to the C.R.D.C., as 'our dream of the future' (fig. 3). This shows a bus shelter and lavatories, a large car park (plate 15) and a new road which would have involved the demolition of the old cottages in Brewer's Yard in order to join up with North Street. This plan was shelved. Perhaps not-so-old residents who waited at the bus stop will recall the entertainment provided by Mr Ridge's parrot as it sunned itself outside on fine days. One of its more startling achievements to those who had not heard it before was a piercing wolf-whistle.

In 1964, a new village plan was the subject of a stormy public meeting. The bus shelter, car park, Mill Lane and the field which rose to Fryern Road were to be swept away (fig. 4). This was the Old Mill Square development and the Stor Meadow and Hawthorn Way housing estates (which had been foreseen as early as 1921, when Bine farm was sold in the break-up of the Fryern Estate). Storrington acquired a new bus terminus, the abandoning of our historic No. 1 bus service together with curtailment of services. A 'new' idea took place in the minds of some local people as rural services were cut: a voluntary service that was something between the old carriers and a private coach company.

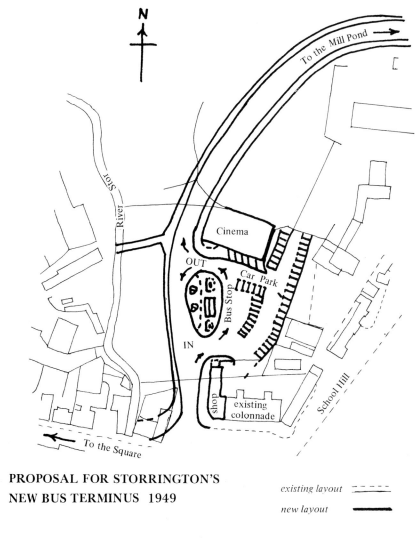

**PROPOSAL FOR STORRINGTON'S
NEW BUS TERMINUS 1949**

existing layout ‑ ‑ ‑ ‑
new layout ▬▬▬

Figure 3

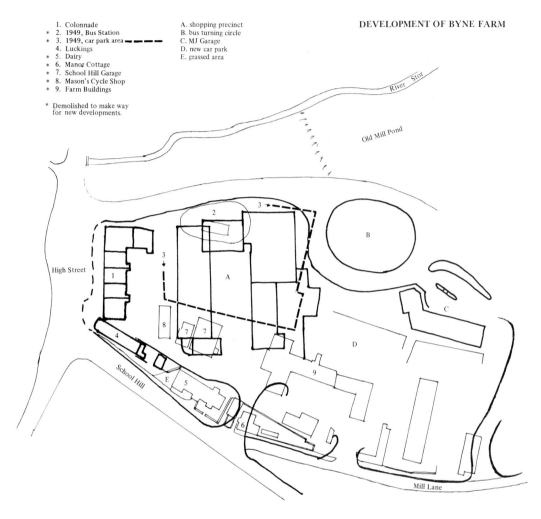

1. Colonnade
* 2. 1949, Bus Station
* 3. 1949, car park area ▄ ▄ ▄ ▄
4. Luckings
* 5. Dairy
* 6. Manor Cottage
* 7. School Hill Garage
* 8. Mason's Cycle Shop
* 9. Farm Buildings

* Demolished to make way
   for new developments.

A. shopping precinct
B. bus turning circle
C. MJ Garage
D. new car park
E. grassed area

DEVELOPMENT OF BYNE FARM

Figure 4

Community Minibus

The Pulborough Minibus, already in use in West Chiltington, where Mr and Mrs Gregg were drivers, started picking up Storrington people when delivering residents of West Chiltington in Storrington for their shopping. They were mainly from Bishop's House, Abbey House and Kingsfield. Pulborough offered their bus for use on a half a day a week in January 1978. The service began with four drivers and four escorts; at that time only 18 people made use of it. By August that year there were 120 using the Pulborough Minibus.

Pulborough then offered to loan their bus on alternate Tuesday afternoons and alternate Monday afternoons; the Sullington Monday Club, an organisation for the benefit of retired people in the parish, used the bus to replace a voluntary service run by people with cars. This service became regular on Monday, 9 July 1979. On Tuesdays, when Storrington people wanted tó leave the village, the minibus would take them to Worthing, where they could go shopping, or stroll around the town or go to the beach. The passengers were drawn from Storrington, Sullington, Thakeham and Washington, although the Worthing journeys collected more from Washington and Sullington than from Storrington itself. Some of them had not been out of the village for as long as two years.

The policy of concessionary bus fares was brought before the Storrington Parish Council for consideration. It was estimated that this would cost between £3,000–£4,000 per year. The Parish Council felt that this was too much, when the minibus would provide a better service: many possible beneficiaries of the concessionary bus fares were out of the range of existing bus services. At this stage, the Parish Council decided to support and promote the minibus for the Storrington and Sullington areas, run by the Community Minibus Association. Storrington voted £1,500 towards the cost.

Horsham District Council bought the new vehicle out of the proceeds of two lotteries, and encouraged its use in other parishes. The bus arrived in June 1979. 150–170 people now use the bus, half of them regulars.

Today, there are many possibilities for the use of Storrington's own bus — collecting and delivering people at the bus station to enable them to go out on their own, possibly tied in with subsidised bus fares. Storrington's minibus benefits from the goodwill of Mr Alan Pockett, who provides a garage for it at the Chantry.

Blacksmiths, Wheelwrights, Harness-makers and Saddlers

Everything needed in Storrington used to come in by road, and in a rural area there were plenty of heavy horses, carts and farm vehicles needing attention. To keep traffic flowing and work in progress, blacksmiths, wheelwrights, harness-makers and saddlers were as essential to horse traffic as the garages are to the motor car.

Early in Queen Victoria's reign, Owen Crowhurst came to Storrington and set up a forge in Back Lane (North Street) next to the end cottage, and extending out to the lane. Back Lane then, was just a track. The blacksmith started work at 6.30 a.m. and finished in the evening according to the amount of work there was, the weather, and the time of year, all of which had a bearing on his job. During hard weather, he would go to the stables and put frost nails in the horseshoes which had spikes to bite into the surface and stop the horses slipping. They were often still working at 10 p.m. when snow was deep, taking off the shoes of the milkman's horse, turning down the heels and refitting then, so that the horse had little 'brakes' on each hoof. Wet weather prevented much farm work, so that would mean a constant stream of farm horses being brought in, and implements; ploughshares needed sharpening or replacing, roadmen's picks needed sharpening and box-sledges used to bring flints from the Downs were tyred with flat strips of iron.

The heavy work and flint roads wore out horseshoes in two or three weeks, and the early blacksmith made his own. Cartwheel tyres also wore out quickly and needed replacing. The Back Lane forge always kept 100 oak faggots ready for this job, which required a ring of fire to be built out in the lane to heat up the new tyre.

Owen Crowhurst had a large family, and his son Alfred Crowhurst followed him into the forge. The Back Lane premises had two forges and there was plenty of work for two smiths. Business, in fact, expanded, and Alfred Crowhurst built a new forge in West Street at the turn of the century (now Swedish Tools), with a house for himself next door. It was the first house in Storrington to have a bathroom, the extension for which was built on pillars from Worthing Pier. His house was built with excellent foundations because Alfred Crowhurst believed in strength and 'one day', he maintained, 'there will be a lot of traffic on this road'. His farsightedness was vindicated when the garden was considerably shortened in the 1960s for the road to be widened. In some things, however, progress could not push him. He would never work with any light but that of candles, even after the installation of electricity.

Alfred William Crowhurst started work in the forge at 12 years of age, the third generation of Crowhursts in the business. His three brothers followed the family trade in Pulborough, Amberley, and West Chiltington. Alfred W. Crowhurst was to see the horse give way to the motor-car, but although it changed his business in many ways it did not make it redundant. Alfred W. Crowhurst was a noted motor-cyclist with one of the first machines to be licensed in Storrington. Many blacksmiths found the motor trade a natural progression of their craft. The 'Collegians' would take their motor-cycles in to him for the handlebars to be adjusted to give them a racing look. He also did a lot of wrought-iron work and collaborated with Paul Hardy to leave some notable examples of his work in the village — the church weathervane and organ screen as well as gates, fire-backs, fire-dogs and fire baskets.

Other things which he remembered making were children's hoops, repaired for a penny, and new skids to bowl the hoop for tuppence. Shoemenders were kept supplied with 'pelts', metal tips for heels (especially heavy ones for the postmen), and horses were still brought in to be shod, though now with ready-made shoes. At one time, Alfred Crowhurst's son-in-law wanted to install an electric blower motor in the forge, but this caused the smith to go into weighty consideration. He declared it would upset the horses. His son-in-law explained that it could go outside and feed air to the fire by a tube. This would not do either, because the old bellows gave Alfred fine control of the draught, he said. This objection could be overcome by a control installed inside the forge. More weighty consideration, and then Alfred said with finality, 'And what would I do with my left hand?'

Over 100 years of 'Crowhurst — Blacksmith' ended in Storrington when the forge closed in 1968. Alfred Crowhurst had many interests in the village; he was clarinetist in the Band, a member of the Village Hall Committee, an original member of the Storrington Volunteer Fire Brigade who could remember the truck they had to 'run and push all the way', and 40 years a churchwarden, eventually becoming Rector's Warden.

Mr Frank Brasington joined Mr Crowhurst in 1946. He had been a smith for over 20 years and covered Parham, Washington, Amberley, Pulborough and West Chiltington as a farrier, making special shoes for show horses, surgical shoes and ring shoes. He recalled the famous Atora oxen being shod at the West Street forge. They were laid on their backs, their feet tied firmly and the shoes fitted as the animals' legs stuck up in the air. Frank Brasington has never fully retired. He has an old First World War army forge in his garden, where he makes wrought-iron items and repairs tools.

There was plenty of work for blacksmiths before the motor-car. George Duke had a forge in Church Street before the building was taken over by the College. John Joyes in the 1920s noted that 'he was a very hardworking man; never thought of taking a bit of pleasure — anything to save money. He built a lot of cottages here, including Duke's Row, Cootham, Spring Cottages and all those in Back Lane'. His old premises are still called 'Forge House', the home of Miss F. Greenfield with Dr Ellis' surgery underneath.

Medhurst was another blacksmith whose forge at the east end of the village can be seen behind the coal cart in plate 12. This forge closed in the 1920s.

To attach a horse to a vehicle, one needed the product made by a harness-maker. Raw materials were supplied by the tannery behind Eastbrook Stores, where Mr Sutherland claims that the ground is still foul from the old tan-pits. Also needed were the rope-makers in Back Lane. The whole length of the road was a rope-walk with high posts at either end for fastening the rope as it was spun. Recalling that the blacksmith at one end used to light a fire anything up to 6 ft in diameter to heat tyres in the roadway, it says much about the volume of traffic!

Mr Joyes noted that George Hughes had the Tanyard, '. . . and used to make leggings which used to be very much worn by farmers and labourers: also made gloves'. Mr Brigden, the harness-maker, had a shop at the corner of School Hill, now Luckings. In the early 1890s it was acquired by Mr Jesse Johnson, a churchwarden for many years. Ron Mitchell was one of his apprentices and worked until 4 p.m., after which he might easily be asked to take a couple of horse-collars up to Lee Farm on the Downs! He found out just how heavy they were.

Mr Percy Dibble started working for Jesse Johnson aged eight, and in 1906 at the age of 14 was formally apprenticed for five years. His weekly wages were 2s. 6d. for the first year, increasing by half-a-crown to 12s. 6d. in his fifth year. Absence through

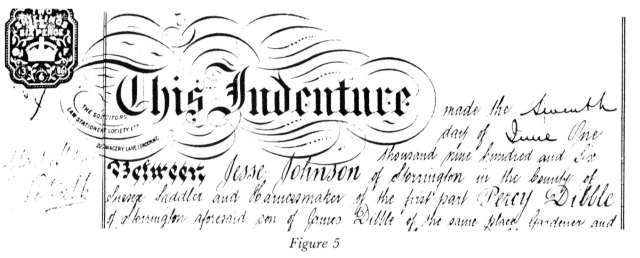

Figure 5

sickness was unpaid. He would not be required to work longer than 7 a.m.–7 p.m. on weekdays, and finished at 3 p.m. on Saturday afternoon. He undertook not to trade as a harness-maker and saddler within seven miles of Storrington whilst Jesse Johnson was in business, without permission. At first he swept up, lit fires and did general work before serious training began. At the outbreak of the First World War, Percy Dibble, three years out of his apprenticeship, joined the Royal Naval Division as a saddler. He returned afterwards to Jesse Johnson, who by that time had three shops, at West Chiltington, Coolham, and Storrington. Percy Dibble went to West Chiltington, returning to stay with his brother, the West Street baker, in the mid 1920s. Later, he moved to North Lane, and in 1937 to School Hill. He visited West Chiltington and Coolham to bring back work to the Storrington shop, where Bill Curtis, another saddler trained by Jesse Johnson, was working.

When Jesse Johnson died, he left the business to the two men, who ran it in partnership. The harness trade declined with the coming of the motor car but the business expanded to include ironmongery, the selling of garden tools, trug baskets, collars, leads and dog baskets, and the making of straps, wallets and briefcases. It became one of those invaluable shops where one could take suitcases for repairs, and have locks and handles attended to. Mr Rapley's father, a locksmith who lived in School Hill, did case locks for Dibble and Curtis. They would tackle any leather work and in our early days of motorcycling, Mr Curtis repaired the saddle of a motor cycle whilst the bike was parked outside his shop. They had the first petrol-pump in Storrington, which was installed on the corner of School Hill.

Another saddler and harness-maker was Mr Dilloway, who was succeeded by Mr Collyer. Mr Mant recalled that he was a Liberal (a terrible thing in those days!) who even put Liberal colours on his pony's whip and bridle. This so enraged certain gentry in the village that they ceased to employ him and made sure than their friends did not give him work either. His trade fell off so much that he had to give up the business. He was followed by P. T. Challen, already by the turn of the century diversifying into a 'cycle and motor depot' and selling Shell lubrication oils and tyres. This was to become Stocker's Garage (plate 29).

One craftsman who was indispensable in the days of pre-motor transport was the wheelwright. Mr George Giles at 'Ormare' was listed as a wheelwright in the 1890s, but the best remembered one was Bridger Woolgar who had a forge and workshop at the top of Manley's Hill, now a restaurant. This was another family business, started in 1880 by Bridger Woolgar and still working until just before the Second World War. His brother Charles Woolgar started in Steyning at about the same time; his sons carried on the business after his death. They built the white-hooded Steyning Brewery carts, which delivered regular consignments of beer to the *Anchor* inn. Plate 70 shows the milk-cart built for John Turner by Woolgar. He also made the waggons for Springhead Farm. Woolgar's pattern-book for the vehicles he built still exists, and shows over 40 carts in exquisite detail and colour. Bridger Woolgar was also an undertaker and coffin-maker. He bought timber, although most wheelwrights had their own sawyers and sawpits. Wood was stacked for 25 years before use, and they guaranteed their wheels against 'fair wear and tear' for *25 years!* Mr Fred Scutt remembers working for Bridger Woolgar in 1922 when he left school. He worked from 7 a.m.–5.30 p.m. blowing the bellows for the smith, Mr Goodyer, who lived in Brewer's Yard, for 2s. 6d. per week.

Garages and Motor-cars

The real change that plunged Storrington into the 20th century and reshaped the village was undoubtedly the switch from horse to horse-power. Its beginnings can be seen in plate 28. Outside the shop are two beautiful early vehicles, a motor-cycle and a car, the first ripples of a flood-tide.

Mr Cripps was in the *White Horse* hotel when he saw his very first motor-car go past. Telling the story when he got home, he just could not stop laughing. After a life-time of horse-drawn vehicles, the motor-car must have looked as though it was running away by itself in clouds of smoke. A driver with no reins to control his vehicle must have looked slightly ridiculous perched up in the driving seat, and his uniform owed much to his predecessors, the grooms (plate 26). The Trotters, owners of one of the first cars in Storrington, had their old coachman taught to drive the Delaunay-Belleville bought for Mrs Trotter. He drove well, but did not like the 'horseless carriage'.

My favourite story, reflecting the very different motoring conditions of those days, is of Father Basil Jellicoe's mother, who lived at Sullington Warren. She would drive into the village, stop in the middle of the road, leave the doors open and the engine running whilst she went to buy fish.

A 1906 open two-seater Ford is among Storrington's early motor-cars. This was Mr Trotter's car, started with a handle, much to Mrs Trotter's anxiety. She was always afraid that the car would run over him. They sold it to a doctor who had previously made his rounds on a motor-cycle, but his patients were troubled by his shaking hands, the bike vibrated so much. A 1908 Metallurgique replaced the Ford, then two Delauney-Bellevilles of four and six cylinders. Alice Trotter drove the smaller one, becoming the first lady

1. SUSSEX WAGGON BED

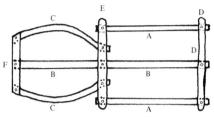

A Side timbers hind bed 5 ft. 5 ins. x 4 ins. oak
B Main timber 4 ins. x 3 ins. oak. Hind bed 3 ins. x 2 ins.
C Side timbers front bed 5 ins. x 4 ins. oak
D Hind dware
E Middle dware } all 6 ft. x 4 ins. oak
F Front dware
o Pin holes, oak pins

2.

MIDDLE TIMBER OF WAGGON BED

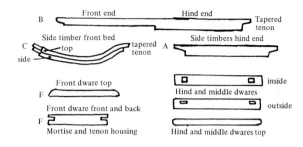

3. SUSSEX WAGGON SIDE VIEW OF BODY

Front section is elevated from the middle dware

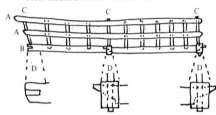

A Top inside lades
B Bed of waggon
C Stay irons
D Front, middle and hind dwares
E Oak staves for fixing side boards

4. FRONT UNDER CARRIAGE

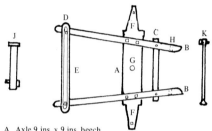

A Axle 9 ins. x 9 ins. beech
B Houms 4 ins. x 4 ins. tapered to 3 ins. x 3 ins. oak
C Front cross key 3 ins. x 2 ins. oak
D Bridge back
E Iron plate on bridge back
F Axle arms, beech
G Main rung hole
H Rod rung hole
K Rod rung, 1 in. round iron
J Main rung, 2 ins. round iron
o Pin holes
☐ Bolt holes

5. HIND CARRIAGE

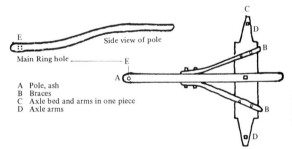

Side view of pole

Main Ring hole

A Pole, ash
B Braces
C Axle bed and arms in one piece
D Axle arms

6. FRONT VIEW OF SUSSEX WAGGON

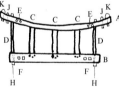

A Summer piece 4 ins. x 4 ins. oak
B Front dware of bed (sketch 1)
C Front staves
D Front stay irons
E Holes for top irons of poles
F Holes for bottom irons of poles
⌂ Top irons for poles
⎍ Bottom irons for poles
K Outside lades
J Inside lades

7.

Long staple and fittings. D.

Rod

1 Tug hook
2 Ridgechain hook
3 Breeching hook

A Rods or shafts
B Keys
C Iron braces
D Long staple with hooks for attaching to harness

8. SIDE VIEW OF SUSSEX WAGGON

driver in Storrington to do so, and taking great pride in her smooth gear-changing.

Mr Henderson at the Chantry had a Studebaker with a specially-built body, and a French chauffeur who drove very fast through the narrow lanes, scaring people and running over chickens. Miss Trotter's first personal car was a 1924 Bullnose Morris Cowley, an open four-seater for which she paid £60 when it was two years old. Before 1914, there were quite a few motor-cycles, Indians for the rich and dashing boys, and also blue and white Douglasses.

By 1910, cars made up one quarter of the road traffic, and the astute tradesman had to reckon with their needs if he was not to be left behind. Mr Challen moved with the times, as did Mrs Powell who opened the very first garage in Storrington in the Amberley Road (plate 27). This picture is thought to date from about 1907. The garage sold its petrol in cans. The Southdown Garage building is still there housing Southdown buses.

Stocker's Garage

Mr Wagstaff Stocker, who first managed the Southdown Garage for Mrs Powell, and then owned it, moved the business to the Square in the 1920s, with a workshop in the White Horse Yard. The garage in the picture (plate 29) is Challen's old harness-maker's and saddlers premises with a whole new shop front. Beside the garages are the new petrol pumps. Pratt's Benzole Mixture *from the pumps* is well advertised, as the old garage had no pumps.

The name was soon changed to Stocker's Garage in order to avoid confusion with the Southdown Garage, Amberley Road. Stocker's employed and trained men who later opened garages of their own — Ralph Saggers, Jim Hues and Mr Ellis. Many started their working lives as grooms. Mr D. Carn remembers starting there after leaving school at 5s. 0d. per week. One of his jobs was scrubbing tyres in the old horse-trough which stood in the White Horse Yard. In winter's ice it was a most unpleasant job, in spite of Mr Stocker's encouraging advice to '. . . get your hands in it boy!'

In 1946 'Wag' Stocker's niece came from London to work for him. Miss Grace Stocker remembers in the early years having to check and count petrol coupons — it was still rationed from the war — before they could get fresh supplies. Petrol for commercial vehicles, having priority over the private motorist, was dyed red, which stained the carburettor, so that it was immediately obvious if a motorist used commercial petrol illegally! One pre-war order from the garage was for a new series E Morris. When peace came, it was one of the first cars to be delivered, and carried Purchase Tax. Miss Stocker very much wanted it for herself, and against the advice of her uncle, who mistakenly thought the 'temporary' war-time tax would be removed, bought it for under £400.

Mr Stocker was a Special Constable in his spare time, and always very active. In the late 1940s his health suffered a serious setback, and Dr Head advised him to get help in running the garage. Miss Stocker's father had started a garage when the first cars appeared, and from the age of about six, her brother Frank had always been in the garage, fascinated by the whole trade. He came to Storrington in 1949 and the business became the joint property of Grace and Frank Stocker in 1951.

The whole family would crowd into one car and go off to collect a new car, returning in two parties. Grace Stocker remembered some lovely summer evenings when these trips combined business with pleasure. A new car was usually kept in the old garage in the Square, but a showroom soon became essential. In 1953 the Co-operative Society put Commercial House on the market, The Stockers bought it and turned the ground floor into a big plate-glass-windowed showroom, although Frank insisted on fitting a steel bar inside the glass, saying, 'One day, we shall drive a car straight through it!' Morris sent down a special new car for the opening of the new showroom.

In 1955, 25 lock-up garages were built in the White Horse Yard. Some were converted stables, and the six where Harwoods now have their showrooms were the old coach-houses. The garages were let for 7s. 6d. per week. Other stables were converted into a workshop. The business continued until 1966, when it was bought by Harwoods, and Grace Stocker retired to Worthing. Frank Stocker still has a part-time job, which is no surprise to those who know him!

Corner Garage – About 1924, Mr and Mrs Ralph Saggers bought a vacant corner plot where the Amberley and Pulborough roads meet, and built a garage. They installed four petrol pumps over 500 gallon tanks, selling Cleveland commercial petrol, National Benzole, Esso Ethyl and Shell. Motorists paid 1s. 6d. per gallon for Shell, including 9d. tax; Shell-mex, the commercial brand, was sold for 1s. 3d. but still carried 9d. tax. During the war, there was only Pool petrol at 2s. 3d. per gallon.

Mr Saggers employed many familiar 'garage' people: Jim Hues and his son Eric doing a Saturday job but later employed full-time, Albert Charman, Harold Bourn, Garnet Haylor and Den Mason. The garage supplied petrol to a Flying Club which had been established at Parham Airstrip. They had no agency for cars, but sold all makes. Albert Charman would go off to Birmingham or Dagenham and drive back with a new car.

In the early 1960s the garage was sold to Mr George McReady, who re-named it *Storrington Motors*. He took on the Ford Agency and started selling caravans under the separate name of 'Chanctonbury Caravans'. On 1 May 1968 he sold out to Mr Monty White from Gray & Rowsell at Bury, whose wife was Margaret Gray. Once again, an 'old garage family' ran the Corner Garage. Mr Norman Whittington, a man who had entered the trade straight from school, came from Gray & Rowsell with him. They developed the existing business and expanded the caravan selling side, and continued with Esso and Ford agencies.

In January 1976 Mr White died, and the garage is now owned by Mrs White with her two sons, Graham and Paul, who work there. Mr Norman Whittington is a director and general manager. The garage and show rooms have been redecorated and the outside has a unified appearance which the old collection of garage buildings never achieved. Among the old features swept away were the iron ladder to the roof, where Storrington's first air-raid siren was installed, and the flagpole which Mr McReady erected.

School Hill Garage – In the early 1920s Mr Peterson opened for business in Mr Gatley's barn on School Hill. He sold a few cars and Red Line petrol until the outbreak of the Second World War. Mr Stocker then took over the premises, and cars were laid up there which could no longer be used by their owners. Shortly afterwards it became an Ordnance Corps workshop, and towards the end of the war it was used to store aircraft parts.

In 1948, the garage was re-opened by Den Mason (a former Corner Garage employee), and Roy Illingworth took it over from him. In 1954 two more Corner Garage men became the owners – Jim and Eric Hues, who ran it until it was demolished to make way for the Old Mill Square development.

They sold new and second-hand cars and had two petrol pumps selling National Benzole. Eric Hues remembers that when the tanks got down to 200 gallons, they ordered 400 gallons from their suppliers, hoping that they would sell at least 100 gallons before the tanker arrived, as the tank capacity was only 500 gallons! They had a delivery about once a week and normal business would be about 600–800 gallons per week. Eric Hues recalls that 800 gallons of petrol in those far-off-seeming days (the 1950s and 1960s) cost the garage about £82 0s. 0d.!

M. J. Garage — Today's new development quickly becomes part of village history. Storrington's most recent and possibly first purpose-built garage is over 10 years old and has seen several changes in that time. M. J. Garage, owned by Michael Williams and Jack Kirk, was designed by David White, who was responsible for the development of Gatley's field. These plans called for the demolition of the School Hill Garage, so a new one which would be part of the new shopping centre was needed.

Before the east end of the precinct could be started, holes were made in the roof of the old green barn that housed the garage to fix the positions of the piles, needed to secure the foundations in the running sand that plagues that part of the village. The new garage was designed with large workshop, staff room, oil and general stores, customers' toilets and manager's office. The original idea included a car showroom, spares sales area and cycle repair shop, but the cycle shop was soon abandoned and the shop leased to Jason shoes.

Since the opening of the garage in 1970 with a splendid 1904 De Dion on show, changes have taken place. Eric Hues, originally manager of the new garage, and Paul Parkin and James Roberts, who were in the workshop, have left. The last two now run the servicing side of the garage as a separate business, and M. J. Garage operates the forecourt. When the first pumps were installed, four gallons of petrol cost 25s., a sum which will not buy one gallon today. There have been three changes of pumps in only 12 years — a measure of how we watch Storrington's history accelerating past us.

1. Rev. George Faithfull 1870–1900

2. Rev. Arthur F. Faithfull 1900–1926

Rectors of Storrington

3. Rev. Richard Faithfull 1926–1942

4. Institution of Rev. W. G. Frostick in 1943

5. Rev. George Mackenzie welcomes a new member of the church

6. Rev. John Norman welcomes the bride

Hooves, wheels and ways

7. Eddistone's Steam Roller driven by James Broadbridge Snr, at Thakeham Road
8. School Hill showing what roads used to be like. Laura Cottages and Sand Lodge had not then been built

9. 'Old Punch' — Edward Edwards

10. 'Young Punch' who died in 1977

11. Family transport for the Mants

12. Carrier delivering coal. Medhurst's forge is just visible behind the driver

13. Carrier's passenger vehicle for
    private parties behind the flats in
    West Street
14. Gatley's field in 1949 (*centre left*)
    (*Worthing Herald* picture)
15. The same view, now the bus
    station and Mr Ridge's garden.
    (*centre right*)

16. Storrington's minibus collecting
    passengers, 1979. 'Jim the
    driver', (Mr Jim Davies) waits
    behind

17. (*left*) The Forges, Back Lane, before 1898. The two chimneys indicate the presence inside of two working forges

18. (*below*) At the West Street Forge, Alfred Crowhurst watches his nephew Edwin shoeing a horse

19. (*above right*) Inside the West Street Forge

20. Frank Brasington at Rowdell

22. Bill Curtis with a saddle which he made

21. Jesse Johnson's shop

23. 1905. Steyning Breweries cart made by the Woolgars

24. 1907. Outside Challen's Saddler's and Harnessmaker's shop. Mr Cripps is driving a cart which looks in need of the harnessmaker's services!

25. Bill Carn, chauffeur, who later drove Southdown buses, in a rare 1912 Flanders car

26. William Pool, chauffeur, with possibly the first car in Storrington, a 1908 Humber

27. Storrington's first garage in the Amberley Road, owned by Mrs Peterson. It is now the bus garage

28. P. T. Challen, harnessmaker and saddler — and Motor Depot
29. Southdown Garages — now with their own advertising signs painted on the wall and new petrol pumps
30. 1929–1930. The Corner Garage

31. Staff of the Corner Garage —
owner, Mr Ralph Saggers
centre front, Jim Hues to his
left and Eric Hues second
from the right at the back

32. Opening of MJ Garages. Mr Williams is in the passenger seat of the 1904 De Dion and Mr Kirk
is in the centre

33. Gasholders, purifiers and condenser towers in the gasworks yard

35. (*below*) Gas Lamp in the Square installed a a memento of Queen Victoria's Jubilee

Taps, knobs and switches

34. North Sea Gas pressure reduction point in Greyfriars Lane, 1979

LIFE ON AN ELECTRIC FARM.

36. On the left, a corner of the dynamo room, on the right , electric milking

37. Overhead mains distribution in Storrington High Street

38. Mrs Skinner at the well of 'Holmwood' about 1920

39. Test boring of the Coldharbour site, 1913

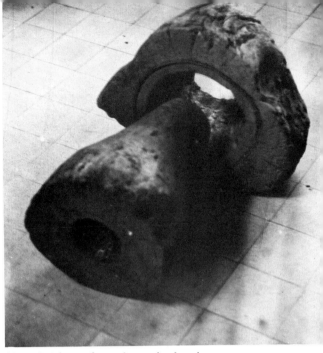

40. Smock Alley pumping station

41. Sections of wooden main showing method of joining lengths

42. November 1979. Some of the staff and equipment at Smock Alley. The old pumping station is the right-hand building

43. Old brick barrel drain in Church Street, broken by modern work

44. Hurston treatment works, April 1978 (*below left*)
45. Fred Hearn and colleagues when he retired. Left to right: Bob Smith, Ken Snoad, Frank Adsett, Alf Maton, Cyril Maybe (*right*)

Emergency and other services

6. Fourth Post Office. Georgian House in Church Street   47. Fifth Post Office, High Street

8. **1920s.** Postmen behind the High Street Post Office in the Co-op. Left to right: Fred Newman, Jim Streeter, Alf Atfield and Mr Lillywhite

POST OFFICE TELEGRAPHS.

Regulation as to Inland Telegrams.

If the Receiver of an Inland Message doubts its accuracy, he may have it repeated on paying half the cost of its transmission to him. In the event of an error having been made, the amount paid for repetition will be refunded on application to the Secretary.

49.   Storrington's first telegram handled by the Post Office, 13 April 1875

50.   Thakeham Post Office in the 1920s

51. Early telephone exchange at the foot of Manley's Hill

52. Site of Storrington's first
    telegraph pole, Rosemary

53. Inside the new automatic exchange. The street cables
    enter underneath the rack on the right

54.   Percy Connor 1948

55.   Edward Post escorting Arundel's civic dignitaries

56.   Ernie Sweeney on duty in Storrington Police Station, August 1979

57.   Terry Smart with the standard specification Hillman Avenger Police car, January 1980

58. Merryweather Engine in use at the Abingworth fire 1911, before Storrington's Brigade was formed

59. Charles Mant says goodbye to Storrington's first manual fire engine as it leaves for the Fire Service Museum in Chichester, 1968

61. Charlie Huffer, one of Storrington's
first firemen

63. On war service with the 60 h.p. Dennis
motor pump, capable of delivering
500 gallons per minute

62. Pre-war firemen in their handsome brass helmets, Charles Mant centre

4. (*below*) Wartime engine outside the old fire station
5. (*right*) Charles Mant receives the King's Police and
    Fire Service Medal from the Rt Hon. Lord Lecon-
    field, G.C.V.O., Lord Lieutenant of Sussex

6. September 1979. Storrington Fire Brigade. John Linfield (Chief) is in the centre of the front row.

67. The Richardson sisters delivering milk
68. This lovely glass-enclosed delivery cart was known as 'the Crystal Palace' to locals

Facing page

69. 1917. Grace Padwick delivering milk to Smuggler's Hut. Ada Miller carrying the churn
70. 1920s. John Turner delivering milk to George Rapley in School Hill, in a cart built by Bridger Woolgar

71. The mill on Kithurst Common

72. Mr 'Snobby' Stringer and family outside his little shoemaker's shop next to the *Cricketers* in West Street, where four cottages stood between the pub and the present row of shops, in front of Twitten Cottage

73. Back Lane, where the ropemakers and harnessmakers were

74. Fish and ice supplier in the Square
75. Mr Towse's Christmas display of meat in his Church Street shop in the late 1800s

76. Ron Ham and Derek Knight outside their radio and electrical shop in the late 1950s. Some of the all-dry radios in the window are now in the Chalk Pits Museum!

77. The newly built Capital and Counties Bank in the early
1900s. Note the cottages behind, and the space to the
right where the Homestead was later built.
78. (*lower left*) Mrs Soffe and sister 'Floss' on the running
board outside The Homestead
79. (*lower right*) Miss Edie Vick outside the Elders

80.   Mr and Mrs Walter Penn in their little shop

81.   The *Crown* inn

82.   1920s. Customers outside the *Crown*

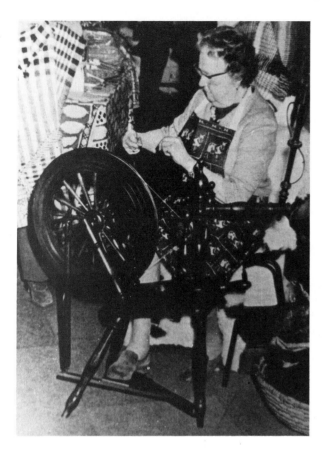

83. Miss Hilda Breed demonstrates hand
    spinning at an exhibition
84. Sand diggers in the Marley pits — as it
    used to be done

85. Crews of Steam Juggernauts

86. Marley's steam juggernauts used from 1928–1936. They picked up their water from available streams and ponds and could carry 10 tons

87. Marley Tile Works seen across Chantry Millpond in the 1920s
88. Bill Bourn with his father's engine

9. Bill Lidbetter, Bert Lidbetter, D. French, E. Towse, W. Bourn in 1940

90. Narrow gauge railway and some of the Thakeham Tile products

91. Thakeham Union Workhouse built on the site of Rydon School
92. Duke's Row, built on the site of the old Storrington Parish Workhouse at Cootham

Storrington at play

93. Storrington's early cricketers

94. Storrington Cricket Club 1937. Hugh de Selincourt is in the circle inset

CRICKET ON THE ICE.

January 8th, 1891.

MR. ERNEST HAMMOND'S TEAM v. MR. CROWHURST'S TEAM.

The inhabitants of Storrington, Sussex, were privileged on Thursday to enjoy an interesting afternoon's amusement in the shape of a cricket match on the ice, which took place about half a mile out, on Chantrey Mill Pond, which was lent for the occasion by the tenant, Mr. Crowhurst, himself a thorough sportsman, who, to improve matters, very generously stopped the "click of his mill" for the day. The chief novelty of the affair was the carrying out of the stipulation of the organising party, viz., that each player should appear in a "top" hat, and whoever conceived this idea must have a keenish notion of the ridiculous, because given a man in a top hat to which he is unaccustomed and start him at cricket in a pair of skates, it shall be very hard lines indeed if there is not a little fun to be got out of him, and the idea was fully realised on Thursday, as in nine cases out of ten when the operator commenced to operate if he did not fall himself his hat did, and when they both came down together, which was pretty often the case, it caused great fun to the onlookers. The hats too were studies in themselves; some real Home Rulers looked as if they had lately done duty at the Kilkenny election; others good old broad-brimmed, long, rough-coated beavers, appeared not to have seen the light of day for years. But to our tale. The respective captains, Messrs. Crowhurst and Ernest Hammond (landlord of the White Horse Hotel), selected fifteen men each, and shortly before two o'clock a start was made on a capital wicket. As the game proceeded the fun grew fast and furious, and the attitudes of some of the performers in their frantic endeavours to secure the ball can be more readily imagined than described. The individual limit of 30 runs was agreed on, and rather strange to relate, one man on each side obtained the maximum. It was a very evenly contested game. Hammond's fifteen ultimately winning by 9 runs. There was a very good attendance, the banks of the pond being pretty well occupied. We noticed members of the leading aristocratic families, representatives of "law, physic, and divinity," tradesmen of all classes, and last, but not least, any amount of the fair sex, who seemed to enter into the spirit of the thing with a deal of gusto. The Storrington brass band was in attendance, and enlivened the proceedings with beautiful airs during the afternoon. There was not the slightest accident and, taken altogether, the match was a decided success, and being of so novel a character we can never hope to look upon its like again. At the conclusion of an innings each the players, headed by the band, marched back to the White Horse Hotel, where, with their friends, they spent a convivial evening. Messrs. Douglas and Linfield acted as umpires. Score:—

MR. ERNEST HAMMOND'S FIFTEEN.		MR. CROWHURST'S FIFTEEN.	
R. Doath run out	2	W. Laker st Joyes b Soffe	4
W. Clifton b Charman	4	H. Crowhurst run out	16
J. Joyes st Laker b Crowhurst	7	S. Searle b Soffe	1
E. Day b Lynn	6	P. Botting st Joyes b Soffe	0
Ernest Hammond c Allen b Crowhurst	5	W. Long c Ern. Hammond b Soffe	5
H. T. Hammond b Charman	3	E. Parlett run out	5
F. Allen run out	0	G. Little b Joyes	9
C. Greenfield run out	5	James Allen run out	7
A. Soffe b Crowhurst	4	P. Floate not out	1
E. Hammond (limited to)	30	A. Towse st Joyes b Soffe	0
W. Grantham b Charman	1	B. Mitchell st Joyes b Soffe	0
F. Herbert b Allen	4	M. Lynn b Soffe	0
A. Woods b Searle	7	P. King st Joyes b Soffe	0
F. Cowper c Crowhurst	10	W. Charman (limited to)	30
G. Ripley not out	0	A. Preslee run out	1
Total	88	Total	79

From "Sporting Life," January 10th, 1891.

95. Account of the famous cricket match on the ice
96. Storrington Football club 1920

97.　The Colts Club, formed for boys too old to be Scouts

98.　The Bowls Club, May 1927

STORRINGTON AND PARHAM
COTTAGE GARDENING SOCIETY.

This Society now includes the adjoining Parishes of SULLINGTON and RACKHAM.

THE ANNUAL SHOW

WILL TAKE PLACE

IN THE COURSE OF THE MONTH OF SEPTEMBER, 1865,

(DUE NOTICE WILL BE GIVEN OF THE DAY.)

When the following Prizes will be awarded:

Class 1. Prizes to be competed for by ALL Exhibitors.

COTTAGES.

Cleanest and neatest kept Cottage
Second ditto
Third ditto
Fourth ditto
Fifth ditto

In awarding these Prizes, the Visitors will take into consideration the number and age of the Children dependent on the Cottager.

GARDENS.

Best cropped and neatest kept Garden
Second ditto
Third ditto
Fourth ditto
Fifth ditto
Sixth ditto
Seventh ditto
Eighth ditto
Neatest and gayest Flower Garden Plot
Second ditto
Third ditto
Fourth ditto
Fifth ditto
Sixth ditto
Seventh ditto

VARIOUS.

Best Collection of Vegetables (6 sorts)
Second ditto
Third ditto
Fourth ditto
Fifth ditto

(These Vegetables must be shown together.)

VARIOUS (continued).

Best Nosegay, grown in Exhibitor's own Garden
Second ditto
Third ditto
Fourth ditto
Best Plate of new Honey in Comb, obtained without killing the Bees
(Given by the Rev. J. Beck.)
Second ditto
(Given by Mr. W. Stanford.)
Best Pound of raw Honey
Second ditto

VEGETABLES.

Best Twelve Kidney Potatoes
Second ditto
Third ditto
Fourth ditto
Fifth ditto
Best Twelve Round Potatoes
Second ditto
Third ditto
Fourth ditto
Fifth ditto
Best Twelve Onions
Best Twelve Underground Onions
Best Six Carrots
Second ditto
Third ditto
Best Six Parsnips
Second ditto
Third ditto

VEGETABLES (continued).

Fourth ditto
Best Three Cabbages
Second ditto
Best Red Cabbage
Second ditto
Best Six Turnips
Second ditto
Best Plate of Thirty-six Dwarf Beans
Second ditto
Best Plate of Thirty-six Scarlet Runner
Second ditto
Best Two Cucumbers
Second ditto
Best Pumpkin or Gourd
Second ditto
Best Bunch of Garden Herbs
Second ditto

FRUITS.

Best Plate of Twelve Eating Apples
Second ditto
Best Plate of Twelve Cooking Apples
Second ditto
Third ditto
Fourth ditto
Best Plate of Twelve Pears
Second ditto
Best Plate of Blue Plums
Second ditto
Third ditto
Best Plate of Green Plums
Second ditto

FRUITS (continued).

Best Quart of Damsons
Second ditto
Third ditto
Best Three Bunches of Out-door White Grapes
Best Three Bunches of Out-door Black Grapes

FLOWERS.

Best Three Plants in Pots for a Window
Second ditto
Third ditto
Best Scarlet Geranium
Second ditto
Best Fancy Geranium
Second ditto
Best Fuchsia
Second ditto
Best Hardy Plant of any kind
Second ditto

CHILDREN'S PRIZES.

Best Nosegay of Wild Flowers
Second ditto
Third ditto
Best Collection of Mosses
Second ditto
Best Collection of Ferns
Second ditto
Best Collection of Grasses
Second ditto
Best Six Bunches of Water Cresses
Second ditto

Class 2. Prizes to be competed for by Agricultural Laborers ONLY.

VEGETABLES.

Best Twelve Kidney Potatoes
Second ditto
Third ditto
Fourth ditto
Fifth ditto
Best Twelve Round Potatoes
Second ditto
Third ditto
Fourth ditto
Fifth ditto
Best Twelve Onions
Second ditto
Third ditto
Fourth ditto
Best Twelve Underground Onions
Best Six Carrots
Second ditto

VEGETABLES (continued).

Third ditto
Second ditto
Best Six Parsnips
Second ditto
Third ditto
Fourth ditto
Best Three Cabbages
Second ditto
Best Red Cabbage
Second ditto
Best Six Turnips
Second ditto
Best Plate of Thirty-six Dwarf Beans
Second ditto
Best Plate of Thirty-six Scarlet Runner Beans
Second ditto

VEGETABLES (continued).

Best Two Cucumbers
Second ditto
Best Pumpkin or Gourd
Second ditto
Best Bunch of Garden Herbs
Second ditto

FLOWERS.

Best Three Plants in Pots for a Window
Second ditto
Third ditto
Best Scarlet Geranium
Second ditto
Best Fancy Geranium
Second ditto
Best Fuchsia

FLOWERS (continued).

Second ditto
Best Fancy Plant of any kind
Second ditto

CHILDREN'S PRIZES.

Best Nosegay of Wild Flowers
Second ditto
Third ditto
Best Collection of Mosses
Second ditto
Best Collection of Ferns
Second ditto
Best Collection of Grasses
Second ditto
Best Six Bunches of Water Cresses
Second ditto

RULES.

All cottagers and small tradesmen living in the parishes of Storrington, Parham, Sullington, and Rackham, and having paid a subscription of one penny, or in the case of children of one halfpenny, before the 1st of August, to Mr. Walter Hemingway, or to Messrs. Botting, will be allowed to compete for the prizes offered; but no gentleman's servant, or master gardener, or person who does not principally support himself by labor, will be permitted to show for any prize, except those offered for the best collection of six sorts of vegetables.

Every specimen shown for a prize must have been grown by the member exhibiting it, or have been in his possession for three months previous to the show; and any member exhibiting any specimen for a prize which can be proved not to have been grown by himself, or to have been in his possession as before stated, will forfeit all claim to that or to any other prize awarded him.

Specimens not included in the published list, if shown by members and bona fide their own growth, will receive prizes if recommended by the Judges.

All specimens intended to be shown for prizes must be sent to the place of exhibition not later than nine o'clock on the evening of the day before, or by nine o'clock on the morning of the show.

All vegetables must be sent clean and washed; carrots, parsnips, and turnips properly trimmed.

Specimens shown by children must have been collected by the children themselves, and by them alone.

The Committee will appoint three Visitors to visit the cottages, and three Judges to award the prizes, and the same Judges will have power to withhold prizes when not merited.

The garden and flower plots will be inspected the first week in July, and all cottagers wishing to have their gardens viewed must send in their names to Mr. Walter Hemingway or to Messrs. Botting, on or before the 25th of June.

Cottagers wishing to have their cottages inspected must give in their names before the 15th of April, and Visitors appointed for the purpose will view the cottages at least twice in the course of the year.

It is confidently expected that no exhibitor will cultivate his garden on Sundays.

Gentlemen and other Friends are invited to send Fruits, Flowers, or Vegetables to the Show.

W. W. MITCHELL, Printer, West Sussex Gazette Office, Arundel.

99. Poster for an early flower show, 1865

00. P.C. Percy Connor inspecting his prize-winning flower show entry

01. (a and b) Celebrating Queen Victoria's Diamond Jubilee in 1897

102. The big procession coming down School Hill

103. The beginning of the Coronation procession in 1953

04. Mr Tom Smith

105. Mrs Louisa Castle (sister-in-law of T. Smith) and her daughter Mary set up housekeeping next to the recreation ground

106. Erecting the big roundabout

107. The Band 1910
Back row, l. to r.: E. Dawtry, C. Mitchell, F. Linfield, S. Moon, G. Soffe, G. Crowhurst, F. Floate, J. Daughtrey, H. Rendell, T. Pickard, F. Piper, G. Hayler, A. Elms, J. Skinner, H. Gibbs
Middle row, l. to r.: Mr G. Trotter, O. Crowhurst, G. Mitchell, E. Elms, Mr Bampton, Mrs Trotter, B. Floate, B. Dibble, G. Daughtrey, J. Hills, A. Crowhurst
Front row l. to r.: F. Crowhurst, T. Dean, H. Wicker, S. Moon, R. Allen, L. Piper, A. Daughtrey, T. Crowhurst, A. French

108. Commercial House 1893, after disastrous Bonfire Night celebrations!
109. Café Chantant — a private entertainment in someone's house. The 'servants' are in fact, guests.

110. Col. Ravenscroft escorts his daughter to church for her
     marriage to Sir Walter de S. Bartelott, Bart. May 1938
111. Described by the *Daily Mirror* as the 'Wedding of the
     Villages' in its centre page spread, this picture of the
     returning bridesmaids gives some idea of the scale of
     the event

112. Audrey and Arthur Reeves
113. Miss K. F. Austin and Mr B. Hood

Storrington at school

114. The village school

115. Village schoolchildren in the late 1920s

> Primary School,
> Storrington.
>
> July 17th.
>
> My dear Mother.
>
> I hope you are
> well I an writig to you from
> school. Tomorrow we start our
> examinations. I am going to try
> very hard. and I hope I shall
> go up to Standard II With.
> love. From.
> Derek

116. Letter written in 1946 by
Derek Aldred. He had the same
teacher as his mother
117. Mr C. R. Waller, headmaster of
Storrington School in his study

118. Sports Day

119. Col. Ravenscroft presenting prizes. This little girl excitedly lifts out the doll she has won, leaving him with the empty box, much to the crowd's amusement!

120. Staff meeting at the village school

121. Mr and Mrs Waller retire, 1964. Mr Carter presents an illuminated address, watched by Rev. G. Mackenzie and pupils

122. Netball team, Rydon School. *Back row, l. to r.:* J. Allen, M. Foulk, Linda ?, P. Summersby; *Front row, l. to r.:* J. Huxley, G. Porter, P. Guile.

123. St Norbert's Roman Catholic School, Kithurst Lane

124. St Joseph's Dominican Convent School

125. Two Dominican Sisters with pupils

126. Mrs Edgell's School at Roselands, July 1911, decorated for the coronation of King George V. Mrs Dora Edgell standing by gate, Violet Edgell holding child on gatepost

127. College students

Storrington at war

128. The butcher's boy who went to war. 17½-year-old Billy Charman in his smart new uniform beside the Plantation. He never returned from France. The trees behind him also went to France as pit-props in the trenches
129. Territorials who joined up as soon as war started

130. Mr Cowdry, Dardanelles campaign veteran, feeding Mrs Gatley's ponies outside the Bine Mill where he worked
131. Miss Lidbetter working in the Plantation during the First World War

132. People chatting in the Square after the peace prayers.

133. Storrington's Roll of Honour

134. Church black-out blind

135. Storrington's Home Guard platoon

Back row, l. to r.: Matt Collier, Jack Daughtrey, Mr Fleming, ? Piggott, Ernest Tambling, ? , Jeff Turner, ? , Derek Austin, John Horn, ? , ? , Ken Edwards. — *Third row, l. to r.:* ? Hayes, ? , ? , ? , Lawrence Beaton, Harold Craven, 'Punch' Edwards, Les Wickens, ? , Mr Pierce, Jack Gilbert (hidden), ? , ? , ? , Dennis Connor, ? , Ken More, 'Shaker' Ford, ? , Jimmy Horton. — *Second row, l. to r.:* Mr C. R. Waller, Mr Rapley, ? Greenfield, Jim Parsons, ? Greenfield, Henry Wicker, John Turner, ? , ? , 'Pongo' Gilbert, Mr Wheatland, ? , ? , Capt. Scarisbrick (Cpl. H.G.). — *Front row, l. to r.:* Anthony Scarisbrick (Capt. H. G.), Jack Chalk, ? Wilkinson (next five unknown), Roy Dean.

136. Home Guard Command

Back row, l. to r.: Romney Towndrow, ? , Cecil Waller, Don Rapley, ? . — *Front row, l. to r.:* Henry Wicker, ? , John Turner

137. War-time firemen with messenger boy (Roy Reeves) in front

138. Firemen parade past saluting base

139. Charles Mant with his war-time control room staff, 1945, on the day the Women's Section was closed down in Storrington

140. Land Girls at Parham
141. Parham Land Girls coping
with winter

142. Factory at Roundabout with the staff who produced ammunition boxes and trays.
L. to r.: George Moore (manager), Mrs Mustchin, Buddy Crabbe, Elsie Manville, Joan ? , ? Gruber, ? Crockford, Basil Skinner, Mrs E. Whitbourn

143. Ashington and Storrington Red Cross outside the First Aid Post, Worthing Road in 1940, awaiting the Duchess of Norfolk's inspection
Front row, l. to r.: Mrs Hewitt, Mrs Joyce Woolgar, ? , ? . — *Second row, l. to r.:* Mrs Burt, Dr Eames, Mrs Ledger, Miss Peggy Ledger, Mrs Coles, ? . — *Third row, l. to r.:* Mrs Wildman, Miss Queenie Hecks, ? , ? , ? , Mrs Funnell, Mrs Lelliott. — *Fourth row. l. to r.:* ? , Mrs Pat Pickworth, ? , Mrs Ormsby (last three unknown).

144, 145, 146. Parham's evacuees

147. Citation from the Queen to
The Hon. Mrs Clive Pearson

I WISH TO MARK BY THIS PERSONAL MESSAGE,
my appreciation of the service you have rendered to your
Country in 1939.

In the early days of the War you opened your door to strangers
who were in need of shelter, & offered to share your home with
them.

I know that to this unselfish task you have sacrificed much
of your own comfort, & that it could not have been achieved
without the loyal co-operation of all in your household.

By your sympathy you have earned the gratitude of those to
whom you have shown hospitality, & by your readiness to
serve you have helped the State in a work of great value —

Elizabeth R

The Hon. Mrs. Clive Pearson.

Some of the Children
from London who lived
at Parham during the
war years 1939-42.

The Officers of 3 (Battle) Wing, 1 Canadian School of Infantry (Overseas)
outside the Officers' Mess (Great Parlour) window, Parham.
Saturday, August 15th. 1945.

Back Row - Left to Right.

Lt.	Roger ...... ?
Lt.	A.J.Grondin. R.22e.R.
Capt.	R.Smith. Regina Rifles.
Lt.	Gordie P. Miller. R.H.C.(B.W.).
Lt.	Frank G.Callaghan. R.H.C.(B.W.).
Lt.	Colin P.Rutherford. R.Regt.of Canada.
Capt.	W.B.Fraser. R.Winnipeg Rifles.
Lt.	Thivierge.

Middle Row - Left to Right.

Lt.	Harry Rayner, Special Service.
Lt.	E.A.Levin. Camerons of Canada.
Lt.	W.J.Deyell. Cdn. Inf. Corps.
Lt.	Jimmy.O.Dutton. Calgary Highlanders
Capt.	D.A.Hay. 1 Cdn. Scottish.
Capt.	Ross Upton. R.Cdn. Dental Corps.
Lt.	Bryan Carruthers.
Lt.	Tommy Caie.
Lt.	Wilkinson. Regina Rifles.
Lt.	Leo Rudolph.
Lt.	Johnny Bond.
.Lt.	Bill Millar.

Front Row - Left to Right

Capt.	Gordie G.Holtby, R.C.A.P.C.
Capt.	Wharton Hood. Q.O.R. of Canada.
Major	Eric G.Byme. Regina Rifles.
Lt.Col.	Ernest Anderson
Capt.	W.Hayne. C.I.C.
Lt.	Thompson.
Lt.	Johnny Gway. R.22e.R.

Photograph by Margaret Ellsmoor, The Studio, 17, Chapel Road, Worthing. Sussex.
(Negative Number 36111 B.)

148. Canadian officers outside
their mess

149. C. R. Waller's National
Registration card

150. 2464 Squadron's radio room 1979
L. to r.: Flt/Lt. John Keegan (C.O.), Cdt. Nigel Golds, Cdt. David Sopp, Flt/Sgt. Andrew Maynard.

151. 2464 Squadron provide a guard of honour for 'Bomber' Harris on his visit to Warnham War Museum

Neighbours

152. Parham House
153. Staff in Lord Zouche's time about 1904

154. Two of Lord Zouche's gardeners, Tom West and Alan Puttick

155. The Pearson children — Veronica on Susie, Lavinia on Chimney, Dione, and Harry on Surprise

156. Lavinia Pearson and Mr Cridland standing on the frozen Fountain Pond

157. Fryern House

158. Interior of Fryern Hall

159. Coach outside the Manor House
Hotel. The coachman is William
Mitchell, Mrs King's coachman

160. Sandgate Lodge in George John Gibson's time

161. Sandgate after rebuilding

62. Mrs Felton who owned Sandgate, with Mrs Rooth, John Rooth her great-nephew and Miss Cook the governess, 1913

163. Canon Henry Palmer

64. Sussexdown

165. The Chantry in the 1920s

166. Capt. J. R. Abbey and Lady Ursula Abbey at their daughter's christening
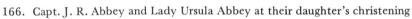

167. Ron (Peter) Greenfield driving a hayturner. Behind him is 'The Bothy' which housed the electrical plant for Greyfriars House. Greyfriars Farm is at the top of the lane

168. Greyfriars, 1925

169. Gerston, 1914
170. George and Florence Trotter

171. Paul Hardy's pen-and-ink drawing in Mrs
      Trotter's visitor's book, 1916

HER BIRTHDAY.

Paul Hardy/Oct 31 1916

172. Laura Charman, house-
maid at Gerston
173. Mr Charman, gardener at
Gerston. Laura and Billy
(plate 128) were his
children

174. Staff at the Abbey
Back row, l. to r.: Horace Packham,
George Searle — *Middle row, l. to r.:*
Mr Charman, Mr Miller, Gabriel
Soffe (gardeners). Mark the footman
in front

175. The Abbey in 1922

176. Reproduction Burmese teak doors in Brown's Lane

177. Alice and Mary Trotter in the Abbey, about 1902

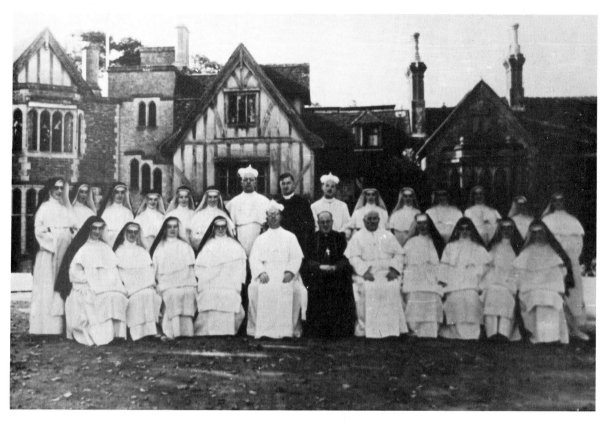

178. The official opening of St Joseph's Convent at the Abbey, 18 September 1953

179. Heath Common, drawn by James Lever

180. The first tractor on Abbey Farm, 1920s

181. Mr J. Norgate at The Abbey, with decorated cart for the 1935 Silver Jubilee

182. Farming at The Abbey, 1936

183. High Street frontage of Bine Farm, between the *Half Moon* and School Hill

184. Fordson type 'F' tractor driven by H. W. D. Tingley in the Mill Field, Hurston Place

185. Lower Hurston Farmhouse

186. Harvesting on Lower Hurston Farm

187. 'Duke' takes a well-earned drink — Lower
Hurston Farm

188. Sullington Farm

189. The date of this picture is uncertain, but the Village
Hall was built in 1894. There is no sign of it here.

Gathering places,
sacred and secular

190. The Village Hall in the mid 1920s with the sign
'Picture Theatre' outside. Mr Pearson, Bill Carn,
Mr Barratt who ran the first cinema and Phil Cripps,
landlord of *The Crown* after the Second World War

191. Cootham Mission Hall

192. Inside the Methodist church

3 . TAPS, KNOBS AND SWITCHES

Gas — Electricity — Water — Sewage

Gas

GAS IS STORRINGTON'S oldest mains service. People who have lived here for longer than 10 years will remember a landmark that has since vanished: two large gas-holders which stood between the White Horse Yard and the Duncton Quarrying Co. property (plate 33). They will also recall a smell of rotten eggs which often pervaded the village.

The Storrington Gas Co. was the earliest gas works here, started in the early 1860s. On 31 October 1861, the *West Sussex Gazette* claimed that Storrington was the 'smallest town lighted by gas in the country. This happy result was brought about by the enterprise of a few of our leading tradesmen, headed by our respected townsman, Arthur Mant Esq., . . . forming a small company for the purpose of erecting a gas-works. . . . Saturday evening last presented our shops and houses illuminated in a way that has forever put the old lamps and candles, not only figuratively, but literally into the shade'. The first secretary of the company for many years was Mr 'Jimmy' Hammond. He was succeeded by Mr Percy Ayling, until the original company collapsed in 1918. Charles Mant, the remaining member of the founding family, received £18 for his block of shares.

In 1871, the parish church was filled with people for the first gaslit service. It was installed, together with gas heating for the winter, for £59 10s. 7d., subscribed by 50 of the parishioners. In 1876, when the church underwent extensive alterations, Edwin Hammond, manager, wrote to Rev. G. Faithfull as follows:

> 'Storrington.
> Dec 1876.
>
> The Revd Geo Faithfull,
> Sir
> 'To lighting and extinguishing the Gas inside and outside of the church. As the New Year is fast approaching and only 2 more evening services in the old I think the time is at hand when I should come to some definite understanding as regards the lighting throughout the year 1877.
> I have done the lighting at the school [in use whilst the church could not be used] and the church since the opening. The expence I strike off entirely — but before entering on the New Year I should like some final arrangement with whom it may concern. To light and put out the gas, clean the lamps find lights and oil etc. for one year including Lent and Advent and taking all weathers into consideration I think it is worth £6 6s. 0d. The lighting I will carry on as usual till the 31 December 1876. I am yrs obty
>
> Edwin Hammond'.

Gas was the first means of street lighting in the village, and although most of the old cast-iron gas-lamp standards were removed to be broken up or sold, one or two old standards have survived in their original positions.

Gas lamps, of course, were an inviting target for vandalism — interference with public property is no new thing! The lights were extinguished, shot at, used as catapult targets to such a degree that there were actually Inspectors of Lighting in Storrington in the 1880s. The Storrington Prosecuting Society published posters offering rewards for information leading to the conviction of offenders — £1 1s. 0d., £5 5s. 0d., and even £10 10s. 0d. on one occasion (fig. 7). This was a large sum of money, far in excess of a week's wages, giving some indication of the severity of the nuisance. Such were Storrington's 'good old days'.

ONE GUINEA
REWARD.

WHEREAS between the hours of 8 and 11 in the Evening of Thursday, the 16th March, some person or persons did damage the Gas Lamp, Lamp Iron, and Lamp Post situate in The Square, Storrington, whereby each person is liable on conviction to a Penalty not exceeding Forty Shillings for each offence, in addition to the damage, or in the discretion of the Justice before whom he is convicted may be committed to prison for a term not exceeding fourteen days.

NOTICE IS HEREBY GIVEN that any Person giving such information as may lead to the Conviction of the Offender or Offenders, shall receive the above Reward of ONE GUINEA, to be paid on conviction.

GEO. FRENCH MANT,

On behalf of the Inspectors of Lighting of the
Parish of Storrington.

Storrington,
17th March, 1882.

FRENCH, Machine Printer, South Street, Worthing

Figure 7

Storrington's old gas-works employed a chemist, Jack Willmott, who travelled between Storrington, Petworth and Billingshurst gas-works, four stokers, a fitter, a yardman, works foreman (still living in the White Horse Yard cottage), and office staff of two or three people, and Mr Thorne the manager. Most of the Storrington staff came here after the Second World War, having served in the forces.

In 1937, the Storrington Gas Co. became the British Gas Light Co. The organisation bought the works, two cottages and the site for £11,939 11s. 7d. Gas made on this site supplied Cootham, Crescent Rise, Thakeham, and the Worthing Road. The British Gas Light Co. was nationalised in May 1948 and became the South Eastern Gas Board (fig. 8). On 10 November 1958, the Engineer of the Sussex Division wrote the following letter to the Storrington works: 'CESSATION OF GASMAKING AT STORRINGTON Further to my memorandum dated 10th Oct. 1958 will you please note that gasmaking at Storrington ceased at 11.30 a.m. today 10th November. Storrington will now receive a bulk gas supply from Portslade works'.

The Estate Officer of the S.E.G.B. wrote to the Sussex Division Engineer on 16 January 1962: 'LAND FORMING PART OF STORRINGTON WORKS I have been advised by the Board's solicitor that the sale of land at the rear of Duncton Quarrying Co.'s premises was completed on Jan. 1st 1962. I recall that you may have some making good to carry out after the purchasers have erected the new boundary wall'. This land was sold to the Hanover Housing Association for flats.

In August 1970 Storrington was converted to natural gas. Pipes were laid diagonally across the hill and fields from Sullington by a route that still shows as plainly as a foot-path in aerial views through the crops. The cross-country route terminates at a pressure-reducing station in Greyfriars Lane (plate 34). The author can remember seeing the work in progress, looking like a wide chalk road, rising and falling over the Downs for miles. The actual conversion took three weeks with a radio communication point in Greyfriars Lane to keep the units in contact. The change-over from town gas to natural gas was achieved in one day — quite a feat of planning and engineering.

Electricity

'How many minor towns and villages can boast of the possession of electric lighting? Steyning has just inaugurated a system, brought into operation by a local company; but news of something still more significant reaches us from the essentially rural parish of Sullington, only a few miles distant.' *Worthing Gazette* 12 October 1921.

The *Gazette* was describing the installation of a private electricity plant at Chantry Mill, the idea of Mr B. J. Hecks, son of Mr A. G. Hecks who owned Manor Farm and the watermill at Chantry. Advised and assisted by Mr F. R Cripps, a consulting engineer from Worthing, Bernard Hecks removed the old water-wheel and installed a 10-horsepower turbine which used 10 tons of water a minute to generate a full load.

The current was carried by means of overhead aluminium wires (to reduce weight) on poles and trees to Sullington Manor Farm. He supplied nine lights to Sullington church, a total illumination of 370 candlepower, utilising the existing oil-lamps. Soon the farm itself was 'all-electric' with vacuum milking pumps — 'a process which it is believed is not to be seen in operation anywhere else in the country', according to a *Gazette* reporter — and electric light in the lambing yards.

In 1922 the Parish Council of Storrington were discussing public lighting for the winter. The Gas Company offered to light 20 or 30 lamps for between £50 and £60; an electrical installation would cost £130 for the first year. The sale of lamp posts would yield £40 to £60, so about £70 would have to be raised from the rates. The enterprising Mr Hecks installed a 30 candlepower electric lamp outside the Hall for the evening, and explained that they could have 20 candlepower lamps if they wished, to reduce the cost by one-third. He also offered 30 lamps for the quoted figure, to cover a larger area and taking in two roads not previously lighted. Mr Rhoden asked for assurance that 'supply would be of a permanent character' and was told that 'there was no chance of the light going out'.

The Parish Council also faced an additional Rate for extensions to the Water Works and anything from £100 to £1,000 was anticipated. Only four people in the well-attended public meeting were in favour of public lighting, and so many against it that 'it was not deemed necessary to count them'. The Chairman concluded, 'I think we all hope that electricity will make its way here, whether by public lighting or not; I think it has come to stay'.

It certainly attracted the interest of some householders and shopkeepers and Mr Hecks was asked to supply them. Miss Queenie Hecks remembered many stormy nights when she and her brother had to come home rather hurriedly from parties and concerts in Worthing because wires had blown down. On one occasion, she and her brother clambered about the Mill pond in fancy-dress to repair broken wires! By 1928 they had brought the electricity supply to Storrington church, but the shaky installations in the village tempted local boys to 'darken the lightness' by shaking the poles carrying the wires. One pole in Brewer's Yard could be shaken with the gratifying result that the Co-op was plunged into darkness! Large houses such as Parham House often had a private generator (page 97).

In the early 1930s the Steyning Electricity Co. extended their service to Washington, and soon Storrington had a reliable public supply with the energising of the White Horse Yard sub-station in 1931.

The author has two old electricity accounts for a shop in Church Street, dated 1940 and 1941, from Central Sussex Electricity Ltd. at Haywards Heath. This company had absorbed Burgess Hill Electricity Ltd., Steyning Electricity Ltd., Seaford and Newhaven Electricity Ltd., and the Uckfield Gas and Electricity Co. The quarter's bill ending September 1940 showed that 70 units of lighting had been charged at 8d. per unit, 1,418

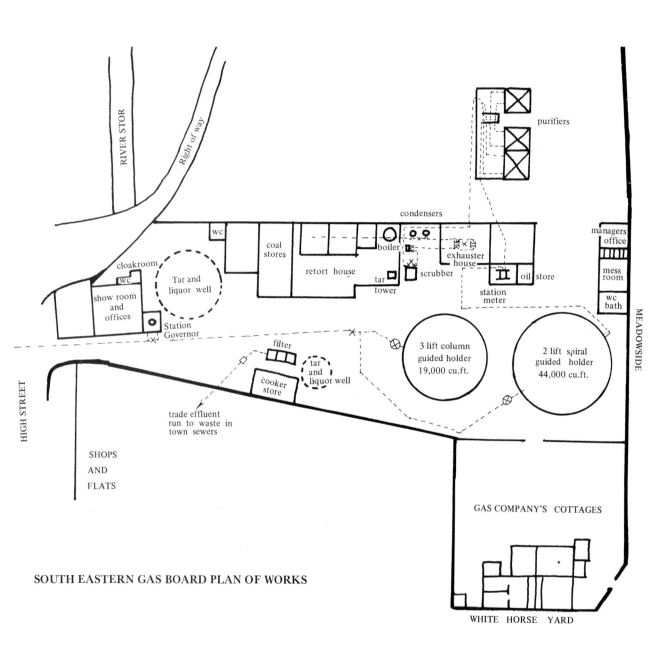

SOUTH EASTERN GAS BOARD PLAN OF WORKS

Figure 8

Industrial power and heating units at 1.65d. per unit plus a meter rent of 2s. 0d. — total £12 3s. 8d. In the winter quarter of 1941 ending 31 March, 105 lighting units and 502 Industrial power units (now increased to 2d. per unit) and the meter rent cost £7 15s. 8d. A special note asked, in view of 'present control of paper', that if the remittance was paid in person and not through the post the enclosed envelope should be handed back to the cashier. This was wartime, when domestic electricity supplies were frequently cut to give industry priority. Greenfields installed a petrol generator to give temporary lighting and refrigeration.

In 1947 electricity was nationalised — it was now too large an undertaking for private capital. Many rural areas such as Storrington were still supplied by overhead cables which were unsightly and the source of much trouble. In 1954, 400 volt overhead cables ran from the pole outside Leatherware passing within a few feet of the author's top window. One particularly stormy night, these cables provided a spectacular firework display, which we did not stay at the window to watch!

As recently as the beginning of the Second World War Hurston Farm Cottages were still without electricity; Mr Knight, of Ham & Knight Ltd., grew up with paraffin lamps at home. He remembers a tractor being hitched to a dynamo once or twice a week to charge cells which produced 60 volt electric lighting for the farmhouse. Mains electricity arrived at the farm in 1957, by which time such installations qualified for a government grant. One of the author's early introductions to rural living was the weekly collection of accumulators brought in for recharging, so that people could listen to the wireless. The small portable 'all-dry' radios finally finished this messy and unpleasant job.

During the Second World War, hundreds of accumulators were charged at R. Vine's shop for Canadian soldiers stationed here. As late as 1958 a customer living seven miles away asked if an accumulator could be charged and delivered to his home every week. The journey included crossing a field on foot, but he was prepared to pay 9d. for the service, he said. He was told that accumulators were no longer charged at the shop, but further questioning revealed that he had, in fact, an electricity supply and he bought a new mains radio. When it was delivered for installation, he was asked where his point was, and said, 'Is that it?' There, sure enough, was a point, with a plug in it 'to stop the electricity coming out'. Many people unused to electricity thought it necessary to keep a plug in the socket for this purpose.

In 1975, SEEBOARD received a European Architectural Heritage Year Award, when it rid the High Street and Church Street of their ugly maze of overhead cables. Three-quarters of a mile of overhead cable and 27 poles vanished during the summer, when the Board invested £8,500 to put the cables underground.

Water

Although today we take tap-water for granted, many people remember drawing water from wells in their gardens, which were tested by the Clerk of the Council and Health Inspector to the Chanctonbury R.D.C. Mr Albert Charman, born in Newtown Road, remembers that the well in front of the cottages which served them all was full of frogs. The boys used to fill a bucket for the old lady in the end cottage, catching as many frogs as possible, leave the bucket in her kitchen and run off, knowing how much she hated frogs! Later, one stand pipe served the same cottages, until the 1930s when piped water was laid on.

In the 1890s, the Inspector found that only 47 out of 163 houses were supplied with sufficient clean water. Thirty-three houses shared eight wells with scanty water, and 51 houses were supplied by 25 wells with discoloured water. Ten houses had six wells with water not fit to drink, three wells supplying 11 houses had contaminated water and three more supplying 11 houses had run dry.

In 1910, a well was bored by Duke and Ockenden for Mr Trotter's new house (pages 105-106), and the water was 73 feet down. The *White Horse* Hotel in the village centre, which is lower, had its water level only 16 feet down, and the school well yielded faintly yellow water, but improvements were only a few years away.

An indenture, 12 April 1915, describes the sale of a plot of land (fig. 9) to the

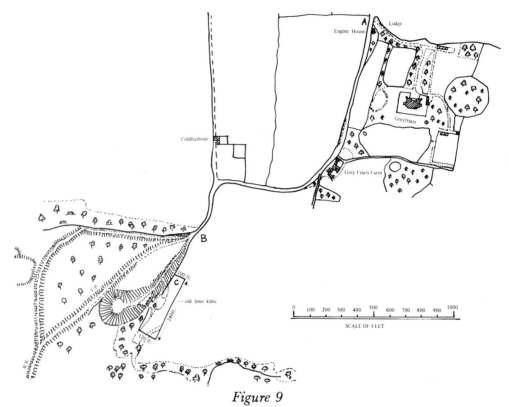

Figure 9

Thakeham R.D.C. by the Rt. Hon. Darea, Baroness Zouche of Haryingworth, of Parham Park, for the sum of £15, 'for the purpose of constructing a borehole, reservoir and other works for supplying the Parish of Storrington with water . . .'. The land is described as

'all that piece or parcel of land (with four large trees and under growth thereon) measuring in length from north-east to south-west one hundred and twenty feet or thereabouts bounded on all sides by other land of the vendor and which said piece of land is identified by four boundary stones fixed at the corners thereof . . .'

The deed also allowed all who had right of access

'either with or without horses, cattle carts or carriages laden or unladen to use the road to the area together with the right or easement of constructing placing or laying, maintaining a line of pipes in and under the said road or way for carrying and conducting water from the said waterworks, with such valves surface boxes and other apparatus as may be necessary . . .'.

The purchasers were also permitted to

'open up the soil thereof for the purpose of inspecting, maintaining, cleansing, repairing or enlarging the said pipes and apparatus doing as little damage as the circumstances permit and restoring the surface as soon as possible thereafter . . . and the purchasers hereby covenant with the vendor, her heirs and assigns that the purchasers will execute such repairs from time to time to the high-

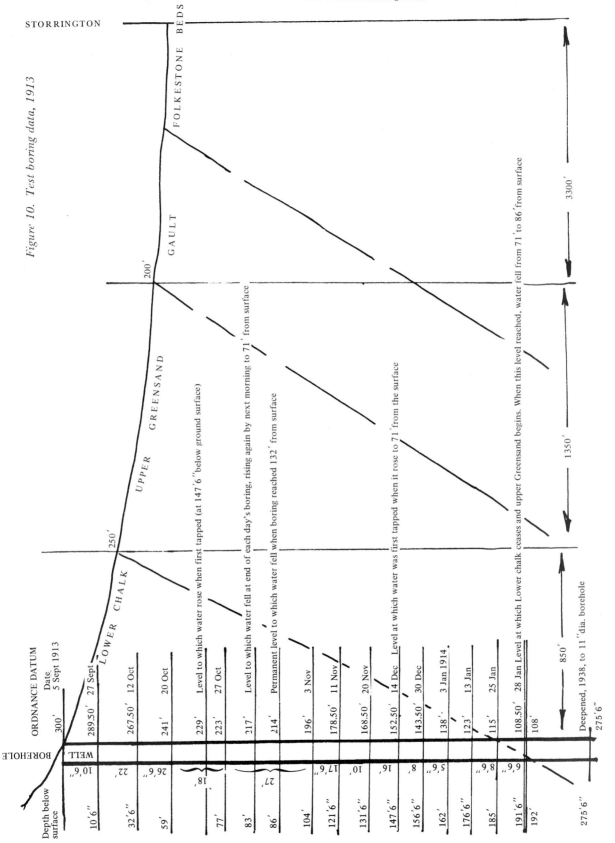

Figure 10. Test boring data, 1913

way . . . between point A opposite the entrance to Greyfriars and point B on the said plan as may be necessary by reason of the traffic put upon the said highway by them . . .'.

In 1913, test boring produced the data in fig. 10. The engineers and their drilling rig (plate 84) are seen in Coldharbour with the temporary engine shelter in front of a collapsed limekiln. Coldharbour is 300 feet above sea level, the level where many springs emerge along the Downs. An artesian borehole, producing water continuously because of natural pressure could deliver 75,000 gallons per day and it was planned to supply the village up to 260 feet above sea level. Thakeham R.D.C. built a covered service reservoir, with a 6 inch pipe from the pumps and a 4 inch main to the village. By 1916, Storrington had mains water, but the present mains are thought to date from 1933 when a new scheme was installed by local men and unemployed Welshmen, who came for work and settled here. An additional borehole was drilled at Coldharbour in 1925, but the power was found to be insufficient to raise water to Sullington Warren.

Thakeham R.D.C. was abolished in 1930, and Chanctonbury R.D.C. assumed responsibility for the water supply. During World War II, Storrington's mains were extended and in 1941 two new boreholes were sunk at Smock Alley through the lower greensand at 92 feet above sea level to a depth of 274 feet. In 1953 Coldharbour became the property of the North West Sussex Joint Water Board, and in 1958 the old pumping station was demolished. The North West Sussex Joint Water Board became the North West Sussex Water Board in 1959, to be replaced by the Southern Water Authority when the industry was restructured in 1974. Two years later an amalgamation of the Authority's North West Sussex Water Division and its West Sussex Drainage Division formed the present West Sussex Water and Drainage Division of the Southern Water Authority. The story of water is a continuous cycle; sewage is cleaned and water recycled after use.

Plate 41 shows sections of old wooden water mains, recovered locally. Very early supplies of piped water were laid on, not primarily for domestic use but for fire-fighting. The fire brigade of the day would turn out to a

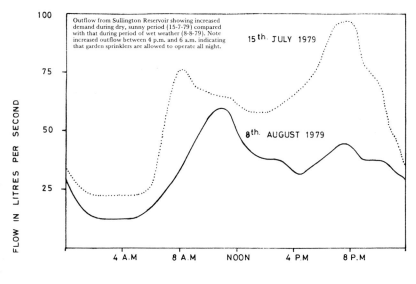

Figure 11

fire, and if the property in trouble displayed a sign outside that it was insured against fire, the firemen would dig down to the wooden main, drill into it and fit their equipment. Afterwards, a wooden plug was fitted to the hole. If the unfortunate property did not have the requisite insurance, the brigade stood and watched the conflagration and the efforts of the local bucket chain to extinguish it. As things got out of hand, the firemen offered insurance at inflated rates, which increased the longer the delay in employing them. It was not unknown for rival brigades to fight over a client!

Sewage

People who lived in Storrington before the Second World War will remember that one service which arrived 'within living memory' was mains drainage. They recall coming home from dances and entertainment late at night and meeting Storrington's 'midnight violets' or 'midnight mail'. In those days, most people's sanitary arrangements were simple earth closets or cesspits, which council employees emptied at night. Mr Rewell, a real village character who lived in a cottage next to Thakeham workhouse (now the site of Rydon School), and his assistant Fred Hearn from Cootham did this unsavoury task in the Storrington area. Fred Hearn cycled from his home to Thakeham and back twice daily, beginning work at 9 p.m. and working until 4 a.m. when he went home for a break and then starting another shift from 1 p.m. until 5 p.m. when household refuse was carted away to Water Lane or Cinerator Lane for burning. The longer night shift was for emptying nightsoil from the village into a cart and taking it away and burying it. Mrs Hearn remembered the time when Mr Rewell lowered a lantern into a cesspit to see what he was doing and the accumulation of gas down there roared into flame and burnt off his long white beard and eyebrows. Mrs Hearn had the presence of mind to cover the afflicted area with vaseline, and thanks to her timely remedy, Mr Rewell's face healed without a mark.

Mr Rewell brought his horse-drawn 'tumbril' to empty cesspits when requested. One resident remembered the horse and cart being drawn up under his bedroom window, where the horse stamped all night with impatience at his long stand. Mr Rewell would lower a longhandled deep ladle into a cesspit to empty it — a job taking the best part of the night and three or more journeys. The horse, despite its unpleasant job, was a beauty which Mr Rewell kept in tip-top condition and its coat really shone, as many people testify.

The village school at this time had no hot water, only two basins and cold taps for the whole school of over 200 children. Their lavatories were outside, nothing more sophisticated than buckets which froze solid in winter. Twice a week, Mr Rewell and his horse and cart called at the school, and he slopped the very full buckets across the playground to empty them into the cart. Mr C. R. Waller, headmaster, managed to get eight flush lavatories and main drainage laid on as soon as it became available.

On 18 April 1934 an enquiry was held under the inspector, Mr F. G. Hill, with the object of compulsorily acquiring land and to sanction the borrowing of £16,000 for sewage works and disposal. The case for the council began with an account of the drainage system which was hair-raising to read. No-one knew the origin of Storrington's drains, although they were confidently dated before 1894 and the birth of the District Councils. Old brick barrel drains served the village centre (plate 43), Church street, West Street, High Street, and School Hill. Originally intended only to carry away surface water, they had gradually become foul sewers and the public water supply of 1916 had vastly increased the volume carried by the old drains. Most of them discharged raw sewage into the open river Stor opposite the Gas Works, which was then carried 200 yards to the Mill Pond, justifiably described by the Council official as 'one huge settling tank or cesspool'. Only the continual flow of fresh water from the source of the Stor, along the stream and into the Mill Pond enabled the system to continue for so long; in effect, the sewage draining into the river had a large natural flushing tank. The West Street drain was not continuous, but had a break near the Comrades' hut and another drain delivered sewage through a filter into a ditch opposite the village pond. This wandered through meadows, joining the Stor at Spierbridge. The Council regularly cleaned the ditch near the filter, but it was only a minor alleviation of an unwholesome system.

Some School Hill house drains emptied into a ditch which joined the Stor between the

Gas Works and the Mill Pond; others emptied into a High Street drain discharging into the Stor. 'The drains generally in School Hill are unsatisfactory' the Council reported with masterly understatement, 'and it is proposed to replace them with new sewers'. Added to this burden of pollution, there were a number of direct connections to the stream!

The Mill Pond effluent, carried by our little river, meandered 'within a few yards of Fryern House' according to the report, through Hurston Street and Hurston Place Farms to join the Chilt at Wickford Bridge, draining the old 'Wickfield Levels'.

This was the drainage system of the 'built up' area of Storrington. Mr Alfred Ham, father of Ron Ham, remembers coming to Storrington on behalf of his firm, J. Dillistone of Worthing. They were employed to paint the old chapel beside the stream opposite the Gas Works on a site now grassed over. This awkward job meant standing their ladders in the stream to reach the roof. The weather was hot, and Mr Ham felt quite ill from the stench. Knowing sewage entered the stream at that point, it is hardly surprising! The Council, with these unsavoury facts to hand, consulted engineers, Messrs Howard Humphreys & Sons, who prepared a complete scheme for main drainage for all of Storrington, Cootham and the west of the parish. It was estimated that the scheme would cost £30,000, and the Council felt that the special rate of over 4s. in the pound was an intolerable burden which ratepayers could not be expected to bear.

The engineers were given new instructions to discontinue the pollution and provide a maximum number of new sewers at a minimum cost. A sewer plan was produced using the old brick sewers and connecting them to a main sewer east of the Stor. Branches to serve various roads and areas all joined this main sewer at appropriate places, and the main sewer followed roughly the course of the Stor west of the Mill Pond, across two fields of Hurston Street Farm to where nearly six acres of land would be acquired to build an outfall works. The works would operate by gravitation making pumping machinery unnecessary. Cost was very much in mind as the ratepayers would have to foot the bill! The scheme as outlined would cost £16,000. The report noted wryly that there is no likelihood of contributions from the owners of property!

Storrington went on main drainage in 1935, the work being done by the firm of H. J. Paris and the original drainage scheme and works were constructed by 1936–37. In March 1957, the Council sent the Minister reports about additions and improvements to the system, including the provision of main drainage to Cootham, Warren Hamlet, Warren Slip, Thakeham etc. and additions to the works in Hurston Lane.

Warren Hamlet, 64 houses and 14 prefabs were drained to three small treatment works which discharged a common effluent into the stream in Water Lane. There was also the new school, Rydon, to consider and parts of Thakeham. These three treatment works were to be abandoned and a pumping station built to deliver sewage straight from the school and Thakeham into a new main sewer draining to the works. Warren Slip's small pumping station delivered to another at Windmill Copse, so this could be abandoned and a direct connection made to a new sewer crossing the fields to Fryern Road and Hurston Lane. New sewers were proposed for Worthing Road, Thakeham Road, Mill Lane and Fryern Road, which would join up with the Thakeham, Warren Hamlet and Warren Slip sewers in the new outfall south of Fryern House and the works.

All of Cootham had cesspools except the council houses at the north end of New Town Road which had sewers into a tank. This discharged its effluent over the land. A simple system was proposed of 6 inch sewers gravitating to a pumping station, where it would be lifted to a new sewer behind Hurston Lane. The Council house sewers would be connected to the new system and the tank demolished. The authorities assumed that the population of Cootham would eventually be 500, and the new Storrington works took this figure into account.

An eventual population of 1,740 persons was estimated for the works built in 1937, at 20 gallons per head per day. By 1957, with a rise to 1,974 persons, it was observed that the flow had more than doubled in dry weather alone and the works were obviously inadequate; site operation and maintenance had become so difficult that the area was saturated with sewage.

New plans for the works calculated a population growth over the next three years from 1,974 to 4,725 including the new areas and the school, with an estimated sewage production of 184,375 gallons per day in dry weather, an increase of almost 100,000 gallons per day. And so the gentle giant in Hurston Lane came into being — a treatment plant that works hand in glove with nature and uses no energy except its own. Hurston is one of the last open sewage works left, and the whole site is managed and maintained by two men: Frank Adsett with 15 years' service and John Hearn with 10 years' servce at the works.

The extended Hurston works were designed to cope with a dry weather flow of 296,500 gallons per day. In 1971-72 an investigation was carried out into the main drainage of Heath Common. This area lies between Storrington and Ashington works, both of which in 1971 were working very close to capacity. Both plants had also been designed to accept enlargements, but neither could cope with the Heath Common needs alone, so it was decided to share the area between them.

The report anticipated that by 1981, the Storrington area would have a population of 6,000 persons, 5,440 in Storrington and 1,160 in Heath Common, allowing 2.7 persons per dwelling. The Heath Common area, bounded by Hampers Lane on its eastern side, would drain westerly by gravity and be connected to the Storrington sewer at the Rock Road-Hillside Walk junction for treatment at the Hurston works. The capital cost was estimated at £15,000, plus £28,000 for extensions to the treatment works. The works layout would be completed using the available land to the best advantage. The authorities at the time of the 1971 report thought that the figures given would be the maximum growth for the area.

In the report of 1934, water consumption per person had been estimated at 30 gallons per day. Now, the figure is 50 gallons per head per day, indicating the extent of the sewage disposal problem. As the authorities put it, 'When it comes to spending money on things like sewage disposal, no one wants to know. It is always swept under the carpet'.

4. EMERGENCY AND OTHER SERVICES

Post Office — Telephone — Police — Fire Service

Post Office

IN 1857, THE FIRST TELEGRAM was handled by Storrington's Post Office, going from the Ship Street, Brighton, office to Mr George French Mant, solicitor. The present Post Office has this telegram and kindly allowed me to photograph it (plate 49). The first telegraph boys were Mr Skinner and Mr Arthur Chapman. Mr Tom Atfield of Pulborough was the mail-van driver, and his last collecting-box was an old wooden one near Wiggonholt church. Storrington was transferred from Petworth to Worthing in 1953, and since 2 October 1978 our mail has been distributed from the mechanical sorting office at Redhill.

The earliest recorded Post Office was built by William Battcock (receiver) in West Street, now Cullen's warehouse. By the 1850s it had moved to a little office next to Poland's and in the 1920s John Joyes wrote, 'John Battcock kept the Post Office which was where Mr Penn's shop now is [*see* page 49]. He had two daughters, Mary Ann who did the office work, and Sarah who was deaf and dumb delivered all the letters at that time: a good many living in the outlying places had to fetch their own letters. Hurstpierpoint was then the Post Town for Storrington, they came through Steyning and were then brought from there by dogs, until the time that the use of dogs was prohibited, which I think was about seventy years ago. After that a man used to push a truck to Steyning and back — that I well remember'.

The Post Office moved to Church Street in 1875, to the shop of E. W. Hammond (Now Carina Hair Fashions). His daughter ran the office, and a directory entry of the time states: 'POST, MONEY & TELEGRAPH OFFICE — Postmaster Edward Hammond. Letters from Pulborough arrive at 7 a.m.–12.30 noon. Sundays 7 a.m. Despatched 10.20 a.m. and 6.30 p.m. Sundays 10.30 a.m.'.

At the turn of the century, the Post Office moved to Georgian House (plate 49) and in 1929 Storrington Post Office moved to the back of Ivens, Kelletts & Childs in High Street (plate 47), now Rosemarie. People went through the shop and up three steps to the cramped Post Office counter.

In 1952 the authorities bought Mr Mant's house, 'The Dawes', in West Street and its grounds for £4,759 0s. 0d. This building was featured in the daily newspapers in 1958, when the Postmaster General wrote to Capt. Henry Kerby, admitting that the building should have been pulled down when it was bought, 'but that is being wise after the event'. 'The Dawes' was very dilapidated and proved very expensive. £2,600 was spent in adapting it for use as a Post Office, with subsequent maintenance costs and £6,000 for a new garage. There was a very bad fire which started in a large central cupboard spreading rapidly through the house and roof. Storrington Fire Brigade, together with the brigades from Worthing and Findon, did fine work in saving the property, but water seriously weakened the old structure. It was not long before staff had to abandon most of the rooms, owing to falling ceilings and rotting beams. A visiting Post Office official went into a room normally kept locked and his foot went straight through the ceiling, showering plaster and nearly himself on an elderly customer at the counter. A new public counter had to be installed elsewhere in a heavily-shored-up room. A prominent

'Mind the Step' sign warned customers what to expect. There was a steep flight of steps to reach the counter. A further £2,500 was spent in converting the new garage into a temporary Post Office whilst a new building was erected.

The Postmaster-General claimed that the authorities were right to buy 'The Dawes' as the price was reasonable and they were desperately short of office space, but 'The Dawes' should have been demolished at once and a new building erected. The new purpose-built Post Office was in service by 1964 and became a Crown Post Office. It employed four clerks, 13 postmen, a postmaster, and had a fleet of seven vans.

Outlying districts had small Post Offices at one time. There was one at Cootham Common, where the 'receiver' was Mrs Laker. Later, Mr Mustow ran the office next to Flansham Cottage, until it moved to a building next to the Mission Hall. Mr Walker, postal historian and author of *The Postal History of Sussex*, has two postcards dated 1917 and 1924, handstamped COOTHAM.

In 1904, Thakeham had a sub Post Office, the letters coming through Pulborough. It was a delightful Post Office–General Stores in a grade II scheduled cottage — an inside wall is dated 1658. In 1904 the grocer, Mr Samuel Evernden, was its sub-postmaster. The longest serving one was Mr 'Jack' Skinner, who took over in 1925 and retired 50 years later. The early telephone stood on the counter and a metal plate outside informed people that calls could be made from the Post Office. Callers asked the postmaster for the number they wanted and he got it for them, entering it in an official book and collecting the charge. If it was not local, he asked the exchange how much to collect. In the early 1930s, the Post Office installed a public telephone kiosk outside, but in the past 10 years this has been moved to one side.

Mr Skinner served in the Far East during the Second World War, and his wife ran the Post Office and general stores. Whilst in a small town in India, he wanted to send a telegram home. The telegraph office was in the railway station, and the Indian clerk noted the address, 'Thakeham, Pulborough' and was told that the telephone number was a West Chiltington one. There was obvious doubt in the clerk's mind, despite assurance that it was correct. Reaching under the counter, he produced a British Post Office Guide (in that remote outpost of the Empire!) to check that Thakeham, Pulborough really had a West Chiltington telephone number.

After the war, it became necessary to have extensive roof repairs done, and Duke's of Steyning were called in. The front of the building was plastered over, and this was bulging and clearly in a bad state, so Mr Skinner asked the contractors to strip it off. This revealed the lovely old beams which are now such an attractive feature, and a small window. At one time, the staircase had risen just inside the front door and was lit by the hidden window. Extensions built at the back at a later date included a new staircase.

The post-box was emptied twice daily and once on Sunday at 3 p.m. by the postmaster, who date-stamped each letter by hand and set aside the local ones. These were handed separately to the postman when he came from Pulborough to collect them, and he delivered them as he went on his way, emptying boxes on the Storrington route. When Worthing became a General Post Office, this was no longer done. During Mr Skinner's long service in Thakeham, many changes took place in Post Office business. Letters first went for 1d., increasing by degrees to 1½d., 2d., and 2½d. over the years. The single biggest revolution in Post Office business was the introduction of Giro.

Early business included the sale of stamps and postal orders, payment of old age pensions (10s.), sale of broadcast receiving licences, and dog and gun licences. The dog licence (7s. 6d.) was renewable every February, and gun licences every July. As it had been a family shop, there was no other building in Thakeham suitable for use as a Post Office, so the business was transferred to Storrington.

The old cottage appealed to Mr and Mrs Goldsack from Hove as soon as they saw it, and they liked the idea of opening it up again for business. Mrs Brenda Goldsack opened the traditional village store on 2 January 1980, and in accordance with Post Office practice that section opened the following Monday, 7 January.

Heath Common also had a sub Post Office at various times between 1958 and 1975. Mr Douglas Wright, the grocer, ran it for a year, resigning in August 1959. It was then abandoned until August 1966, when Mr Charles Foster became postmaster. Two years later Mr Maurice Bunting took over until 1973, when he was succeeded by Mr William McKenzie, Heath Common's last sub-postmaster. The office closed in 1975.

The Telephone Service

The beginnings of Storrington's telephone service are not easy to trace. A small paragraph in the *Southern Daily News* of November 1913, states that there was talk 'some time ago' of Storrington being connected to the telephone service. Originally, Storrington should have been connected to the Pulborough exchange, but this was opposed by subscribers who thought they had more links with Worthing. The postal authorities disagreed with them. The Thakeham Guardians did not wait for their decision, but installed a private wire between the Workhouse, the Clerk's Office and the Medical Officer's residence, for the Master, '. . . to obtain assistance more promptly in the case of a refractory pauper or of sudden illness'.

One clue is the telephone pole in 'Rosemary' (plate 52) with its plate DP1, indicating it as the site of the nearest pole to the first exchange. It is post office practice to number poles from the exchange outwards, so the first pole from the exchange would be 'distribution point 1'. Charles Mant remembered the first exchange being in the Church Street Post Office (plate 46) run by Miss Childs, with very few subscribers — 'The Dawes' had number 18, 'The Geddings' was 25. The exchange itself was probably just a switchboard operated by Miss Childs, which Mr Mant thought was opened in 1914. When the Post Office moved from Church Street to the Co-op (plate 47) the exchange moved to the house at the bottom of Manley's Hill, owned by Mr Charman (plate 51).

It consisted of a 4-switchboard manual exchange, installed in the front room of the cottage where the caretaker-operator, Mr Frost, lived; a ringing machine which started slowly when a number rang; the supervisor's desk; a distribution frame where the external cables terminated; and miscellaneous apparatus screwed to the wall over the fireplace. The hallway contained racks of apparatus and batteries. There was a great deal of 'open wire distribution' in the area, such as bare wires through trees, and on stormy nights the operators got little rest because the lines appeared to call every time bare wires touched together!

The public call boxes needed no money to call the operator, and there were no buttons, just a refund chute. The familiar buttons A and B were introduced with the new exchange. The original exchange required batteries at each subscriber's telephone to energise the microphone. These were Leclanché-type cells needing periodic topping-up, which was one of the engineer's routine jobs; the more obliging customers did their own. Later, the exchange was modified to feed transmission current to the telephones. One engineer remembers in the mid-1960s finding one customer still topping up the redundant cells! Space in the exchange was so limited that, working on the distribution frame, the engineer could break the glass fuses behind by turning with less than extreme care. It was a frightening place in a thunderstorm, with lightning flashing across the equipment, but in fact was exceptionally safe because everything was well earthed.

The girls worked in shifts, two working eight hours and others doing morning and evening with several hours off in between. Telephones at the time had no dials. Customers picked up the handset and asked for the number, and because they spoke directly to the operator, one old lady always said, 'Can I speak to Mary?' and the operator put her straight through to her niece who worked in a local office. It was at this time that we came to Storrington and, living over the shop, found it necessary to have incoming calls blocked after shop hours. We were often called by the friendly operator with the query: 'It's your mother, all right if I put her through?' We never needed to remember local numbers either, but could just ask for 'Greenfields' or 'the Council Offices' and be connected without further trouble. 'Storrington 1' was the telephone box which used to stand at the entrance to the Co-op Yard; 'Storrington 2' was Goacher's Nurseries at Rock. When the Ashington exchange came into service, they should have been connected to it, but were permitted to remain with Storrington and keep their distinctive number. To have been routed through Ashington would have given them an unfamiliar three-figure number, but with the coming of the automatic exchange, 'Storrington 2' finally had to go.

In 1940, an underground cable was laid along the Downs from Chantry to Devil's Dyke, and a switchboard was installed at Storrington's fire control station.

One of the operators of the 1950s, Muriel Kent, now officer-in-charge of day staff at Horsham, remembers the happy and friendly old exchange with affection. In the summer when their window was open on to the street, it was not unusual for a customer to look in and report a fault, or hand in a box of chocolates for services rendered. The engineer before the Second World War was Arthur Pope, succeeded by Sid Knight who later became mayor of Worthing. George Gigg and Colin Smith were followed by David Rudram, engineer from 1959–69, who saw the changeover from manual to automatic exchange on 15 June 1960, at 1 p.m. exactly.

By 1958 the old exchange had become very busy indeed with 700 lines. The new exchange was built at the top of School Hill with automatic equipment. The changeover had to be almost instantaneous. All underground cables had been diverted in advance, keeping the old exchange working at the same time. The cables were then 'teed' together in an underground jointing chamber (in a most unorthodox manner) at the corner of School Hill and High Street, at which critical time any fault would have caused chaos, but luck was with them. A short period of no incoming calls to the old exchange was arranged by prior publicity, and it was disconnected by inserting 'wedges' into a break-jack frame. When this was completed, similar wedges were removed from the new exchange. Immediately this became operational, a team of operators made calls to every subscriber to test the lines. Storrington had very few faults. The old exchange pole, DP20, was really at the end of its working life and was in a very bad state. The batteries (to supply the exchange in the event of mains failure) were housed in a shed in the garden.

The new exchange opened with 900 lines. There are now 2,800, and though it has trebled in size, the much extended equipment is again full and awaiting further extension. The building was constructed so as to be extendable upwards whenever this became necessary, and the land next to the fire station has also been acquired for future needs. Alec Bonsall replaced David Rudram in 1969 and, one year later, Bob Bashford became the Storrington engineer.

The impression on entering the exchange is of a vast area, spotlessly clean and smelling of sun-warmed polish. There are large racks of identical equipment, wired with neatness and precision, reducing thousands of wires to order and beauty. There are strange sounds of unattended machinery — chirps, clicks, buzzes and the chatter of metal contacts. It took one year for Ericsson to build, and the exchange serves an area from Rackham to Washington and part of Thakeham, north to West Chiltington, Wiggonholt Common and Redford Cottage. This de-humanised mechanical connection of disembodied voices is all a far cry from the old lady who used to pick up her telephone and ask a sympathetic operator to 'put her through to Mary'.

The Village Policeman

The earliest recorded policemen in this area were listed in the dispositions and numbers of West Sussex Constables 1857, one year after the passing of the County Police Act. Storrington's village Policeman was P.C. (third class) 51, William Tribe, who, in common with constables for many years, had much with which to contend. Storrington had been in the habit of running its own private law enforcement agency, and local worthies did not give up their powers easily. Letters were often written to and by the Chief Constable at Petworth without reference to the village policeman, complaining of probable nuisance by forthcoming Bonfire Night celebrations or complaints against local residents or the constable himself and other small local matters which should have been well within the capabilities of the village policeman. One such letter is a good example of this attitude.

'C. Carew-Gibson,
Sandgate.
Feb. 23 1878

On receipt of your letter, I went over to Thakeham and I saw the pig sty. Most certainly P.C. Oates was very wrong in removing any of the slabs without your leave, and I told him so. He assured me that the floor of the closet was very much out of repair that it was unsafe for him and his wife to go to, and he states that all the slabs he removed at any time were used for the repairs of the floor, and one or two that he placed at the back of the closet on the outside. He expressed to me at the time, great regret, and I have received the enclosed from him this morning. I will remove the man if you wish it, but he has done his duty at Thakeham quite to my satisfaction and I have not, at the present time, any man I could send, there being no accommodation for children in the cottage. I will order the P.C. to pay the value of the slabs he used for the closet if you wish it. In the event of removing P.C. Oates from Thakeham I hope you will allow me to become the tenant of your cottage on behalf of the County as I have been told that no other cottage can be obtained and I think you will agree with me that Thakeham is not a village that should be without a policeman.'

Not surprisingly, the turnover of constables in Storrington was fairly rapid; they often stayed for less than a year. Daniel Ellcombe (1860–62), George Benfort (1864–68) and William Stillaway (1867–85) were three exceptions to the 15 or more constables who served in the first 28 years of the Constabulary. In 1887, constables worked a seven day week. They were not assisted with rent in West Sussex unless it exceeded 3s. per week, and it was not until 1895 that the first police cottage was built at Thakeham. Police housing was appalling as the letter indicates. A constable who started with a good character from another force was paid 2s. 8d. per day, which meant that a labourer was better paid! A policeman earned 15s. 8d. for a seven-day week and a labourer 15s. for six days.

The records are not complete, but our first long-serving and well-remembered policeman appears to have been Percy Connor, P.C. 132, who served in Storrington from October 1923 until 1939, when he retired. He came to a village with no police house or station, although after the First World War a constable's pay had increased to £3 10s. 0d. per week. His home in Amberley Road was rented by the Police Force. He was the first one to move into the new police house when it was built in North Street, and was later joined by a second policeman, P.C. Field. There was, by then, a telephone in the police houses, and 'Storrington 22' reached the local policeman. The P.C.s wife was not allowed to work and must take telephone messages whenever her husband was away from the house. She had to admit the Inspector on demand to inspect the house. Mrs Connor walked miles with messages; once from the Amberley Road to the West Sussex Golf Course at night, and back. She carried tea and food up on the Downs to her husband, when he and others were searching for the man who shot P.C. Jex, another Storrington police constable. This was in 1934 when P.C. Jex disturbed a burglar, described as a 'second Charles Peace', who shot him and escaped. P.C. Jex was taken to Worthing Hospital. Leonard Rowland Hill, the burglar, took to the Downs where he went into hiding, breaking into houses for food, clothing and anything else he could find. He never saw another newspaper, and believed he had killed the policeman.

It was during one of his burglaries that he was disturbed again and the hunt was on. A massive cordon was thrown around a 10-mile radius of the Downs. Mrs Michael Sadlier was staying at a local hotel when she was roused and asked to bring her bloodhounds. The dogs picked up the fresh scent at once and tracked up the hill, through undergrowth and hedges, to within two miles of Myrtle Grove. They cornered Hill, and as the police dashed in to arrest him, a shot rang out. The gun that had wounded P.C. Jex was turned on its owner. Hill was taken to Worthing Hospital, where he died without having spoken, in a bed close to that of P.C. Jex. The policemen taking part in that manhunt were armed.

The routine work of the village policeman was not as exciting, fortunately. P.C. Connor (plate 54) was very much part of village life. His children went to the village school, leaving at 14 and starting work; his elder daughter went to the Chantry as nurse-maid to the Scarisbrick children at £2 per month. Percy Connor was a leading light in the Storrington Horticultural and Handicraft Society, and supported the summer show extensively. A cheese-hater, he won one of the famous Sullington Cheddar Cheeses! He was a great sportsman and won cups for cricket, football and golf, and ran the football club dances.

Percy Connor became a legend in Storrington and people still recall his great patience and his ability to catch villains. He was always about when the pubs closed to see that all was quiet, and if he had an enquiry afoot, he would see the late night bus crews who were often able to give him information. If he was chasing someone, he often called on Mr Peterson of the School Hill Garage, and they would drive about in an old motor-car. George Goring also liked to be called in on a chase. During the General Strikes of 1921 and 1929 he was among the West Sussex policemen drafted to Wales to help keep order.

After the war, he retired from the Force, and collected Council rents and private debts. His patience and knowledge of his area served him very well. Once he sat outside a privy for two hours waiting for a debtor, who had fled there to escape him, to come out. Percy Connor collected his money! He knew which trustworthy people in the village to call on for help, and he was perfectly able to deal with 'roughs' and erring children. At the age of 74, he threw out single-handed some drunken gypsies who had gate-crashed a dance. His ¾-acre garden in Georges Lane was a showpiece that people would come to see. He won the *Amateur Gardening* Bronze Medal in 1948, and the Storrington and District Horticultural and Handicrafts Society award, a silver cup, presented by his daughters in his name, for the best beginner's entry in the annual show.

It sounds strange today that a policeman was obliged to ask a private motorist for transport in emergencies, but his beat was extensive for a constable on foot or bicycle. The police Velocette was not introduced until after the Second World War. The beat included: 'Amberley Road 200 yards west of Paygate-Pulborough Road where River Chilt meets road — Monkmead where Chilt meets road — and again W. Chiltington Road, Smock Alley at junction of Threal's Lane — north to W. Chiltington and Thakeham Road — 200 yards west of Danhill crossroads — continuing N.E. to Blue Idol — then S. crossing Coolham-Thakeham Road to ½ mile south of Coolham crossroads — then S. through Nightingale Farm and easterly crossing Danhill-Ashington B.2133 at Lancing Brook — south to Warminghurst Church — Hampers Lane — Barns Farm Lane and Cobden Farm — west to Lee Farm — north to Amberley Road'.

Police communications — the vital link between a country policeman and his head-quarters — have reflected the changing years. At first, a point on the beat was prearranged where messages could pass from one area to another. Mrs A. E. Cripps saw the policemen meeting at Peacock Tree where she grew up. The children used to chant, 'Heffer, Pullen, Foots and Legg!' Pullen was the Pulborough sergeant, and she thought that Legg came from Thakeham or Washington.

The West Sussex Constabulary was slow in installing the telephone. Perhaps the acquisition of three new and one second-hand bicycle by headquarters in 1897 was considered progress enough. In 1904 principal stations had the telephone and policemen were expected to be at public call boxes at a stipulated time every hour, and to wait for five minutes for headquarters to call them. Between the First and Second World Wars, the telephone was installed in their homes. Mr Edward Post recalls '. . . one thing that was a great benefit at that time was the fact that we had a manually operated Telephone Exchange . . . All these people [the operators] were very good to us. We had to make points at certain times at telephone kiosks around the district . . . Always, if we were late, the operator would ring at intervals to try to contact us — usually to say that the sergeant had rung from Steyning to see if we were at the point. If they could not get us that way, they would ring the house and leave a message thus we could phone in with our excuses before we were queried. There were operational benefits too — I recall one night when the operator rang me to say he was getting a call from Gatley's office and that no-one was answering. I had time to get up, dress and make my way to the scene just in time to catch a man leaving by the office window with the contents of the safe. He never knew how I came to be there at that moment but, in fact, when he climbed in the window, he knocked the receiver off without knowing and this automatically alerted the operator to the number calling and he knew no one should be there at that time of night. We do not get the same service from S.T.D.'.

P.C. Edward Post (plate 55) came to Storrington in 1948, replacing Mr Brockhurst, so sadly killed in a road accident during his retirement. His senior partner was Percy Penfold, who had the motor-cycle, while P.C. Post had a bicycle. When P.C. Penfold was promoted and transferred, P.C. Post had the motor-cycle and his new partner P.C. Middleton inherited the bike. There were just two police houses at that time, one with a very large garden which helped considerably with rations, as they had their own vegetables, chickens and even a pig at times. At Christmas, the Hon. Clive Pearson sent the policemen a quarter of venison, which was very welcome.

They lacked a proper office, causing considerable inconvenience to the policemen's families and sometimes testing their ingenuity. A spate of burglaries occurred throughout a whole winter when P.C. Post was working single-handed. The thief worked on wet and windy nights to cover any noise he made, although there was never any sign of a break-in. One night Mr Post who had been out until 4 a.m., was called by a lady who had seen a man in her bedroom. After interviewing her, he decided that his villain would be likely to head for Spierbridge:

'I raced around as quickly as possible. When I was going back towards the village, I approached the lane that ran beside the greengrocers near the Legion when I saw a dark figure emerge from the lane. This shape (it was little more than that in the dark) raced off like the wind — it had to be the chap I wanted so there was no way he was going to escape from me to give me more sleepless nights so I pounded after him. It was soon obvious that he was wearing only a jersey, trousers and plimsolls, all black, whilst I was in full uniform with a cape and boots. I was about 10 yards behind him when he got to the allotments which were behind the recreation ground and then the going became really hard and I was not gaining on him at all. The sticky mud of the allotments slowed us up and I was almost on the point of collapse when he suddenly stopped and held his side gasping for breath. I could not speak — in fact I could hardly stand so I threw my cape over his head and tucked both under my arm. We stood like that holding on to one another for some minutes sinking into the mud, while the wind blew and the rain poured down. Eventually I was able to walk him back to the house and neither of us uttered a word the whole time.

It must have been one of the strangest arrests ever and it shows the impracticability of the Court ruling that a policeman must inform a person at the time of his arrest why he is being arrested. Having got him home, all I found on him were a pair of gloves and a ring which I suspected came from the burgled house. I phoned for C.I.D. to come (that was going to take at least an hour) and I wanted to reassure the people that all was well at last, and to check over the ground we had covered to see if he had dropped anything. There was no cell at the house and no-one except my wife and daughter asleep upstairs. I improvised by sitting him in a chair in the small office, bent him forward and handcuffed him under the seat by his wrists, then I left him and went out again. I figured that, if he could get off the chair and out of two locked doors, he deserved to go but he was still there when I got back over an hour later. He was not comfortable but was fast asleep which was more than I was!

I found a few more pieces of jewellery where we had struggled . . . Det. Sgt. Arthur Ellis (C.I.D.) arrived later. We went to the man's house about 7.30 a.m. and there we found an Aladdin's cave. It appears that he always went for cash, food, drink and a few odd pieces to give his family but he seemed to take away everything he could carry. Under his bed were piles of property, some quite worthless but including the ration books of the occupiers of the houses he had burgled which helped to clear up some 35–40 offences, some of which he could not remember. It appeared that he toured the same houses every windy night but he only entered those where a window, even a fanlight, had been left insecure. On leaving he closed the window and left by a door with a Yale lock — hence no sign of entry. I knew that more than one householder sacked the cleaning lady on suspicion that she had taken their property — how unfair!

One funny incident out of this amongst others. There was a nice house . . . on the corner of Amberley Road. The occupier . . . kept his whiskey etc. in an old grandfather clock which had no pendulum. I saw him after the second theft of whiskey . . . and we agreed it would be wise to change the place of storage, but he agreed I could lay a trap. I obtained several dummy bottles used for display purposes from Geoffrey Greenfield and I put them in the clock. Needless to say, they disappeared one night, so that did not help much. However, when we were recovering the property from under the culprit's bed, I found all the dummy bottles intact except one which had lost about 2 inches of liquid. I asked him about these and he said, "Did you put that in the clock? That was a rotten trick — I was off work for a week after I had drunk it." The liquid is a vile concoction which does not cloud'.

Mr Post evoked the period immediately after the Second World War with his recollections of additional duties in the late 1940s and early 1950s. Barns Farm Camp was in use as a resettlement camp and hospital for Poles and other nationalities. The village policeman helped with screening and immigration procedures and alien control in the district for the Home Office. There were miscellaneous fire-arms about, thanks to returning servicemen with 'liberated' trophies, abandoned relics of the Canadian 'occupation' of the area and of course, shells, bombs and other nasty relics of pre-invasions training on the Downs. Crime also reflected the times. Mulberry House was the Food Office, and ration books and coupons were valuable loot, causing great embarrassment to the local police when the building 'next door' to the police houses was burgled!

Mr Post was the first constable after the war to be promoted to sergeant when he was put in charge of the Arundel section in 1951. An illustrious career has seen him in Cyprus, as Inspector, Chief Inspector, Assistant Chief Constable of Surrey and Deputy Chief. He was invited in 1975 to become Chief Constable of the Port of Liverpool Police Force, and he formed and commanded that force. This led to an invitation for him to become Security Consultant to the government's Port Authority in Sierra Leone. Edward Post has also been involved with the E.E.C. The possibilities are unlimited for a Storrington village constable!

Senior stations were linked up during the Second World War when radio was introduced, controlled from Chichester. The two big radio masts on Burton Down have existed for over 25 years, relaying police transmissions which today are controlled from the communications centre at the Lewes Headquarters. Police radio, like domestic radio, has followed developments until the idea of radio in a police car is as normal as our own car radios, but once it was a very new piece of police equipment. A vivid description of a car chase and the first use of mobile radio comes from Edward Post and it would not be out of place on the television screen, except that it is all true.

'Sidney Ridge . . . a friend of mine for well over 30 years, telephoned me late one night to say that some lads had broken the glass of his display cabinet outside his shop in the Colonnade. I had only just passed through the village and no-one was about so I went straight back there but there was no sign of anyone. Just then my friend Harry (Joe) Murgatroyd, who was a Traffic Patrol driver based at Steyning, came along in his brand new Riley patrol car which had just been fitted with radio for the first time . . . I thought the lads were from Findon or Worthing and they might take someone's car, which was their favourite transport home after the last bus had gone. We decided to patrol the Washington road in the car to see if we could spot them, which we did for some time without success. Before giving up, we decided to run through Findon to the Worthing boundary — against orders as both were outside our division . . . Just after we had passed the Findon roundabout, a large 3–5 ton Army truck then used by War Ag. came out of the W.A. depot and swung very fast into our path and nearly rammed us. We could see two lads inside so we turned, overtook them and jumped out to stop them. They drove straight at us, with the engine revving very fast and both Joe and I dived gallantly into the ditch. This did not please us at all so we drove after the lorry which had turned into Findon village and defied all our efforts to overtake. Eventually, it took a minor turning which we knew went only as far as rough down-land so we thought we had them trapped. However, they drove straight onto the Downs — terrain for which the lorry was designed but not our patrol car! We kept on its tail across country — easily the roughest high-speed drive I have ever experienced and there was no way in the dark we could tell where we were or in which direction . . . We alerted all other units by radio which I was operating . . . not an easy task when one's head was continually thumping the car roof . . . Joe drove magnificently and never let the lorry get away from him.

We must have driven thus for some 40 minutes . . . and in our headlights, we could see huge clouds of dust, rabbits etc. racing all over the place and showers of sparks flying as the lorry hit stones and boulders. It was not doing the car much good either. I did not realise I was using the radio but I was told later by the Control operator that it sounded like a Wild West Show — it certainly looked like it . . . Eventually we found ourselves on tarmac with lights below us and we recognised the narrow lane that ran down into Steyning where it joined the main road . . . the lorry was completely out of control on the steep hill and increasing to a frightening speed but fortunately at 2 a.m. not many people were walking towards the Downs!

There was a triangular grass island at the junction ahead and . . . houses on the other side of it — there was no way in which the lorry could stop and we envisaged it ploughing into the houses. However, we had forgotten the stout wooden pole on the island which carried electricity cables. The front of the lorry hit this at great speed and reared up. There was a blinding flash and it caught fire . . . Joe went to the passenger door where he pulled one man out and I went to the driver's door. I got it open but the man in there was unconscious and I could not move him. I called Joe and we both tried to pull him out but the lorry was high off the ground and flames were all around us. With much heaving, eventually he came and we managed to smother the flames on him and ourselves with the lorry seat cushions.

We learned later that we had nearly severed his foot which was jammed in the pedals in pulling him out . . . Steyning was in total darkness as the pole carried the main power cable but people came from the houses to help, including a doctor. We all went off to Southlands Hospital but Joe and I were virtually unhurt. In fact we felt quite well until we realised that we had grabbed the metal doors of the lorry before we knew whether it was alive with current or not.

The injured man recovered but was crippled and he stood trial at Worthing a year later. We were highly commended by the Court and later were presented with certificates of the Carnegie Hero Trust Fund by the Chairman of the Steyning Branch. It must have done us some good in spite of the mess we made of the patrol car, as Joe and I were promoted within the year'.

Ted Post's promotion took him to Arundel. He had been a very popular village police-man, and his friends threw a farewell party for him, at which he was presented with a special edition (the *only* edition) of the *Storrington Examiner* (Fig. 12). It was signed inside by many local people.

We remember the snowy February night — our first in Storrington — when we saw late at night P.C. Tom Wright pacing reassuringly along the road with his cape white and his footprints marking his path behind. Now the village policemen (there are four) patrol in a Hillman Avenger, a mobile police station equipped with radio, first aid, resuscitation equipment and other facilities that get them quickly to an incident with all they need to deal with it or to summon assistance. The following list gives some idea of the variety

The Chanctonbury Cornet & Storrington Examiner.

END OF A POST CHAISE

Vol. 7 Nº 1   August 1951   Registered at Stationers Hall as a nuisance paper.

Editorial.

Treetops Storrington.

In an adjoining column we announce the news of Mr. Post's transfer to Arundel; but our real regret at his departure is mollified at the news of his promotion. As we wished to signify our respect and affection, invitations had been sent out to such as had not been arrested, to subscribe towards some token of this general feeling. The response was also general, and, to a certain extent significant, in that subscriptions were received from such Bodies as the Poachers Protection Society; the Downland Distillers and Moonlight Distillers of Sullington Bottom; the Cockfighters and Crown and Anchor Board Amalgamated Union of Heath Common; the Worshipful Company of Practitioners in Night Legerdemain; and Coiners and Stationers Guild. These tributes as well as those from the Westminster Glee and Fiddlers Society have been returned to the senders.

TED POST LEAVING STORRINGTON

Police Constable Post, on his promotion to the rank of Sergeant, is to be transferred to Arundel.

POST POSTED

Boy! Hand me my Jemmy!

and range of duties, that for today's village policemen are 'all in a day's work'. Accidents; assaults; missing persons; fete arrangements, including parking; criminal damage; lost property; traffic cones wanted; loose horses; intruders; collapses; drunks; fake heart attack (a free lift!); domestic accident; empty premises; cows, straying; an unexploded paint tin; abandoned cars; alarms; obscene phone calls; colorado beetle; fires; sheep worrying; bombs; lost property; baby shut in car; a bogus meter reader; court processes executed and so on.

One of the oddest 'arrests' made in Storrington occurred when a double-decker bus drove round North Street, stopped outside the police house and its driver got out and banged on the door of P.C. Goacher's house. It was 11.30 p.m., and the policeman was in bed after a day's duty starting at 5 a.m. He woke up to the throb of the bus engine outside and the driver trying to rouse him. Some troublesome youths were on the bus, refusing to get off and there had been a lot of similar trouble on the late buses. P.C. Goacher pulled a pair of trousers over his pyjamas and went down to sort it out. Most of the youths gave no further trouble, but one took a lot of getting off the bus. This and other offences resulted in an appearance at Steyning Court. P.C. Goacher took a long time to live down the subsequent headlines about his odd 'arrest': 'P.C. in pyjamas reports local youth'.

He also recalls the lively time they had with local lads and fireworks leading up to Bonfire night. On the night of 5 November they were especially vigilant. He and P.C. Bristow were watching from the Square, while the troublemakers were across the road by Stocker's showrooms. At 10.45 p.m. when Mrs Bristow came out to speak to her husband, she went across the road and told the boys 'in no uncertain terms' to go home. To the amazement of the group of policemen (there were extra men because of the bother) they went!

P.C. Ernie Sweeney, AS910 (plate 56) had first-hand experience of the extreme problems the local constable might face. In Jubilee Year (1977) he was stationed at Pulborough, and was out with his family on a free evening. Crowds on Pulborough Recreation Ground were celebrating with fireworks and a bonfire, when he was told of a gang of men who were terrorizing bystanders. He went to see and they came at him with cudgels, planks with nails, and a steel car park chain. P.C. Sweeney disarmed one man and tackled the one wielding the chain. Other off-duty policemen then arrived to help, but one of the gang had the steel chain around Mr Sweeney's neck causing him to lose consciousness. He recovered in the First Aid tent, having been hit around the head, punched and kicked. At the trial, Judge John Gower asked that his commendations of the three policemen, especially P.C. Sweeney, be put before the Chief Constable.

P.C. Sweeney's number, AS910, reflects the change which took place in 1968, when the East and West Sussex boroughs were amalgamated. After that date, police numbers began with 'A' for male and 'B' for female police officers, followed by their surname initial. The first Storrington policeman with such a number was Leslie Towse, AT538, who came in 1968.

The Specials

The Special Constabulary was formed to help the regular police in the event of a national emergency. Mufti-clad and untrained, quite a few local men became Special Constables; traders, professional men and independent gentlemen were all listed in a beat book, together with a note saying which of them had cars that were available for police purposes. Another useful thing for a 'special' was to have a telephone, but before World War Two this was rare. One of the earliest warrants issued was to Mr Crowhurst, the blacksmith.

When war broke out, there was a useful body of men available for police duties, relieving regular policemen from routine work. They have been compared to Civil

Defence Volunteers with police powers and responsibilities, working during weekends and at night without pay. After the war, their numbers were reduced drastically, although the remainder do receive instruction. This, however, is less than a regular policeman at the beginning of his career.

Edward Post recalled one Special Constable

'...whose name is lost in time. He was a very small man who was a farm labourer living at Thakeham. One of my tasks as a motor cyclist, particularly on Saturday nights, was to race around all the pubs around closing time to see that everything was quiet and to see if the gypsies ... were celebrating in one. By the time I arrived at the Thakeham pub, it was quite late but my Special would be waiting for me outside. He was not a good dresser — he always wore his uniform cap at a rakish angle with the strap under his chin, had half his buttons undone or missing and wore brown boots — his only pair. I was always sure that he spent all of every evening inside the pub and only nipped out when he heard the motor cycle, but I never could catch him out'.

The Fire Brigade

Fires in Storrington at the turn of the century were either fought with buckets of water, or a telegram summoned the Steyning Brigade which would harness up its horses and gallop headlong to answer the call. One hot August day in 1911 the windmill on Sullington Warren caught fire as flames raged across the gorse and heather (*Storrington in Pictures*, plates 217–218). Everybody turned out to fight the fire, which endangered the school and other property. At 1.45 p.m. the Steyning Brigade was telegraphed. They received the message at 2.52 p.m. and galloped over at top speed; the fire horses had been drawing carriages to give Steyning people rides, and had to be taken unceremoniously out of the shafts and harnessed to the engine, leaving the passengers stranded! The fire was brought under control but the Warren and underlying peat smouldered for weeks and had to be watched until heavy rains finally extinguished it.

In 1912 when Greenfields used to cure their own bacon, their paraffin store and smoking shed caught fire in the early hours of the morning lighting up the whole street with the flames. Charles Mant, sleeping in his bedroom at the front of 'The Dawes', woke to find he had a grandstand view of the fire. He realised that he was the first to see it and rushed out into the street yelling '*FIRE!*' at the top of his voice. A bucket chain was organised from the scullery pump of 'The Dawes' and rainwater tanks were also used, and Charles Mant sat on the wall passing buckets. The fire spread to a building in Selden's yard where Mr Peterson kept a motor-cycle and sidecar. This was soon in flames and the petrol tank exploded with a roar, driving Mr Mant off the wall. Sand and earth from Selden's yard extinguished that fire and the water chain subdued the one in the smoking shed. The firefighters were entertained and refreshed in Charles Greenfield's house and it was voted a successful night's work.

In 1916 the question of fire appliances for the village was raised at a Parish Council sub-committee meeting, at the request of Head Special Constable Mr T. Dove-Keighley. The members were Mr F. Hodson, Mr W. Rhoden and Mr Wicker. The clerk wrote to the village insurance societies inviting them to subscribe towards the cost. Two years passed. They approached the Town Clerk of Worthing, enquiring the cost of Worthing Brigade's attendance at fires, but decided that they could not pay the retaining fee required. Thirteen months later, a fire brigade sub-committee was formed with Dr William Fulton, Miss Petre and Mr F. Piper, and soon they had bought a stand-pipe and hose — but no handcart to carry them! In July 1920, a hose-truck was purchased from Worthing Brigade, and Mr Bridger Woolgar became the first Chief Officer. Miss Petre then persuaded Mr M. Plowman of Lady Place to become Captain, and the fire equipment was kept at his home. The first Fire Brigade consisted of Engineer F. Leggatt,

Firemen W. Quait, A. W. Crowhurst, Owen Crowhurst, C. Huffer, E. Farrell, H. Elms and P. Malone. They wore their own clothes with a cap, belt, axe, key and a coil of rope.

An engine was deemed unnecessary as there was a very good pressure of water in the mains. Tests showed that they could shoot water to the top of Storrington's highest building, the Monastery. They had just 200 feet of unlined canvas hose which leaked like a sprinkler. Water was supplied 'free of charge' to the Brigade! It was obvious that there was not enough hose and that double the length was needed and it was also recognised that some means of summoning the firemen to a fire was necessary.

Five years later Storrington's best known fireman, Mr Charles Mant, was appointed Hon. Treasurer. The new brigade had by then attended four fires, and at the end of 1925 had proper uniforms and handsome brass helmets. Two years later Mr Mant became the Chief Fire Officer, and purchased the old Merryweather manual engine for £65. The strength of the brigade was raised to 12 men. They had no horses, so an arrangement was made with local traders owning vans — Reeves the carrier, Mr Bryant the coal merchant, Mr Saggers from the Corner Garage, Stockers, Greenfields and others. The first one to arrive attached the Merryweather and drew it to the fire. The insurance company paid £1 for expenses; this was given to the driver. The Parish Council agreed that the previous voluntary attendances by the firemen should now be rewarded by 1s. 0d. per man.

About this time the fire station was built on land owned by Mrs Hare Mant in West Street. This little building has now gone and the site is occupied by a row of shops. Storrington Fire Brigade became affiliated to the National Fire Brigades Association, and in 1928, with 14 men on the strength, took part in the N.F.B.A. competitions. In that year the official register began in Storrington with the following volunteers on the roll:

Chief Officer Mant, C.E.	Fireman Malone, P.
Chief Engineer Leggatt, F.	Fireman Farrell, E.
Second Engineer Crowhurst, A.	Fireman Gilbert, H.
Fireman Huffer, C.	Fireman Lillywhite, T.
Fireman Quait, W.	Fireman Elms, H.
Fireman Bowers, W.	Fireman Peterson, R.
Fireman Reid, G.	Fireman Ellis, S.
Greenfield, R., joined in December.	Fireman Mustchin, W.

They used to hold monthly drills which were keenly attended. When the Brighton Fire Brigade replaced its old unlined hoses, these were passed over to the Storrington Brigade and Mr Mant decided that they would serve excellently for rick fires, where their porousness was a distinct advantage. They were also offered a motorised engine by the Brighton Fire Brigade in 1928, costing £400. Charles Mant wanted this and some more hose, but funds stood at £35. Undaunted, he appealed to two influential people who had recently had fires attended to by the Brigade, and they, together with Mr Mant and his wife, guaranteed a £500 overdraft at the bank. Later, A. E. R. Gilligan became a guarantor.

CD 6510 was a solid-tyred Fiat chassis fitted with a Dennis pump, and was, according to Charles Mant, a wonder, remaining in service until 1940. Its gigantic hose-lockers for 4,000 feet of hose so delighted the brigade that they arranged a demonstration in the Square, damming the river Stor by the gas-works and shooting four jets of water straight up in the air. The show was greatly enjoyed by people who turned out to see the new acquisition. One man, however, was rather less than pleased afterwards. Mr Lurcock's drapery business was in Commercial House next to the White Horse Yard, and the wind, not allowed for by the enthusiastic firemen, had brought all the water down behind his premises, washing the garden soil into his yard and piling 18 inches of mud and water against his back door. When Mr Lurcock opened the door to let the cat out, all this mess was released over his kitchen floor. He was livid, and only pacified when the firemen cleared it all up and scrubbed the floor clean.

The overdraft on this engine was cleared by 1933, and another engine purchased from Croydon, a 60 h.p. Dennis with a Bayley Fire Escape. In 1937 Fire Chiefs were assembled to discuss the procedure in the event of war. The Fire Brigade Act was passed in 1938 and 1,400 volunteer and other fire services in the country became the responsibility of local councils with rate support. The Council signed a contract with Storrington Fire Brigade for them to carry out their duties for £393 per annum — the average cost of running the brigade over its past 10 years. Charles Mant became Honorary Chief Officer for the Chanctonbury area. On his advice, Storrington acquired its third appliance, a new Bedford truck with hose-box and extension, and a Worthington-Simpson pump towed on a trailer.

Volunteer firemen had regular jobs elsewhere, and were summoned by a bell outside the Fire Station; they would down tools and run at its sound. During the war, call-boys cycled to firemen's houses for night-calls; one of them was John Linfield, later Chief Officer with 27 years' service. They could turn out in under 15 minutes. During the day they were summoned by the air-raid siren, sounded by the girls in the control room when notified by telephone of imminent raids.

Fred Scutt in 1938 joined the Fire Brigade, then the Auxiliary Fire Service, and became a full-time fireman for the duration. There were six of these full-timers. Machines had to be dispersed when the air-raid warning sounded, and he remembers many nights spent on Sullington Warren which was his dispersal point.

The A.F.S., augmented by extra volunteers wearing dark blue arm-bands and the steel helmet of all defence organisations, practised drawing water on Sunday mornings at the village pond. The first fire control room was at 'The Geddings', staffed by volunteer operators trained by Mrs Mant; Mr and Mrs Gilligan, Miss Morris, Miss Mortimer and Miss Langhorne worked during the day, and Mrs Mant was the night operator. By the time of Dunkirk, both day and night were very busy. Mr Mant recalled that he and his wife were not out of their clothes for weeks on end. On 4 September 1940 all units and control rooms were at full stretch with aircraft crashing all over the area and the brigade doing a magnificent job. Mrs Mant made tea for the crews in addition to her telephone duties. In 1941 the Home Office took control and local fire brigades were nationalised as the N.F.S. (National Fire Service). The appliances were bought by the Government, except for the old Fiat which was sold to Tom Smith for scrap, and the Merryweather manual engine which was presented to the W.S.C.C. as a museum piece.

Charles Mant's control room behind 'The Geddings' was requisitioned by the Home Office, together with the Fire Station in West Street which stood on his land. Full-time control room girls staffed the telephones — Miss Mitchell, Mrs Mant, Audrey Powell and Mrs. Leggatt. Mrs Mant was promoted to Leading Firewoman in recognition of her fine work. Apart from fire and air-raid messages, they were also informed when the ammunition trains were due at Amberley Station.

Civilians did fire-watching duties during the war. Mrs Gatley remembers her stint of duty at Prynne Gatley's office. Others recall a small hut by the Mill Pond which was set on fire to give them fire-fighting practice. Routine drills, supplemented during the war by lectures on water supply, respirators, oil fires, hand signals, ladders and fire risks, continued alongside their war work.

The control room staff were disbanded after the war, having made a valuable contribution during those difficult years. In 1947 Charles Mant retired after 22 years' devoted service, when the W.S.C.C. became responsible for the Fire Brigade. He was awarded the King's Police and Fire Services medal, the ceremony of investiture being held at Chanctonbury House by the Rt. Hon. Lord Leconfield, G.C.V.O., Lord Lieutenant of Sussex.

Charles Mant was called upon in June 1949 to advise when a heavy cart-horse fell into a well, and the brigades on the spot had no lifting tackle. This led him to design a special lifting sling for heavy animals in distress, also fitting a padded hood over the animal's head to reduce its panic and struggling, so often the cause of trouble.

Edward Post, who lived near the fire station, remembered the turn-outs:

> 'Roley [Greenfield] was in charge of the part-time firemen whose sole appliance was garaged in a shed opposite the police houses. Most of the firemen worked in shops etc. in the village and on Wednesday afternoons and Sundays not many of them were available so it was not unusual for a policeman or anyone else to make the number up. Fortunately, calls were not numerous and I gave up attending them when I went on the appliance to a heath fire once and they left me to walk back!'

We always rushed to the window when the fire siren sounded. We would see the various firemen coming from all directions on bikes, in cars, on motorcycles; the first one in drove the engine out, and others could be seen struggling into their uniforms on the back. We often had a pair of socks waved to us as they raced past on their way to a fire.

In 1958 a new fire station was built on School Hill, and two engines were accommodated there. They have a tower and a rest- and lecture-room and the latest in fire-fighting equipment. The part-timers have their own personal call system, and with their private cars can turn out in response to a call in record time.

Equipment, training and speed of attendance are all greatly improved in the 60 years since Storrington bought its first hose truck, but the spirit and dedication of men who risk their lives every time they fight what Charles Mant called 'the common enemy' is the same as ever.

5. STORRINGTON AT WORK

Traders — Industries — Craftsmen — Workhouse

Tradesmen and Craftsmen

MR JOHN JOYES came to live in Storrington in 1855 when he was six months old. In 1929 he made notes about some of the things he could remember, recalling those trades and crafts that had already vanished. There were, for example, 60 working windmills within a radius of 10 miles of Storrington when he was a boy, whereas by 1929 there was not one. The Domesday Survey lists 'two mills of 11 shillings' for the manor, so that windmills around Storrington have a recorded history of over 1,000 years.

John Joyes was a miller like his father before him, owning the mills up to 1879. He ran the Black Mill belonging to Mrs King of Fryern, which was on Byne Common, now the corner of Fryern Road. The only traces left of this mill are the names 'Windmill Copse' and 'Mill Lane'. Wooden windmills with their internal friction were a natural fire hazard, and this particular mill burnt down one hot night in the 1870s. A red-hot millstone was said to roll down the hill and bags of flour became red-hot.

Mr Joyes also ran the Byne water-mill (*Storrington in Pictures*, plates 143–147) which survived until the 1970s. The flour was delivered to the barn next door to his bakery in West Street. The Chief Constable wrote to Mr Joyes regarding the obstruction caused by his carts at late hours. He also sold wood and coal, and employed 'Toby' Cooper as a delivery-man. According to Mr Rapley, he was usually in a thoroughly black state by the evening, and his wife Charlotte told him of it on one occasion early in their marriage, suggesting that he should get a wash. Toby, who was a little deaf, eventually grasped her meaning and said, 'What's the good of washun now gal, I'm gwine cart coal agen termorrer'. After the First World War, Joyes' Bakery was sold to Mr Jim Dibble, and 'Dibble's' it remained until a few years ago, although bread is still baked on the premises. Mr and Mrs Joyes also had a corn-chandler's shop in Eastbrook, later run by the two Miss Joyes. Mrs Virgo Snr. remembered that if no-one was there and she stood very quietly, a mouse was sure to come out sooner or later. Miss Rankin recalls seeing Mr Joyes sitting by the fire in his shop, putting seeds into little packets.

During the First World War the water-mill ground flour for Worthing. It was carried in waggons drawn by two horses which could pull two to three tons of flour at a time. It was sieved through silk screens stretched over frames and Mr Cowdry who worked for Mr French (who ran the mill after John Joyes), recalled that it was 'lovely flour'. Local farmers provided enough grain to keep the mill working. Mr Cowdry also remembers the rats jumping onto his shoulder to get at the meal. They kept cats to control them and one particularly beautiful ginger cat would sleep on the mill-wheel! The overshot wheel worked by water pouring into cups and pushing it round, and children used to ride on the revolving pole taking the drive. An old hatch could pen the water back as far as Brewer's Yard, and if the pond was full it would flood the Yard and gasworks. After a particularly bad flood, the river board made a new escape chute. This mill was worked in conjunction with Chantry Mill (*Storrington in Pictures*, plates 100–112) which used the same stream. The last farmer to use the mill was Mr Tom Gatley, who ground cattle-feed there during the Second World War and Mrs Gatley remembers having to deal with ration cards. Since the mill went out of use, young Mr Gatley grinds animal feed by electric machinery at the old Barns Farm Camp.

Many people were sad to see the old mill demolished but, in fact, great efforts were made by the developers, Storrington Contractors, to preserve it. They had drawn plans showing the mill still standing, but converted into a house or flats, or even a restaurant. The foundations were tested and surveyed several times, and much thought was given to the problems involved in preserving the building, but the site suffered from the fact that the river had made the ground unstable, and the foundations were rotten. The mill needed underpinning, the fabric was decayed and the building derelict: the expense was enormous. An East Sussex museum rescued all that could be salvaged of the mill machinery, but the iron mill-wheel was so badly rusted that even the museum could not preserve it. The mill pond, in accordance with the original plans, was restored and now gives pleasure to many people who enjoy watching the birds that have established themselves there.

The Sullington Mill on the Warren (*Storrington in Pictures*, plates 213–219) was run by John Quait in the 1880s, together with Chantry Mill. This white windmill burned down in 1911. Mrs Crowhurst ran them both until 1903, after which it remained empty and derelict.

Another Black Mill stood on Kithurst Common, and was not demolished until 1923. It was a landmark that could be seen from across the village pond. It had been worked by the Crowhurst family for three generations, together with a bakery in West Street in the little row of cottages which stood next to the *Cricketers*, and have now gone. When paying their bill, customers would be given a glass of beer or a bag of buns. In Mr Rapley's schooldays, children going to school across the meadow used to call there. The old oven door was so warped that the baker sealed it with dough, and the children were given this when it was cooked! Crowhurst's also sold wood and coal, but how such an unlikely trade came to be associated with millers and bakers, I have no idea.

There was another bakehouse in Storrington next to Peterson's Garage in School Hill. This made cakes for a teashop — now Manley's Restaurant.

In his notes of 1929, John Joyes also recalled other vanished craftsmen:

'Charles Paige was a Cooper; lived in the Square where Stocker is. He used to make tubs, barrels, baskets and a lot of other things not wanted now — it is all galvanised things from big factories . . . Mrs Churchell, bootmaker, lived where Mr Wickens' house now stands. The old lady was a widow; she had several sons all brought up in the trade; you could always see about ten working in the shop: they made boots for miles around. I don't suppose there is ever a pair of boots made in the parish now; everything is massed production, which I think is the cause of a lot of unemployment. No Churchell left in the parish . . . James Wagstaff, bootmaker. His shop was where Heath View now stands opposite Miss Latham's. He also employed several hands, like the Churchells. There is only two of them left now — Thomas, a son, who is over eighty, and a sister. They live in Back Lane'.

This bootmaker's was the first of the shops past Twitten Cottage, and the men used to sit making boots by the fireplace in the cellar. They had to walk to Pulborough for leather, fetching it back in a wheelbarrow. Between the *Cricketers* and these shops were four tiny cottages, the first of which belonged to 'Snobby' Stringer, the shoemaker (plate 72). Another of these old cottages was used by Mr Wheeler for his shoe-shop.

Before Unigate Dairies were established, there were several local suppliers of dairy produce. Mr Richardson, dairy farmer, who lived at Water Lane, had a milk-float drawn by a pony called Joey (plate 68). He was in business before the First World War. Milk was delivered twice daily by his two daughters. In the days before refrigeration, the milk had to be delivered when it was very fresh, or made into butter and cheese. It was carried in churns and measured into customers' jugs with long-handled measuring ladles.

Mrs Ada Miller came to Storrington in 1916 to do a milk round for the Padwicks of Merrywood (plate 69). Later, she worked for Mr Richardson. The morning milk round began at 7.30 a.m. and ended about 11 a.m. Then the churns had to be washed and at 2.30 p.m. she began a second round. At 4.30 a.m. the cows were fetched in to be hand-milked before the morning round. Mrs Miller recalled that 'you couldn't see them but they breathed on us!'

Cootham folk were supplied with milk by Mr Parsons at 'The Laggs', who also sold butter made on the farm. Another local farmer, John Turner, also kept dairy cows and had the first dairy shop in the Square in 1927 (now Arun Travel). After the Second World War, his shop was sold first to Mr Ashby, then to Mr Stubbs who ran it as a fish-shop. Errand boys cycled to Rowdell, Fryern, Chantry, Greyfriars, Gerston, Parham, The Abbey, Greatham Manor and Wiggonholt Rectory with ice and fish in the baskets of their trade bicycles which were fitted with oil lamps. One retired gentleman who started his working life as an errand boy still remembered the cold dark rides he was obliged to do in winter.

In 1954 the shop was bought by Jim Barratt and Glynn Cripps, who reopened it as a dairy. They soon realised that people working in Storrington needed somewhere they could get a midday meal and opened up the back room of the dairy as a café, which rapidly became popular. They served appetising meals and soon acquired regular customers from the local shops and offices. Although Barratt & Cripps took over Storrington Dairies during the last years of food rationing, there were ample supplies of butter and eggs in this area. One memory we have of 1954, when we were first married, is of taking our ration books into the dairy to establish ourselves as regular customers, and being able to buy a *complete half-pound of butter*, and bacon and eggs, without anyone bothering about the paperwork! This was unimaginable luxury.

Ridgewell's was another dairy, situated in School Hill, but it soon ceased trading and Storrington Dairies began to run their deliveries from there. They took delivery of bottled milk from Southwick Hill Farm Dairies, which drew its supplies from local farms, and had five rounds, covering Storrington, Roundabouts, West Chiltington, Nutbourne and Thakeham. Amberley Castle Dairy sold farm-bottled milk from Jersey cows, and amalgamated with Storrington Dairies in the late 1950s. The dairy sold general groceries, local honey and eggs, until 1962, when Storrington Dairies sold out to Unigate.

Next to the dairy stands a shop which has grown up with a 20th-century invention — the wireless. It had been a butcher's shop, then Barnes the hairdresser's, and later Mustchin's cycle shop. In the late 1920s it became a radio and electrical shop belonging to Ron Vine. Ron Cripps used to go in on Saturdays whilst still a schoolboy to put accumulators on charge and do other odd jobs, and Glynn Cripps also worked there for a time. Mr Peterson of the garage was a great friend of Ron Vine. He would put on private film shows for his friends — early silent movies of Charlie Chaplin or the Keystone Cops. Later, Ron Vine ran the cinema in the Village Hall with Sid Ellis. The seats cost 6d. and the film was shown in three or four parts to give the operator time to change reels. Two lads, Gordon Woods and George Barnard, were given pocket-money to operate and rewind the film by hand, so that Ron Vine could slip away. One night when the boys were left in charge, a slip in the mechanism clawed a row of jagged holes along the middle of the entire reel of film. Undaunted by this appalling accident, Ron Vine spent hours ironing the film flat again to return to the hiring company. He was a happy-go-lucky individual who saw the funny side of most situations. Power from a portable generator on a lorry outside supplied the projectors, and the night that the lorry and contents caught fire while they had slipped away again only resulted in their great merriment as they watched the inferno!

Mrs Virgo remembered her son George staying out late every night to '. . . play about with wireless with Ron Vine!' The factory-made set was a rarity in those days. People made their own, and often the components, too. George Virgo made his first radio with a cat's whisker and crystal, cutting up a tea-chest with a hacksaw to make a cabinet with two doors. Mrs Virgo remembers a horn loud-speaker, and the neighbours coming in to listen to this great novelty. Ron Vine installed a wireless for one old lady, erecting the usual long wire aerial in the garden, and leaving two wires coming in at the window for connection to the set. The lady asked when she could use her new wireless. 'Straight away — we'll switch it on now.' 'Oh I can't do that. I haven't written to the B.B.C. yet to ask for the music.' Apparently, she believed that the two wires went all the way to the B.B.C. (like the telephone!). One man who remembered buying his first wireless from Ron Vine was Dick Cothard who came to Storrington every year with Tom Smith's Fair. He thinks it was actually built by him.

Accumulators, filled with acid, were a necessary source of power to early listeners, and there are many tales of holes burnt in carpets, furniture and clothing after being splashed. One was *never* allowed to carry an accumulator on the bus. They needed charging about twice a week, and were brought into the shop for this purpose, which took about three days. Often people bought two accumulators and they would bring in the 'flat' one and collect the recharged one at the same time. One customer, obviously unaware of this fact, put his accumulator on the counter, saying, 'I'll wait for it'. During the Second World War, accumulator-charging became a major part of the week's work. Canadian troops brought in all of theirs to be charged.

The electrical side of the business included lighting in the Village Hall, special lights for concert parties and Dramatic Society productions, the lighting for the annual Flower Show, and the decorative lights on the tree in the Square at Christmas.

It was at the beginning of the war that a 10-year-old boy called Ron Ham came to Storrington to stay with Ron Vine. He spent most of his fortnight in Ron Vine's workshop, fascinated by the things going on there, and he went home with some unusual souvenirs — a valve, odd components and a circuit, from which he built himself a short-wave receiver. This was the forerunner of hundreds of pieces of equipment that Ron Ham has built since, including a radio telescope, whose big aerials fascinate people as they walk up to the Downs.

In 1954, we returned to Storrington, first to manage and then buy the radio and electrical business in partnership with Derek Knight. It is now the second oldest firm in the village. The radios and components that Ron Vine sold, and even the sets that were stocked by us in the 1950s, are now exhibits in the Chalk Pits Museum at Houghton!

Next door was the first bank in Storrington. In the 1890s the Capital and Counties Bank rented one room of a house in West Street (later called *Banksia*). Mr White, the manager, attended twice weekly. The little flint bank in the High Street (plate 77) was built soon after this. The Capital and Counties Bank was amalgamated with Lloyd's Bank in 1918, and the present building was erected on the site in 1927. They extended their premises in the 1960s to cope with their increased business.

After the bank is 'The Homestead', built by Abner Soffe in 1907–8. He was a shoe-mender and a well-known village character, with a workshop next to Wicken's draper and men's outfitter (the present Bookshop). He built a house on the site (later Tucker's), and then built 'The Homestead' where he took up residence and opened a teashop and tea-garden. 'The Homestead' had a toilet for the convenience of customers, which was something of a novelty in those days. Abner Soffe would not allow it to be used by those who had not had their tea in his premises, and would tell them so in no uncertain terms! He was well known to the College boys, and would 'accommodate' them when they found themselves short of cash. He built Finlay Cottages in the Pulborough

Road, named, it is said, after the racehorse that enabled him to finance the venture. Two more quaint old characters lived next door in 'The Elders' (Leatherware), Henri Vick and his sister. He was an undertaker with a coffin workshop at the bottom of School Hill (now T. Stocker the plumber). He had a handcart on which he would collect the bodies of his 'customers', wheeling them back to School Hill. Edie Vick kept dozens of cats.

Tailoring is another village trade that has vanished. In his notes John Joyes commented, 'George Hews tailor, lived at which is now Mrs Faithfull's [Orchard Way] in Church Street: he had a first-class business, kept on a lot of hands — no country tailors now — it is all ready-mades'. Mr Rapley added that in 1934 there were nine or 10 tailors and 10–14 bootmakers whereas now there is not a single one.

He also recalled an early watch and clock-maker, Teddy Eldridge.

> 'He . . . was in business for many years and very clever too his only trouble being that he was very apt to get in too much elbow drill. He lived and carried on his business in my early days in the small shop now used as a radio shop by Mr Vine, later moving to a room next to the Blacksmith shop which was situated in the space between the *Anchor* Inn and Stream Cottage. He ended his days in School Hill, in the house which was at one time a Public House, to wit the *Railway* Inn at which he combined his business with his wife who carried on a little general store'.

However, the best-remembered watchmaker was Walter Edward Penn, who had a shop in West Street, next to Polands. Mr Penn came to Storrington just after the turn of the century. When plate 80 was taken in 1937, he was 82, the oldest working clockmaker in England. There are some of his timepieces in the village still. Mr Penn died during the Second World War aged 87.

Cootham

Miss Hilda Breed of Flansham Cottage is well-known as a weaver. She studied weaving and specialised in teaching crafts. Shortly before retiring she found 'Flansham Cottage', originally two workmen's cottages, named after Flansham Manor near the coast. She bought a huge loom and some interesting Yorkshire weaving apparatus. At the same time the cottage was altered; a workshop was built in the garden to house the loom. Miss Breed retired to Cootham in 1963. She makes tweeds and soft rugs, among other fabrics, and uses the wool of Jacob's sheep for its delightful range of natural creams, black and greys. She has developed a unique method of dyeing thread to produce interesting colour mixtures. A bar holds the warps over dye buckets on the stove, so they can be moved along from one colour to another. Hand-spinning enables her to vary the textures of the thread. Miss Breed produces beautiful and unique fabrics, some of which have been made into the soft furnishings for her cottage.

The Crown Inn

A central feature of the hamlet of Cootham is the old *Crown* Inn. This was kept by Mr and Mrs Ware, the grandparents of Miss Gladys Rogers, prior to the First World War, and before that by her great-aunt and uncle, Mr and Mrs Davey. A curse allegedly rests on the head of household of *The Crown*, because a resident drowned himself in the boggy ground at the bottom of the garden where it joined the stream. An old coaching inn, *The Crown*'s original buildings ran north and south at the end of the present establishment. Crown Cottages, where Miss Rogers lives, used to be the stables, built in 1688 when Cootham was all wild common-land. It was also alleged to be 'Smuggler's Stables' — there are many tales of smugglers in this area.

When Parham had a pheasant shoot, *The Crown* supplied the beaters' lunches. Mrs Ware roasted 36 lb of best sirloin and Dibble baked special long loaves. There would also be mounds of cut-up cheeses and crates of beer. Mr Ware fetched a farm waggon from Parham and the packed lunches and beer were loaded on board and driven to the park. Mrs Ware was a fine cook and her food had a high reputation. A plate of bread and cheese (today's Ploughman's Lunch) cost only 4d. and for 6d. it was served with her home-made pickles.

At the east end of Crown Cottages was a hut where George Greenfield mended shoes. He took in the boots and shoes from the workhouse which stood on the site of the present Duke's Row. At the other end, where Miss Rogers lives now, Mrs Greenfield had a sweetshop in her kitchen window. The sweet jars were kept on shelves up the stairs. Three sisters, Kate, Ada and Sid Greenfield kept the Duke's Row grocer's shop, run from the front room of the little cottage next door to what was later to become Cootham Stores.

Mr Charman, one of an old Cootham family living in Newtown Road, did the baker's round for Stillwell's in the High Street. In the morning he took the pony and cart round, and in the afternoon he used a handcart to do the Church Street area. Loaves and small items, flour-box and scales, were kept in the top and large loaves in the bottom. In bad winters ponies had to be rough-shod and he carried a small iron hook to de-ice their hooves. On one occasion when he was at Greyfriars with the pony and cart a peacock suddenly screeched from behind a hedge. The pony took off and did not stop until it reached the village, with the cart bouncing along behind. On his way down after it he met a friend who had seen it go by, and he assured him that nothing would stop that pony before he reached his stable.

Local Industry

The Sawmills

Mr William Bourn came to Storrington in 1915 and started the sawmills in Thakeham Road. During summer they did contract work, taking their equipment to such places as Lord Leconfield's estate at Petworth and to Midhurst. From November to March they worked in the sawmills and bought in timber to saw up, mainly elm for coffin boards. When on their way to fulfil a contract they must have looked like a small travelling fair on the road — there was a steam engine, a truck with sawbenches and other equipment, and a caravan for use as living quarters. Two men drove the engine, one rode in the caravan to pull the string if traffic wanted to pass and let the driver know, and one man drove the car back. During the Second World War there was no more contract work. William Bourn and his new partner were in a reserved occupation doing war work. They produced timber, coffin boards and did work for the army.

Father and son were working shifts to keep the sawmills in production from 6 a.m.–10 p.m. and they began to modernize their equipment, first converting the machinery to run on electricity. The old steam engines burnt bark and sawdust and ran entirely on waste, but every year they needed to be stripped and serviced. In the 1940s they changed over from circular to band saws. Mrs Bourn remembers that after one saw had been un-used for eight weeks, they found that a blackbird had nested on it. She was allowed to raise her brood before the saw was used again.

After the Second World War the sawmills bought in English timber which was either cut to order or kept to mature; it was mainly oak, elm, ash for building and fencing, and as furniture timber for sale to contractors. Mr Johnston was the sawyer from 1949–69, and Mr Boyd their saw-doctor. About 14 men were employed in all. One steam-saw was still in use at this time.

The site of the old sawmills which closed down in 1969 is now marked by the name 'Timberlands'.

Thakeham Tiles

The story of Thakeham Tiles must start with the story of a remarkable man, Mr Frank Knight. Kentish born, he came to Worthing at the beginning of the First World War and later made his home in Storrington.

Mr Knight was physically handicapped (although he made light of his disabilities), having arms that ended at his elbows and legs that were useless below the knees. He had special pads made so that he could walk on his knees, and was able to write, do the joinery for his building work until his teeth had to come out, drive a pony and trap, keep bees and canaries, 'play about with wireless' and photography, give shows of his glass plates, and paint exquisite watercolours, including botanical subjects of such detail and beauty that they would have graced any text-book on the subject. A favourite saying of his was that there was 'not such a word as *can't*'. His painting was shown in 1890 in Raphael Tuck and Sons' Exhibition held at the galleries of the Royal Institute of Painters in Watercolours, where it earned him an impressive diploma and cash prize of £3 3s. 0d.

In the late 1920s he started a sandpit on the Thakeham Road site, and in 1933 registered the firm as Thakeham Tiles Ltd., where roofing tiles were made for the houses he built. His original building is still in use, and his son continues to work there.

At first, sand was dug out by hand and loaded into the trucks of a 24-inch narrow-gauge railway, which were pulled by a petrol engine made on the site. This ran the sand into the old shed where the tiles were hand-made. Mr A. L. King bought the works from Mr Knight, and began to make building blocks there until the outbreak of the Second World War, by which time two more sheds had been erected. Production stopped and, like so many places during the war, the works were used by Canadian troops as a transport division with lorries and tanks stored and maintained there.

In 1946 Thakeham Tiles re-opened, but the old sand-pit was worked out and roofing tiles were no longer made. Building blocks and decorative garden walling are produced now and the business has greatly expanded. There are five manufacturing sheds making a wide variety of garden walling products, paving slabs and screen walling. The sand comes from a pit at Midhurst, together with some marine sand. The firm employs 70–80 people from Storrington, Littlehampton and Worthing. It is incredible just how much is made at the works. Mr Bevis, the manager, was himself surprised when a new computer stores record was introduced and all the products needed a part number: there were 150–160 separate items!

They supply their blocks all over the south-east of England from Kent to Dorset and as far north as Hertfordshire and North London. The fleet of lorries on the road is currently eight, with six delivering products and two bringing in raw materials. Several lorries delivered tiles before the war and one 1936 Bedford was in service until 1956. Since then, the fleet has built up until fleet number 37 was added in February 1980.

One feature of great interest at Thakeham Tiles was the narrow-gauge railway, which attracted enthusiasts from specialist societies. This track, two engines and the skips were replaced by roller conveyors, and the rolling stock and track were donated to the Chalk Pits Museum at Houghton at the end of 1980. 'Thakeham Tiles No. 3' and 'Thakeham Tiles No. 4' now attract great attention as they chug along the re-laid track, delighting boys of all ages.

Marley Tiles

This industry in Chantry Lane began in 1927 making roofing tiles. In those days it was a 'rough place'; the work was filthy and dusty, and several men died from the effects of the dust. During the depression in the 1930s many people came down from the north to work there. It was the second works of the Marley Tile Co. of Marley Banks in Kent. They used large steam juggernauts (plate 86) to move their products, the sand from their pit in Chantry Lane had to be dug by hand, the men filling the trucks that ran on a narrow-gauge railway which the men pushed along. The fifth man from the left in plate 85 (back row) is Charlie Randall, who helped start the Marley going and finished as chief engineer of their motor transport. The engines were used up to 1937, after which diesel lorries were put into service.

Late in 1939, the works closed down for the duration of the war, but by the following year they had re-opened, their production being geared to the needs of war. This included roofing tiles, prefabricated buildings for the army, and before the Invasion, parts of the revolutionary Mulberry Harbour.

Since the Second World War, they have diversified, and now make aluminium products, roofing slabs and kitchen furniture, garages, greenhouses and concrete products.

The Workhouse

Sometimes, people could not earn their living, or found themselves temporarily unemployed. Before the days of the Welfare State, local charity was the only alternative. On 1 May 1835, the Board of Guardians of the Thakeham Union Workhouse met to arrange the running and staffing of a workhouse (Fig. 13). The old Cootham and Thakeham parish workhouses were valued and sold up, and elderly paupers moved to the new Thakeham Union Workhouse. By 1882, the expenses for supplying the needs of the workhouse averaged £45 per week, which included provisions, clothing, repairs and other necessities.

The workhouse premises were inspected regularly and reports made. In 1883, Local Government Board visitors reported a 'bad smell' in the female receiving ward (which was traced to damp clothing), and more dampness in the male receiving ward which had been out of use.

Casual vagrants seeking temporary lodgings were expected to work before leaving, usually on highway maintenance or flint-carting. The relieving officer made small payments of out-relief to those suffering temporary hardship, such as 'own illness — blood poisoning'; 'kicked by horse'; 'wife's illness'; 'in decline'. Orphaned children, where possible, were placed with foster-parents who were paid from Union funds with an added 10s. per quarter for clothing and school fees, and when the children left school they were placed with suitable employers or apprenticed. Children seem to have been a cause for genuine concern, as one item for outfitting two little girls before boarding them out insisted that the £4 10s. 0d. was to be spent in Greenfields on *new* clothes.

In 1911, Storrington had a population of 1,186. In the half-year ending 30 September 1918, nine were on out-relief and eight in the workhouse. The dietary consisted of breakfast, dinner and supper. Sunday breakfast for men was 8 oz. bread, ½ oz. margarine and 1 pint of tea. Women received 6 oz. bread, ½ oz. margarine and 1 pint of tea. During the rest of the week they had 6 oz. bread and 1½ or 1 pint of gruel. Dinner on weekdays consisted of 4 oz. bread and 12 oz. potatoes or other vegetables, roast beef, corned beef, bacon, suet pudding, pulse soup or meat pudding. Alternatively, there might be 8 oz. bread and 3 oz. cheese. Supper was invariably bread, cheese, broth and tea. Men doing parish work began at sunrise and finished at sunset. The pay was 7s. 0d. per week if married, or 6s. 0d. if single. Those only capable of working inside were employed in grinding corn or picking over vast quantities of junk which came from London's East End, to make a kind of coarse rope from oakum. Potatoes, peas, pigs and hay were all produced by the workhouse and sold to supplement funds.

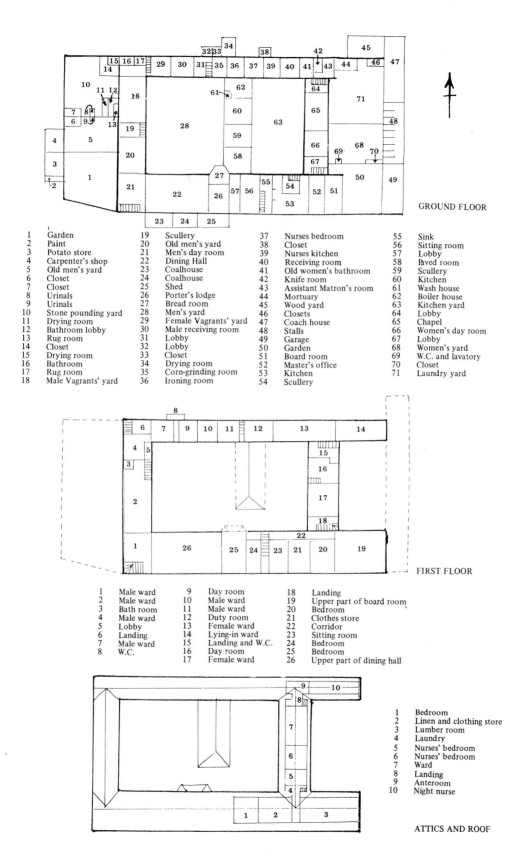

GROUND FLOOR

1	Garden	19	Scullery	37	Nurses bedroom	55	Sink
2	Paint	20	Old men's yard	38	Closet	56	Sitting room
3	Potato store	21	Men's day room	39	Nurses kitchen	57	Lobby
4	Carpenter's shop	22	Dining Hall	40	Receiving room	58	Paved room
5	Old men's yard	23	Coalhouse	41	Old women's bathroom	59	Scullery
6	Closet	24	Coalhouse	42	Knife room	60	Kitchen
7	Closet	25	Shed	43	Assistant Matron's room	61	Wash house
8	Urinals	26	Porter's lodge	44	Mortuary	62	Boiler house
9	Urinals	27	Bread room	45	Wood yard	63	Kitchen yard
10	Stone pounding yard	28	Men's yard	46	Closets	64	Lobby
11	Drying room	29	Female Vagrants' yard	47	Coach house	65	Chapel
12	Bathroom lobby	30	Male receiving room	48	Stalls	66	Women's day room
13	Rug room	31	Lobby	49	Garage	67	Women's yard
14	Closet	32	Lobby	50	Garden	68	Women's yard
15	Drying room	33	Closet	51	Board room	69	W.C. and lavatory
16	Bathroom	34	Drying room	52	Master's office	70	Closet
17	Rug room	35	Corn-grinding room	53	Kitchen	71	Laundry yard
18	Male Vagrants' yard	36	Ironing room	54	Scullery		

FIRST FLOOR

1	Male ward	9	Day room	18	Landing
2	Male ward	10	Male ward	19	Upper part of board room
3	Bath room	11	Male ward	20	Bedroom
4	Male ward	12	Duty room	21	Clothes store
5	Lobby	13	Female ward	22	Corridor
6	Landing	14	Lying-in ward	23	Sitting room
7	Male ward	15	Landing and W.C.	24	Bedroom
8	W.C.	16	Day room	25	Bedroom
		17	Female ward	26	Upper part of dining hall

1	Bedroom
2	Linen and clothing store
3	Lumber room
4	Laundry
5	Nurses' bedroom
6	Nurses' bedroom
7	Ward
8	Landing
9	Anteroom
10	Night nurse

ATTICS AND ROOF

Figure 13. Plan of Thakeham Workhouse

Local people obviously cared about those in need of the shelter of the workhouse, and many entries in the minute books record their provision of extras and treats. Gifts of cakes, jam, papers from the Pulborough Reading Room, 13 armchairs for the old men from Mrs Wright of Brook House, regular outings and teas from Mrs King of Fryern and Miss Asprey of Cobb Court, entertainment at the workhouse and at the Storrington Flower Show appear in the books. The Guardians often voted extra Christmas Relief to those receiving out-relief, although sometimes a few votes defeated this kindly proposal.

A most interesting gift was made in 1925 by private subscription. This was the Institution wireless, a four-valve Marconi receiving set (to be installed before Christmas) with five loudspeakers, which was, in fact, one of the first wireless sets in the village. The Guardians also installed a telephone (*see* page 32) at a time when the village was still making up its mind whether it wanted the service installed. For £50, the Postmaster General offered to buy up the private lines, the telephones and poles, to take over the maintenance, provide an extension between the clerk's office and the Institution with *unlimited free calls*, and to connect the Institution with the exchange.

These are some of the brighter aspects of the Workhouse, but before Social Security, when the Workhouse was the dreaded alternative to destitution, people did not willingly give up their independence to live on parish charity. The case of Sarah Lawson shows what it really meant to the unfortunate individual.

In 1908 Sarah Emily Lawson, described as 'a lunatic', came into the care of the workhouse, and steps were taken to remove her to the Lunatic Asylum at Chichester. Her property was sold to defray some of the Union expenses which were £15 19s. 9d. for examination, removal, lodgings, maintenance, clothing, medicine and care. In addition, there was the cost of the removal, £4 6s. 7d., and maintenance at the Asylum from 1 January to 31 December 1908 — 366 days at 1s. 7d. per day, totalling £28 19s. 1d. Ratepayer's money was not spent until the last penny of a pauper's resources had been exhausted. Sarah Lawson had £52 12s. 5d. and £2 8s. 0d. due from the Prudential Insurance Co., £3 1s. 3d. from the 'Lion Slate Club' at Ashington and three shares of £5 in the Tayside and Floor Cloth Co. This, of course, was her savings and not cash in hand. Mr James M. M. Erskine J.P., signed an order to Mr Percy Ayling, clerk to the Guardians, for the seizure and sale of her household goods and effects. An inventory was taken, filling three typed pages, of her furniture and crockery, bedding and clothing and 'odd pieces of stuff', right down to the blacklead and brushes used to polish the grates and 'sundry bottles and jars'. Not a corner, a drawer or cupboard was missed. These goods were put out to tender and sold for £12. Sarah's husband repaid £2 15s. 0d. of the debt, and the balance due after the sale was £19 13s. 7d.

Storrington folk seemed to accept the presence of Workhouse inmates walking about the village on various errands as naturally as any other residents. Many remember individual paupers, and although often feeble-minded, some were real characters. Charles Mant tells of Arthur:

> 'At Christmas time, Arthur used to play the game quite a bit — He would stop you in the street, hand you a Christmas card and very solemnly wish you a Happy Christmas—The proper thing then was to give him a couple of shillings, wish him a Happy Christmas and hand the card back — Arthur would then carefully rub your name off the card and "work" it on someone else — He was supposed to be "daft"! but very cunning'.

Mr Mant also remembered seeing the tramps walking through the village to the Workhouse for a night's sleep, having walked from Westhampnett Union, Chichester or Petworth Union.

Between 1866 and 1930, 36 babies were born in the Workhouse, the last in 1930. It is a mere half-century since the Workhouse closed down, and its remaining elderly residents sent to Easebourne. It is one part of Storrington's history that has vanished without regret.

6. STORRINGTON AT PLAY

Cricket — The Village Show — Great Events — Fairs — The Band

Cricket

THE CRICKET CLUB was founded in 1793 and some illustrious names have been part of our cricketing history: John Hammond, the Sussex and England cricketer who lived here and is buried in the churchyard, his grandsons who kept the name of Hammond alive in the annals of village cricket; Arthur E. R. Gilligan, captain of Sussex and club president; and of course, Hugh de Selincourt, captain in the 1920s and '30s and author of such classics of village cricket as *The Cricket Match* and *The Game of the Season*, in which Storrington and its cricketers appear under the lightest of disguises.

An early book on cricket records the first matches played by a Storrington team — one on Henfield Common in 1793 and another on Storrington Common in 1798. Subsequent records are lacking, however, apart from a scorebook which lists a game with Priory Park, Chichester in 1856, and another in 1887.

Three famous matches were played on the ice during hard winters. One was in 1859, played on the village pond between 'sliders' and 'skaters', and another in 1867 between J. Linfield's XI and W. Hammond's XI. The most famous of all was the 1891 match between Ernest Hammond's XI and Mr Crowhurst's XI, played on the frozen millpond at Chantry. This gala event was reported in *Sporting Life* and is reproduced in plate 95. A great deal of hilarity was caused by the ruling that all players had to wear top-hats. Mr George Rapley was asked about this famous match in 1937 when he was 81 years of age. He recalled, ''Twas great fun, 'cept that I got a lovely smack on the face with the ball. No, haven't got my top hat now. Sold it to my son. Had several, you know. I was an undertaker.'

Anything seems to have provided an excuse for holding a comic cricket match — the Armistice, coronations, or just because people felt like it. Matches were played between 'sweeps' and 'bakers', between ladies and gentlemen, when only the ladies were allowed proper bats, between people in all kinds of fancy dress who paraded to the cricket ground with the band in joyful attendance.

The heyday of cricket in Storrington was recalled by Mr C. R. Waller, who remembers finding a letter on his doormat informing him that he had been elected to the committee of the Storrington Cricket Club the moment he entered his newly-purchased house in 1932! He first played at Horsham the following Saturday. Hugh de Selincourt was captain, with whom he later became firm friends. He remembered the famous victory against Bristol Wayfarers, an all-day match in which the visitors batted all day until tea, scoring 240 runs. Storrington had two hours in which to beat them, and with a quarter of an hour to go, they needed over 40 runs. C. R. Waller and D. Clarke were in and at the last over the score was close: only three runs were needed. The boundary was not marked then and C. R. Waller hit the ball hard to the Spierbridge Corner, where the ground dropped away 8 feet. 'We ran and ran — he seemed to pass me many times both from the front and rear and must have run five whilst I ran four. The scorers credited us with the necessary three runs which was legitimate; the bails were off and we had won'.

Another time was when Hugh de Selincourt took the first nine wickets of a match, and his side decided that he should have the tenth. The wicket keeper moved back in

55

case he was tempted to stump the last man, and C. R. Waller deliberately bowled wide on the leg side. The batsman hit the first ball and they ran. Fine leg hurled the ball in and he was run out by yards, foiling the kindly plot!

The Storrington Cricket Club was unique. The team played with white-painted stumps and their opponents were always amused by their lack of boundary lines. 'We ran out everything to the hedges and ditches and fives were common towards the north side. The ball pitching in the hedge was only four and had to be hit literally "out of the ground" for a six!'

Col. Ravenscroft presented the club with a flag-pole and Union Jack, which featured in the 'Colonel's Match' referred to by Hugh de Selincourt. In the early 1930s C. R. Waller designed the swan, and a Horsham sign-writer produced the first flag. Soon they had caps and ties as well. In the late 1930s Eric Hues, then a 14-year-old schoolboy, took his place in the team and gave a good account of himself. In a match against a London side in 1938 he made a last-wicket stand with Leo Gilbert for 44 — as much as the whole visiting side had scored. He was also goalkeeper for the Storrington football team against Bognor Wednesday. Hugh de Selincourt presented him with an inscribed copy of *The Game of the Season* for Christmas 1936.

One final story from Storrington's cricketing history: Brown was batting at the bottom end at Storrington and snicked the ball through the slips. The batsmen ran, the ball just crossed the boundary and the bowler's end umpire signalled four. The ball was returned to the wicket-keeper and as Brown was out of his ground, the bails were taken off with an appeal for run out. The square leg umpire gave Brown out. Brown protested that the other umpire had signalled a boundary. 'Ah,' said the square leg umpire, 'he is in charge of his end and I am in charge of mine and you are out.' In the score book it was recorded that Brown had scored a boundary and was run out off the same ball. (*Storrington Cricket Club Magazine, 1974*).

The Storrington Show

The Storrington Show claimes to be one of the oldest in the county. Reference was first made to it in the *West Sussex Gazette* of 7 April 1864:

> '*Cottage Gardeners' Show*. We understand that a show of fruit, vegetables and flowers, grown by cottagers, will take place in Storrington in the month of September next. Prizes will also be given for the best kept garden. This will be the first show and a good competition will be expected from the neighbourhood'.

The Show report in long columns of purple prose on 22 September 1864, began, 'Nothing succeeds like success'. Mr Hemingway, promoter and honorary secretary of the new show certainly had a triumphant event to his credit, and the *Gazette* reporter gave rapturous details of the show. Sixty exhibitors had sent their choicest productions, 'ladies and gentlemen of the two parishes' had sent fine collections of fruit, vegetables and flowers and to add to this, the ladies had created some beautiful and delicate devices — a shield of dahlias, stars and rosettes of flowers and festoons of hops and ivy. Mr Goatcher had sent ornamental trees and Mr Marsh a very beautiful model garden. The show was 'largely patronised by the gentry' and crowded with visitors both afternoon and evening. The band of the 8th Sussex played and the church bells pealed as prizes were distributed in a marquee in Rev. James Beck's garden. The *Gazette* with a sidelong glance at the proposal for a branch railway which would have had a station in Storrington, concluded,

'. . . the Storrington Show may have gained such a position and name that Mr Hemingway, if the railway be then completed, may have to apply to Mr Geo. Hawkins for special trains for the accommodation of visitors to the Storrington and Parham Show . . .'

The next year's show had all the appearance of a well-established and popular event, as the poster (plate 99) shows. The rules reflect the social structure of the village perfectly; those permitted to enter were:

'All cottagers and small tradesmen living in the parishes . . . having paid a subscription of one penny, or in the case of children one half-penny before the first of August to Mr Hemingway, or to Messrs Botting, will be allowed to compete for the prizes offered; but no gentleman's servant, or master gardener, or person who does not principally support himself by labor [sic] will be permitted to show for any prize . . . Cottagers wishing to have their cottages inspected must give in their names before the 15th of April and Visitors appointed for the purpose will view the cottages at least twice in the course of the year'.

This competition was for the cleanest and neatest kept cottage, and those submitting their homes to such inspections were offered seven prizes which would keep them in fuel for a year — £1 10s. 0d. down to 10s. 0d.

By 1867, an item in the *West Sussex Gazette* shows that needlework was now to be included. The new Sullington School had been opened and on the occasion of a visit from the Inspector, the Rector of Sullington addressed the children:

'. . . A few words were then addressed to the girls on the importance of needlework, and the rector told them that he hoped they would carry off some of the prizes that would be offered at the forthcoming flower show at Storrington because so many servants in the present day failed in obtaining places through their ignorance in this essential part of a girl's education'.

In the early 1870s, the Rev. Henry Palmer brought his new bride to Sullington and she was invited to present the prizes at the show for that year. This would have entailed her handling many coins, so Mr Hemingway had them washed in readiness.

The annual show was held for a further 10 years, and then it lapsed. The next show was not held until 1905. A thousand people attended in the field opposite the Abbey, and it certainly made a vivid impression on little Alice Trotter, whose family lived at the Abbey at the time:

'The flower show was one of the great events of the year in our village in Sussex. The preparations were exciting, as the marquees were erected in the field and the exhibitors bearing their plants, vegetables, and butter, arrived and began searching for places on the shelves. The far end of the marquee was always reserved for three displays from the most important houses in the neighbourhood and the head gardeners were keen to win the coveted first prize from their rivals. As these gardens possessed large hothouses, many rare and tropical plants could be shown and the effects were truly magnificent. Points were awarded for artistic display, so it was not always the show of rare plants that won, as the general arrangement counted as well.
'Vegetables were scrubbed until they literally shone and the butter, from pale yellow to deep amber, looked particularly inviting. The judge, armed with a knife, would slice it thinly for texture and taste. I remember our cook being very disappointed at having failed to win on account of making her pat square instead of round. Of course, there was a tea-tent, always charged with bustle and gossip. And various competitions, such as guessing the weight of a pig. The weather always seemed perfect on the day though I remember one year when there was a terrific thunderstorm during the afternoon and a man, sitting outside his cottage door, was struck by lightning. Not the least part of the excitement was the evening's entertainment. The local village band, which was founded by my father . . . played for dancing on the green, one of the most popular numbers being the Valeta. Mrs A. de S. Georgano (née Alice Trotter) (*This England* Magazine).

The 'cleanest cottage' class was not revived, but the 'best-kept allotment or garden' class was extended so that four prizes were awarded, as well as one for the best 'window garden'. There were two medals awarded by the Agricultural and Horticultural Association Ltd., for the two most successful exhibitors who had purchased 'One and All seeds and manures' in that year. Dr Mudd was the secretary and treasurer, supported by a 'distinguished' committee. There were 87 people on the subscribers' list, contributing a total of £59 4s. 6d., which financed the show and left a balance over. Tents, including carting and putting up, cost £7 6s. 0d., with an additional 10s. 6d. to hire a tent from the Rural District Council. This, except for prize money (£20 11s. 0d.), was the greatest expense. The band, which then had 35 members, was hired for £3 10s. 0d. The open classes were keenly supported and contested by the big houses in the district — Grey-friars, Sandgate, the Abbey, Little Thakeham, Parham, Fryern, Chantry, Cobb Court, Apsley and Brook House.

In the following year Dr Mudd noted in his prize book that there were 587 entries and that 350 feet of tabling had been filled. The *Southern Weekly News* reported that it was a much better show than the previous year, although the 'new feature of the show' the needlework section, was not a success — 'There being a marked and unaccountable paucity of entries'. Perhaps the schedule was a little lacking in tact and interest: 'women over 65' could enter a crochet cross-over or hug-me-tight; 'women and girls over 15' had to make such uninspiring items as men's shirts and calico nightgowns; and the children's entries were to consist of 'marking', calico nightgowns and patching in print, calico and flannel! The show ended with dancing to the music of Storrington Military Band, which had enlivened the afternoon.

The show continued to be successful. In 1907 there were 660 entries requiring 420 feet of tabling, which Dr Mudd noted was 'quite full!', while in 1908 the *West Sussex Gazette* reported the show to be breaking all previous records for attendance and exhibits, which were up to seven hundred and fifty. A new attraction that year was a baby show. One dozen of Storrington's new population were entered, and seven of them were awarded prizes. Young Robert Dawbarn, aged between three and nine months, and his older colleague, George William Quait, 9–15 months, received winner's prizes of 15s. It was a good year for boys!

Statements of account and subscription lists exist for all the shows held from 1929 onwards. By that time, the old cottage gardening society had become the Storrington and District Horticultural Society affiliated to the Royal Horticultural Society, with 12 vice-presidents, who were local landowners and rectors, and with an executive committee of 17 people and four officials. In 1933 the subscription list recorded separate collections from Storrington, Cootham and Hurston, Roundabouts, Parham and Rackham, Thakeham, Warminghurst, Heath Common, Chantry and Sullington.

In the years up to the Second World War, the cost of putting on the show remained stable. The marquees at that time cost £28 10s. 0d., but the money received from subscriptions had nearly doubled.

In 1937 a new Handicrafts committee was formed and ran itself and the handicrafts entries with little reference to the executive committee. In 1938 their exhibition filled 40 feet of tabling and more space was required. In the following year 288 handicraft entries were attracted to the show.

During the war the show was dropped, but in 1944 the Horticultural Society was busy planning its post-war show. The handicraft sub-committee, under Mrs Blanche Langton, O.B.E., met on 4 December in the W.V.S. room. The 1945 president was Lieut.-Col. Ravenscroft, assisted by 15 vice-presidents, most of whom had held office before the war, and an executive committee of 15 'old names'. The hire of the marquees had risen to £52 11s. 8d. Food rationing and shortages of all kinds had to be remembered when the handicraft committee planned their schedule.

Washington joined the subscription list in 1948, and in 1950 the society became the Storrington and District Horticultural and Handicraft Society. In 1951 John Wolstenholme, that year's president, gave a handsome silver challenge cup to the handicraft section. It was their first major trophy. Rationing had eased by 1953 and the ladies filled their schedule with classes for iced cakes, meringues, sweets, savoury snacks and sausage rolls, and allowed competitors to use their own favourite recipes for Victoria sandwiches and fruit cakes, instead of the economy recipes previously included with the schedule. In that year, Mr E. S. Elliott became Chairman, after running the sports section under the chairmanship of the Hon. Clive Pearson. In the same year it was decided to have the show, traditionally held on a Wednesday (to fit in with early-closing), on a Saturday instead. Mr Elliott told the A.G.M. that he doubted if the committee would ever want to hold it on a Wednesday again. The handicraft entries rose to 466 in 1955, and in 1957 they formed the greater part of the show.

In 1956 a major change took place. The Society instituted paid-up membership instead of subscription, with a minimum membership fee of 2s. 6d. They also held their first autumn show for chrysanthemums, which in fact was discontinued in 1959. Mr Taylor, who was Hon. Secretary for three years during which he had done much to revitalise the show, died. His widow donated the Horace Rea-Taylor Memorial Cup and this was awarded for the highest points in the cookery classes.

Perhaps the vintage year for the post-war society was 1972. The season began with a spring show in the village hall. In May the B.B.C. 'Gardener's Question Time' team visited Storrington and the Rydon School was hired for the occasion. The Handicraft committee laid on a buffet tea for the visitors which was greatly enjoyed. The summer show that year was an excellent one, with the added attraction of a Pony Show and Gymkhana organised by Mrs Kirker-Head. The marquee, however, cost £153 to hire, and many saw the writing on the wall. The expenses of a large village show were escalating beyond the society's means, and stalwarts who had helped with the heavy preparations were getting older. Many newer members were simply not available until the Saturday of the show, and much preparation had to be done during the week, especially on the Thursday and Friday. The Handicraft committee merged with the executive committee in 1974. The show had long been made up of more or less equal numbers of entries from each section, and the collaboration was more practical. In that year the marquee hire cost £282.98, and it was obvious that the society could not go on holding the big outdoor show.

The Spierbridge School was the experimental venue of the 1975 show, and then it was moved to the Priory, to which had been added a fine new public hall and kitchen. This, with the space in the cloisters, enabled the society to continue holding a big show.

Mr Elliott resigned as Chairman in 1976. The year 1977 was Jubilee Year, and he pointed out that it was almost his own Silver Jubilee as Chairman. Those at the meeting were not to know that he was terminally ill, and he died early in the following year, after many years of loyal and devoted service to the society.

Today, the village has changed. There are no longer large houses and estates employing many gardeners, and most people's gardening is a weekend and evening pastime in small gardens. The society has kept pace with the changing way of life. More social events are held throughout the year, and the show schedules reflect the changes in gardening. Entries do not require as many vegetables per class, and new and inexperienced gardeners are given every encouragement.

New residents with new gardens find that the Storrington and District Horticultural Society offers a quick introduction to Storrington and its people, and a source of information and help for the problems that beset the amateur gardener.

Great Events

Storrington has always been exuberant in its celebration of great events. One such occasion was the Golden Jubilee of Queen Victoria, which Canon Palmer described in a letter to his mother.

'22 June 1887
'Dearest Mother
    The day passed off with great credit to those who had the conduct of the arrangements here,
and to the enjoyment of those who were invited . . . We got the hay barn prettily decorated with
festoons of evergreens, Rhododendrons and ferns and pictures and flags made by the children
waved from all corners.
    At twelve I had a church quite full and there we had the N.A. the short authorised service with
Whitfield's Anthem – Psalm 133 – I gave a little extemporar [sic] address on the Text "Dei
Gratia" (on all coins) from the lectern, but as there were no reporters you will get no written
report of it. The whole was over in ¾ of an hour and then all came down to the Barn and the feast
lasted from 1.15 to 3.15 cold except the pudding. G. [George Gibson, Sandgate] gave the mutton
and put up the tables and C. [Charles Pickersgill-Cunliffe, Sullington Manor] the pudding and a
small pig (whole) and beer and I the beef and paid for the cooking. The boys [H.P.s] pupils gave
a glass of wine all round and pipes and tobacco. After dinner I gave "The Queen" and made them
all respond in a shout with three cheers which were lustily given. After that "Rule Britannia" and
another patriotic song were sung and then lawn cricket and other games. "The young contending,
while the old surveyed" – By five o'clock your tea was made ready. Made in the copper – buns
marked V.R. to which about 100 sat down, of all ages. About 70 dined. As no other healths were
allowed, yours was not given, but I think the donor was known.
    After this there were presents and medals for the children, sent by Chattie [Mrs King, Fryern]
and the whole party came onto the lawn, and very pretty it looked. Gradually they drifted away,
some going down to join the sports at Storrington. After a scratch supper we all went up on the
Downs and saw the Bonfires and Fireworks, which were very beautiful. No less than 46 were
counted. May and Cicely [Lady Caldecott and sister] rode Bobbie by turns. We got home by 12
and today did not breakfast until nine . . .'. (Fig. 14).

Ten years later there were more celebrations for an even rarer royal event – a Diamond
Jubilee. The day began with an hour's bellringing and the Union Jack flying from the
Church tower. The Village Band turned out to play, and Divine Service was held. In
Dixon's field (below the bank in the churchyard, where the 'Old Pillery Gardens'
attached to Mr Dixon's house stood) Rev. George Faithful allowed a tent to be erected,
made by James Mead of Clapham. Inside, dinner for 400 had been laid out, 680 lb.
beef, potatoes, plum puddings, with 'what was considered a proper amount of beer and
other beverages'. After demolishing this mountain of food, races, tug-of-war and greasy
pole were the order of the day, during which the ladies arranged tea, bread and butter,
and cake. Burgess Hill band played for dancing until 9 p.m., when a 'small quantity of
beer' was served, the National Anthem was sung and three lusty cheers given for the
Queen. Mrs King of Fryern presented the children with medals. The Jubilee was marked
by the installation in the Square of a beautiful gas lamp (plate 35).
    Mr J. Parsons remembers the big bonfires in Parham and on the Downs to celebrate
the relief of Mafeking and Ladysmith in 1900. The hill known as Spion Kop at the top
of School Hill was given its name after Bridger Woolgar, Sam Huffer and Bert Medhurst
(all blacksmiths) 'fired the anvil' on the hill as a celebration. This seems to have been
the village cannon – the blacksmiths poured gunpowder into the hole in the end of
the anvil, packed it with a fuse and hammered in chalk. The fuse was lit, and hopefully
the spectators withdrew to a safe distance! The tradition of firing the anvil is said to be
very old. (Fig. 15).
    One of the most spectacular celebrations was for the Silver Jubilee of 1935, for King
George V and Queen Mary. 'Storrington's greatest day in history' proclaimed the headlines, 'Carnival parade nearly a mile long, and big torchlight procession'. Even the weather
added sparkle and that May day was described as wonderful.
    The day began, traditionally, with a peal of bells and a church service, and many of
the congregation wore fancy dress ready for the day's events. The big parade was marsh-
alled in a field in Nightingale Lane by Mr Hecks and others. Pictures were taken as it
processed down School Hill by a photographer who set up his equipment in a bedroom
of The Anchor, where he had a grandstand view of the cars, trade vehicles, fire engine,

THE STORRINGTON JUBILEE COMMITTEE,

IN ACCOUNT WITH THE SUBSCRIBERS.

1887. June.		£	s.	d.
Of 2 at £10	...	20	0	0
Of 3 at £5	...	15	0	0
Of 1 at £3 3s.	...	3	3	0
Of 3 at £3	...	9	0	0
Of 1 at £2 2s.	...	2	2	0
Of 11 at £2	...	22	0	0
Of 1 at £1 10s.	...	1	10	0
Of 5 at £1 1s.	...	5	5	0
Of 16 at £1	...	16	0	0
Of 1 at 10s. 6d.	...	0	10	6
Of 9 at 10s.	...	4	10	0
Of smaller sums	...	8	3	7
		£107	**4**	**1**

1887. June.		£	s.	d.	£	s.	d.
Dinner for 400	...	47	0	6			
2/6 each to 25 people unable to attend		3	2	6			
		50	6	0			
Deduct for "ruins"	...	2	0	0			
					48	3	0
Teas for about 850	...				12	1	0
Sports, Balloons, &c.	...				14	0	4
Band	...				6	0	0
Tent	...				8	0	0
Printing	...				2	16	0
Police	...	0	10	0			
Bell Ringers	...	0	10	0			
Stamps and Stationery	...	1	0	0			
Printing Imperial Institute Meeting	...	0	10	0			
					3	10	0
Printing these accounts	...				0	10	0
Wagstaff's stable burnt	...				3	3	0
Balance in hand	...				10	0	0
					£107	**4**	**1**

GEO. FRENCH MANT,
Chairman.

HARRY T. CHALLEN,
Hon. Sec.

Fig. 14. Storrington's jubilee expenses

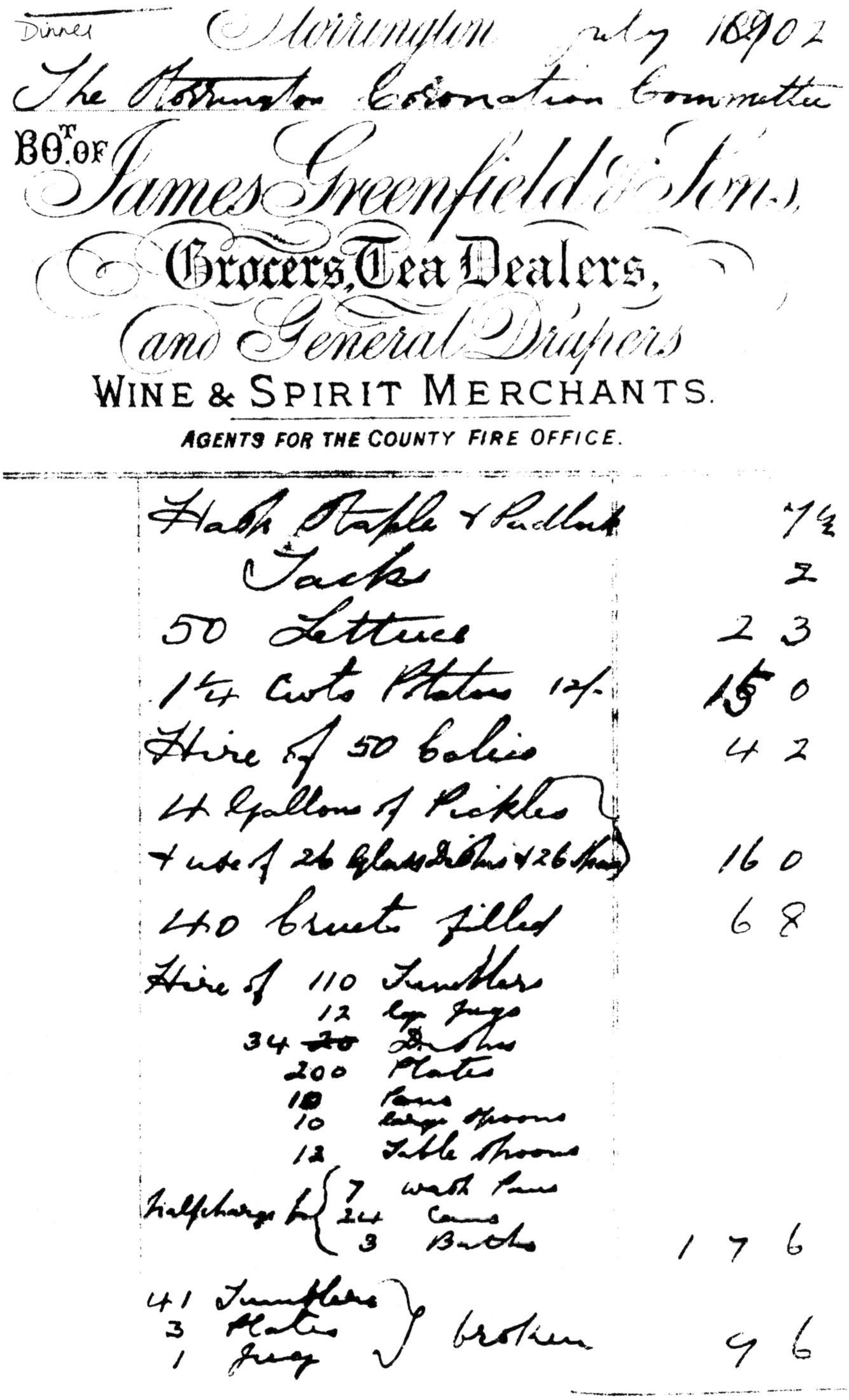

Dinner Storrington July 1902

The Storrington Coronation Committee

Bot. of James Greenfield & Sons,

Grocers, Tea Dealers, and General Drapers

WINE & SPIRIT MERCHANTS.

AGENTS FOR THE COUNTY FIRE OFFICE.

Hasp Staple & Padlock			7½
Tacks			2
50 Lettuce		2	3
1¼ Cwts Potatoes 12/-		15	0
Hire of 50 boilers		4	2
4 Gallons of Pickles & use of 26 Glass Dishes & 26 Spoons		16	0
440 Cruets filled		6	8
Hire of 110 Tumblers, 12 Cup Jugs, 34 ~~20~~ Dishes, 200 Plates, 10 Pans, 10 Large Spoons, 12 Table Spoons; Half charge for 7 Wash Pans, 24 Cans, 3 Baths	1	7	6
41 Tumblers, 3 Plates, 1 Jug broken		9	6

Fig. 15. 1902 Coronation dinner account from Greenfields

waggons, cycles, prams, pedestrians and riders as they made their way to the recreation ground. Mr Waller and Col. Ravenscroft had prepared this for judging, and the band played and the onlookers sang.

Children's sports followed, and tea was provided by the W.I. The children had Jubilee mugs, medals and flags. After tea a comic football match was played and Mr R. Vine relayed the King's message to the crowds. A procession with 200 torches and the band marched up to Kithurst, where a huge bonfire had been built by Mr Mant and the Fire Brigade; this was one of the chain of beacons which could be seen for miles. Mr D. Rapley had organised a Silver Jubilee Ball, held at the Girl Guides Hut, which went on from 10.30 p.m. to 2.30 a.m. and at which 200 people danced the night away.

Queen Elizabeth II's coronation in 1953 was another occasion for parades and celebrations. The village was dressed with flags and Mr R. Vine, asleep in the early hours of the morning, was awakened by voices shouting outside, 'Ron! Ron!' When he eventually aroused himself there were two village merrymakers outside, shouting up to let him know that he hadn't got his coronation lights switched on! The top of this decorated shop is just visible vehind the bus in plate 103. The Parish Councils of Storrington and Sullington circulated a programme showing a new factor in national celebrations — television. Television had been slowly becoming more popular since the war, and the day-long coverage of the great event by the B.B.C. Outside Broadcast service brought the heart of the celebrations into every town and village in the service area. Everyone wanted to see the Coronation take place, but a great many people had not then got television receivers. Ron Vine installed a set in a hall for the elderly.

Fairs

One eagerly anticipated summer event was the old fair which used to visit Storrington. Mrs Cripps remembered her schooldays in the 1890s, when there were two annual fairs, on 13 May and 11 November. She bought many penny gingerbreads at these fairs, '. . . all covered in hundreds and thousands'. Mrs Cripps saw the end of a tradition going back to 1400, when the Calendar of Charter Rolls records the

'Grant of special grace to Thomas earl of Arundel, and his heirs, of a weekly market on Wednesday at their town of Storghton in the county of Sussex, and of three yearly fairs there one on the feast of SS Philip and James, another on Wednesday in Whitsun week and the third on the feast of St Martin in the winter'.

John Joyes noted that

'two fairs were held at Storrington up to about thirty years ago, which was about the time the weekly auction markets started, which gradually did away with all the fairs . . . I have seen bullocks reach from the Comrades' hut down to Mr Wickens' shop [The Bookshop] and part of the way up Church Street. The Square used to be full of tents selling toys, sweets, and other things, shooting galleries etc. At that time the triangle in front of the *White Horse* was Manorial property. The Duke of Norfolk was the Lord of the Manor, to whom owners of tents had to pay one shilling for the 24 standings but now that part is passed over to the district council'.

Three travelling fun fairs used to visit Storrington regularly: those of Tom Smith; Matthews; and Harris of Ashington; as well as circuses. They would set up (plates 105 and 106) in a field by the stream and at Foxmead, the corner of the Amberley Road (not then built up), Gatley's field, beside the wheelwright Bridger Woolgar on Manley's Hill, or beside the windmill in Kithurst Lane, and of course, on the recreation ground.

The best-remembered fair was Tom Smith's from Steyning. Starting out at 6 a.m. they would have set up the fair by 12 noon in Storrington. The big roundabout was erected in two hours by six men, and taken down in one and a half hours. More than six men would get in each other's way, and less than six was not enough. The fair had horses and steam engines which drew thousands of gallons from the village pond. It was all brightly lit by naphtha flare lamps and later by Blanchard lamps using paraffin and air which burnt by a mantle. By 1920 they generated their own 110 volt electricity for lighting.

Tom Smith (plate 104) was a well-known character, always dressed in black from boots to hat. During the First World War he bought horses for the government, vetted by Charles Mant. He lost two or three sons during that war, and the fair closed 'for the duration'. About twenty years ago he sold the dodgems and the family now live on a caravan site at Shoreham.

In winter Tom Smith traded as a scrap merchant, and the local garages found him very useful in obtaining spares. His reputation among local traders stood high, because he visited them all before the fair left the village to see that no money was owed them. If it was, the trader was invited to identify the debtor, and Tom Smith took it out of the man's hide!

The fair had many attractions such as a fat lady and boxing booths, and it also brought the first 'wall of death' to the village. Spectators climbed the steps to see motor cycles and motor cycles with sidecars ride round the 'wall', and money was offered to anyone mad enough to ride in the sidecar.

Mr Richard (Dick) Cothard ran some of the side shows. He and his son now live in Steyning, where they have converted an old organ into the traditional fairground type, making every bit of the decoration and carving the figures themselves. Young Mr Cothard built the machinery that plays old music books; and drums, trumpets, cymbals and organ music all belt out of this lovely instrument as the old concertina music book unfolds through the 'reading' mechanism operating bellows and drumsticks.

Mrs A. de S. Georgano (née Alice Trotter) recalled the fair which always accompanied the village show:

> '. . . there was the fair, complete with old-fashioned steam roundabout, swings and coconut shies as well as hoopla. I vainly tried to win a goldfish in a tiny bowl but my hoop never landed around it without touching. I thought this most unfair.
>
> Then there was the test of strength; the lusty village lads would swing the heavy mallet and bring it down with a thud in their endeavours to send the weight soaring upwards where, if it reached the top, a bell would ring. And how few succeeded, whereas the gypsy boy manning the apparatus seemed to do it every time with the greatest of ease. Was there a trick in it, I always wondered?
>
> When we were bundled off to bed we lay awake listening to the blaring from the roundabout, vying with the music of the band, while lights could be seen from our windows making dancing patterns on the walls and floors. The sounds of revelry gradually died away, darkness invaded our room, and we fell asleep to dream of all the fun and excitement of, for us, the best day of the year'. (*This England* magazine).

Cattle fairs were held on 11 November. Cattle, horses, sheep and pigs were penned by hurdles from West Street, through the Square to School Hill corner. There were roundabouts and sideshows in front of Mulberry House and more in Parlett's field behind the White Horse Yard. Mr Charles Mant remembered his father representing the Lord of the Manor taking the tolls. These were charged for every animal, stall-holder and for the fair people, and were collected from them by an old man called Frank Figg who also posted bills. On fair night he was usually 'well oiled' and gave Mr Mant a good deal of trouble in agreeing the money he had collected with his accounts. The standard excuse was 'I baint no Skollard'.

Storrington in those days presented a vastly different appearance, with no yellow lines or traffic; and with all the shouting, noise and bustle of the fair and animal noises in the main streets, with gypsies and dealers trotting horses up and down to show their paces, and an influx of people attending this annual event.

Cattle pens were cleared at noon and more stalls set up. There, people could buy humbugs and fairings, 'babies' — a flat child-shaped cake suitably marked with currants and peel, pickled salmon, a most useful commodity before Storrington had a fishmonger, 'squirts' or tubes filled with water for shooting at people, peppermints, hard-bake and sweet loaves. The fair people stayed in the area for a few days afterwards, selling brushes and brooms, leather, velvet and boots from door-to-door. Charles Mant, like Mrs Cripps, saw the end of an old tradition; 11 November would be remembered as Armistice Day in the coming years.

The Storrington Military Band

According to Mr Rapley,

The Storrington Village Band was preceded by a band composed of monks and lay brothers from the Premonstratensian Priory. This band numbered nine or ten performers all playing on brass instruments and its rehearsals were held in a temporary shed on the site now occupied by the Monastery Church. Before very long this band had ceased to exist, principally owing to deaths among the players. The Prior's interest, however, did not cease with the cessation of this band, and when the village band appeared he not only subscribed to its funds, but invited it two or three times a year to play in the Monastery grounds, and liberally rewarded its efforts.

The village band was formed on 1 February 1904 by Mr Trotter who lived at the Abbey. Helped to some extent by public subscriptions, but mainly from his own resources, he provided the instruments as well as the music. He played both the oboe and trombone and superintended the practices on Mondays and Fridays. Later on, Mr Bampton came over from Christ's Hospital and coached the Band on Wednesdays. The rehearsals were held at first in Dr Lee's house, 'Southdown', which was then empty. They moved to the old malthouse in Lady Place grounds, and subsequently Mr Trotter rented a site from the Monastery on the waste ground facing the church and erected a wooden room there. When the Village Hall opened its hospitable doors to the band, this wooden room was sold to the Thakeham R.D.C. and removed to the top of School Hill, where it became their Council Offices.

At the outset, only two or three of the Band knew anything about music, but energy and enthusiasm soon overcame all difficulties, and when the band was only 10 months old, it gave its first concert in the Village Hall on 14 December 1904. In preparation for the great event Mr Smith from Queen's Hall, London, came to coach the performers. At his own expense, Mr Trotter had been sending one of the clarinet players to London for lessons, and one month or so after this concert he took the Band to Brighton to hear Sousa's band which Sousa himself conducted.

In June 1906 the Band, which had started with brass only, but had by this time added reed instruments, entered for a contest at Horsham. The result was not altogether happy, as the judge advised them to go home and learn to play in tune. In 1907 they gave two concerts at Pulborough and one at Steyning. As the years went by, the Band played at church parades at Washington and Arundel and at Flower Shows as far afield as Southwater.

During the First World War, several Band members were called up for active service and some were killed. Mr Trotter left Storrington, and the secretary, Mr Harry Gibbs, died; the Band went through a period of suspended animation. At the end of the war, Mr C. Mitchell of saxophone fame, revived the Band and acted as Bandmaster with Mr Gordon Mitchell as secretary. The latter was soon succeeded by Mr Ewan Goff, who had always taken an active interest in the Band, being a useful clarinet player.

Mr George Daughtrey succeeded to bandmastership, and a new career of undiminished prestige followed. The Band played at Flower Shows at Pulborough and Bognor, church parades at Broadwater and even Worthing, and in 1920 at Stopham Regatta. The Band was first in uniform in 1923, a symbol of its increasing recognition in Sussex. Not only was Stopham employing the Band at the Regatta and Conservative rallies, and Wisborough Green for its gymkhana, but even Lancing thought its presence necessary to the success of their Flower Show.

Village folk recall with pleasure the concerts in the Square which were once a regular feature. Mr J. Parsons, an ex-bandsman, remembers that they always played Christmas Carols at Greyfriars, Parham, Washington and all round. It was a big day for them. Mr Parsons played the trombone and was with the Band for 30 years, finishing after the Second World War. Mr Carn's memory of the Christmas carol visits made by the Band, are of stopping at Fryern Lodge, where his grandparents, Mr and Mrs Mitchell, lived. They played a couple of carols there, knowing that Mrs Mitchell always invited them in for a drink. Her home-made orange wine was well-known for its excellence. The whole Band inside the tiny lodge was a tight fit, but by the time they took their leave and made their way to the big house to play, some of them were well and truly merry.

Charles Mant recalled one notable Christmas when the Band told him that the big houses had subscribed well, but there was little 'hospitality'. Mr Mant, helped by his great friend Lionel Faithfull, invited them to 'The Dawes' for 'a bit of a tune and supper'. In the big kitchen of 'The Dawes' sandwiches, bread, cheese and beer awaited them. Food, music, and more food with the beer flowing freely, and then Charles Mant offered them whisky. After a time, finding the whisky 'taking hold', they wanted to add water to their glasses. The jugs had been filled ready for this by Lionell Faithfull and himself, *but with gin* (then a mere 2s. 6d. per bottle).

Finally the Band, having enjoyed their 'hospitality' enormously, took their very late leave, going home in various directions playing their instruments. some joyfully, some mournfully. The strains of 'Oh, Oh, Antonio' were heard from the Cootham direction at 1.30 a.m. Others, talking at the corner of Brown's Lane, disturbed the Rector living at 'Orchard Way', who threw up his bedroom window with such force to shout at them to go home, that the glass shattered around his head.

Charles Mant remembered it all being rather harmless fun. They could not have known that war would break out in the following year (1914) and that some of those merry-makers would never have another Christmas to celebrate.

7. STORRINGTON AT SCHOOL

The Village School — Spierbridge C.P. School — Sullington School — St Norbert's Roman Catholic School — St Joseph's Dominican Convent — Rydon Secondary Modern School — Private Schools — The College

The Village School

THE STORY OF THE OLD VILLAGE SCHOOL begins in 1763, when Jane Downer left a sum of money in her will to be vested in five trustees with powers to make rules for the school. The money was to teach 20 poor children reading, writing and arithmetic, the Church Catechism and Psalmody, so that they might take part in Church Services. John and Mary Hooper added to this sum to increase the salary of the master on condition that he taught another 10 children. Education in those days was a great privilege, rare for ordinary children, and the most terrible punishment was 'to be struck off the list for EVER'.

By 1868 there were 50 scholars at the school under Mr Alfred Lashmar and paid monitors but after 1875 properly appointed teachers were installed. The school's three rooms were the Boys' Department with 50 pupils under the headmaster, Mr Thomas Moore; the Girls' Department with 40 girls under Mrs Annie Moore; and Infants, 24 under Miss Kent. In 1879 Mr Thomas King took over temporarily. The school had grown considerably, and in that year new appointments were made; Mr Thomas Andrews to the Boys' Department and Mrs Sarah Andrews to the Girls and Infants. These two had pupil teachers to help.

Mrs Cripps attended from 1891-97, starting at five years old and leaving aged eleven. She remembered two Infants' teachers in addition to Mrs Andrews and Mr Andrews. They and their children, Bob and Irene, lived next door to the school. Mrs Cripps lived at 'Peacock Tree', Roundabouts, and walked to School by way of Hurston and Love Lane with her friend Ada Miles from 'Threals', often walking home by way of Greenhurst Lane.

At the turn of the century, the school became Storrington Board School under Mr Henry Caldwell, two assistant teachers and three pupil teachers. A lease was drawn up with the County Council, who took over the school for educational purposes from 9.45 a.m. until 4 p.m. for a nominal 1s. rent per year. The trustees were responsible between 9.00-9.45 a.m. and the premises reverted to them at 4 p.m.

In 1901 Mr Rhoden became headmaster with 160 pupils in four classes. After the First World War, during which many of those pupils lost their lives, numbers rose to nearly 200, and an army hut was added for use as a fifth classroom. Sometimes bright pupils from the school became pupil teachers there. Miss May and Miss Edie Dibble did so. May Dibble retired, but went back during the Second World War when school numbers were swollen by evacuees. Mr Rhoden was aided by Miss Allen, Miss G. Mitchell, Miss Terry, Miss Dibble, and Mrs Beard who taught the Infants.

Mr Rhoden retired in 1932, and Mr C. R. Waller became headmaster of the village school. The school and village gained a valuable resident and a fine teacher who loved his profession. Two years before, the headmaster of his previous school, Central C.E. School, Chichester, wrote him a testimonial, giving high praise of his abilities and character, ending, '. . . any school to which he is appointed will be fortunate, but I hope, sincerely hope, that he will never leave my staff'.

Mr Waller came to a school that had no hot water and no light except the caretaker's hurricane lamp. They closed at 3 p.m. in winter because it was impossible to see to work. In his first year Mr Waller managed to get 10 new windows installed. The primitive sanitation has been described on page 27. As soon as possible, he obtained electric light, flush lavatories and mains drainage. Getting alterations done was difficult because although it was a Council School, the building itself was leased.

Seven years later in 1939, the School Inspector reported to the Board of Education that

'... the children in the infant division give a willing response which is maintained throughout the school in a happy atmosphere — one of the good qualities which makes his school a pleasant one to visit. There is a marked improvement in written composition as regards structure and scope of expression. Art and Craft work continue to show promising development. Good work done in Nature Study and Geography, and attainment in Mathematics are above average ... In general, it is clear that the headmaster has already, by his clear and broadminded devotion to his conception of his duty (both in and out of school) done much to make the school a living centre of interest in the area'.

Mr Waller took children to the Hendon Air Pageant, the Aldershot Tattoo, Hampton Court, Windsor Castle, on river trips and on visits to many other places. He obtained prices from coach and railway companies for his party, and took over 100 children out for less than £1 each for the day. One or two very poor children could not afford it, but Mr Waller ensured that they went anyway. 'They were never a bit of bother', he said.

Another of his great interests was sport. He played cricket for the Storrington Cricket Club, and was 'Brock the Schoolmaster' in Hugh de Selincourt's books. He played county cricket and football, and turned out for any cricket club that was short of men! He soon instituted Sports Day for the children, and made it a memorable day for them, with prizes presented by Col. Ravenscroft. Mr Waller went to the recreation ground beforehand, putting in hours of work marking out courses and putting up tapes. Chapter 9 relates his grand wartime service. He also held a 1925 warrant as a sergeant in the Special Constabulary, and started and commanded C flight 1140 (Chanctonbury) Squadron of the Air Training Corps, preparing many youngsters for air crew. His love of teaching extended to 910 hours of voluntary instruction to cadets during the four years of the Squadron's existence.

Mrs Waller started the wartime school canteen — a pioneering venture that preceded the official school meals service. She master-minded the smooth changeover to the new Spierbridge School canteen. In that time Mrs Waller served one million meals in trying conditions. Mr Waller's retirement was delayed for one year so that he, too, could oversee the change when the new school was built. It was by no means easy, as part of the old school, the Infants, were housed in pre-fabs and only two classrooms were completed, so that only part of the school could move in. He saw the remaining six rooms built and the eight-class Junior School installed and working, although his Infants were still housed in their pre-fabs. Optimistically, Mr Waller pegged out the site for the swimming pool to be installed! A testimonial was presented to him on his retirement, recognising his loyal and devoted service to the school and the community.

In Mr Waller's time 3,000 pupils passed through his hands, 300 going on to Grammar schools. Forty of the latter completed their education at colleges and universities.

Storrington County Primary School

The new school in Spierbridge was officially opened in 1965, but the building was by no means complete on that day. The old village school continued in use for some classes for a further four to five years, while building continued at Spierbridge. Two extra classrooms were built, the hall was extended outwards and the music room and kitchen were added. During extensions Mr Carter took eleven-plus exams while pneumatic drills and machinery worked away next door. Large open-plan classrooms were added to accommodate the intake and infant classes.

The school has an impressive curriculum — the basic three Rs, music, science, P.E., history, geography and plenty of sport: football, netball, rounders, volleyball, swimming and cricket. Four specialist teachers coach the music classes where children can learn to play clarinets, 'cellos, violins, brass instruments, percussion and recorders. The school is proud of its orchestra and musical achievements.

As well as Mr Lidstone, the headmaster, who claims to know every one of the 315-40 children at least by sight, the school has 10 full-time teachers. Two originally taught at the old school and Mr Carter actually started teaching the children of original pupils about ten years ago.

Parents give splendid support to the school, raising large sums of money for extra equipment. They raised £5,000–£6,000 for the new heated swimming pool and then built it themselves, and a more recent purchase was a video cassette recorder. They paid for and erected a covered way, where children could be met in wet weather, and which could also double as a changing area for the pool. In the past 10 years this keen organisation has raised £10,000 for equipment. Fornightly newsletters keep parents in touch, and in March there is an open evening and display.

Spierbridge C.P. School has had three headmasters since it opened — Mr Waller who saw the changeover, Mr Blackwell who took over from him in January 1965 and Mr Lidstone who replaced Mr Blackwell in 1978.

Sullington Church of England School

This little school opened in the 1860s. Mr George Carew-Gibson of Sandgate established it for the children of estate workers, workhouse inmates, Barns Farm, High Titton and Chantry. It was just one room with a fireplace, a slow combustion stove in the lobby and no running water. Drinking water was carried from the big house in two pails on a yoke by Mr Puttick who lived with his family in one of the cottages.

There was one teacher and an assistant. Canon Palmer came to test the children in mental arithmetic. The ages ranged from 5-14 years and they were taught in three groups — Infants, Lower and Upper Divisions. The attendance varied between 40 and 50 pupils, all taught in the one room. Canon Palmer's diary notes:

> 1862. May 25. A new schoolmaster and wife appear today, a rustic couple but more suited to the place than their elegant predecessors.
> 1873. Nov. 28. To school, at which I have been regular for this week from 9.15–10.30 taking Scripture, Catechism and a long division class.
> Dec. 4. To the school! . . .
> Dec. 16. To the school: my Long Division girls are dull. Was not I dull at their age?
> 1884. Sept. 3. Cleared. Brisk N.W. Busy all mg. clearing up lawns. Had our school tea, which, contrary to expectation, gets this fine day. About 50: Tead them in the coach-house.

Sullington School closed in about 1917, when the estate was sold on the death of Mr Felton. Its few remaining pupils went to the village school.

The Roman Catholic School

The tiny school in Kithurst Lane was the work of the newly-installed Catholic Community. The late Mr Piper, possibly the oldest resident to have been taught there, remembered attending the school until he was 12 years old and then going to the boys' school in the monastery until he was fourteen. The teachers at the school were Sisters of Mercy who lived in Fern Road, next to the present shrine.

The late Duke of Norfolk was once a pupil there, and Mrs Ewins sent her sons there when it was run by Father Philip. The only teacher was Miss Stokes and after she died, Miss Robertson took over. There were about thirty children — a mixed school shared by evacuees during the war. A tortoise stove in the middle of the room heated it, and the first boys to arrive in the mornings would get in the wood from the back of the monastery — usually the Anscombes, Gilberts or Ewins, and light the stove.

Soon after the Dominican Sisters came to the Abbey in 1953 and started St Joseph's Dominican Boarding and Day School, Kithurst Lane School closed. The Sisters used to send two of their number to teach at 'The Academy' as they laughingly called it, during the short time that it remained open after 1953.

The building is now used by the Priory Boxing Club.

St Joseph's Dominican Convent

The Abbey, home of Col. Ravenscroft, was sold in 1953 after his death. The Dominican Sisters, an old teaching Order, were invited by the Bishop of Arundel and Brighton to start a new school. The Abbey proved to be an ideal house for the purpose, and the Sisters moved in, opening a mixed boarding and day school in 1953 for children of all ages, although since 1971 it has been a primary school.

The school was first accommodated in the house until the old coach-house was rebuilt and part of it raised by another floor to provide classrooms. These are to the south of the house, and built around a courtyard which makes a hard playground. The first floor of the house was already conveniently arranged for small homely dormitories with four or six beds, with a bathroom and large walk-in cloakroom where the children could keep their belongings. In the old part of the house, the original dining-room facing the garden was converted to an oak-panelled chapel. The spacious gardens give the children plenty of room to play outside and the Sisters are proud of the good health record of the school, helped no doubt by the easy access to the Downs where they can often be seen walking with exercise books and pencils. In the early days of the school they even had their own farm and cows, but now they just grow their own vegetables.

The school averages 40 boarders plus local day-pupils. They have a fine record of achievement in local drama and music festivals and the art and craft work made by the children is imaginative and of a very high standard.

Rydon School

In September 1939 Britain declared war on Germany and among many peacetime activities deferred 'for the duration' was school building. The Government decreed that those already begun should be completed, so the new senior school at Thakeham, taking the place of the old Poor Law Institution which had occupied the site, was finished but the Spierbridge site on which work had not started remained empty.

Named after Henry Walter Rydon, chairman of the R.D.C., the school was officially opened on Monday 3 June 1940 by the Director of Education, Evan T. Davies. The first headmaster was Mr R. W. Bunday who had a staff of six teachers and 213 children. Mr F. C. (Cliff) Mayes had transferred from the old village school, but was soon on active service. The school began with seven classes. The caretakers, Mr and Mrs 'Taffy' Maurice, were installed in their cottage next to the school and Mr D. Rapley described it as 'A modern school such as would have been beyond the wildest dreams of our younger days, a veritable palace of a school, fit for the teaching of Kings and Princes'. There was provision for teaching every subject '... from highly scientific to cooking and laundering'. Everything was in luxurious contrast to the old school of the 1930s — '... Girls' lavatory and cloaks, the latter being fitted with numbered pegs, seating accommodation with wire racks beneath for private belongings, a suitable number of wash basins and also a drinking fountain. The girls' drying room was next visited, where wet clothes are hung to dry with the aid of an electric drying fan ...'. The Art room had magnificent windows giving a north light, and artificial adjustable lighting; and the finest gymnasium in Sussex had '... a marvellous maple floor ...' In addition, girls' and boys' changing-rooms, towel-racks, showers, wood and metal work-rooms with a forge and brazing hearth and electric lathe, a science laboratory and superb Assembly Hall were included among other modern facilities as well as a special kitchen for school meals. Thermostatically-controlled central heating, adjustable to within one degree, was yet another contrast to the days of stoves and fires in the classroom. 'It remains to be seen', wrote the correspondent, 'whether the final results will justify the enormous expense incurred in the building of what is un-doubtedly one of the finest schools of its kind in the country. The answer lies with generations to come!'

The splendid new school, however, had opened as Britain went to war, and its early years were shadowed by hostilities. The children had to learn what was grandly called 'rural sciences', but was actually part of the 'Dig for Victory' campaign and attendant skills. Mr Maurice, the caretaker, remembers one occasion when a place was needed to accommodate troops overnight who were passing through and he was asked to show the officers the boilerhouse which had been commandeered for the purpose. Having seen what they wanted, they left him to see to his duties and lock up. He found it was not so easy to get out, because they had left a guard on the door who challenged him as he came out!

On 29 July the bright new windows were painted with splint-stop, a sticky, horrible-smelling substance that would protect children from flying glass in the event of a raid. On 10 November 1940 a German bomber closely followed by Spitfires flew low over the school buildings and machine-gun bullets passed between some of the children. The air-raid warning sounded 10 minutes later! A splendid total of £163 8s. 6d. was raised in December of that year for War Weapons Week. The war continued to affect the school and by the following midsummer Mr Maurice and the gardening master were called up for service in the R.A.F. Seven evacuees arrived at the school, diverted from Parham. By the end of 1942 evening classes started in book-keeping, shorthand and mathematics. There was also a mild outbreak of scarlet fever, in which six people were infected.

In 1943 the school was machine-gunned at 8.40 a.m. but few children had arrived and no-one was hurt. The police had to interview three boys at school about entering military munitions stores and stealing 'therefrom'. The surprising thing is that they should have bothered to break in at all, as there were all kinds of ammunition deposited in various places in the open! In November 1944, 10 boys were exempt from school in order to help Mr Walden with the potato harvest. The area between the brook and the school comprised little 'Dig for Victory' plots where the boys grew vegetables. The great day came at last in 1945, and the school closed for two days to celebrate V.E. Day (Victory in Europe). By July all the remaining evacuees had returned to London. Gradually the staff began to filter back to the school as they were 'demobbed' from the Forces.

By 1946 children over the age of 11 started coming in from Pulborough, as well as students from the Bognor Emergency Training College, for their four-week period of teaching practice. Later, children from Coldwaltham and Nutbourne joined the school and by 1949 children were also coming from Sutton and Bury.

Rydon School has had five headmasters: Mr Bunday, who was there when it opened until 1953; Mr H. S. Duffin, who remained until he went on sick leave in 1966,

Mr Cliff Mayes who acted for Mr Duffin during his illness and then took over as head, followed by the present head, Mr Williams, who came in 1969.

The school has also changed its 'label'. In 1939 it was Storrington Council Senior Mixed School; towards the end of the war it became the County Secondary School, and in 1952 it was amended to Rydon County Secondary School. Since 1969 it has been Rydon Intermediate School, but Mr Williams prefers just 'Rydon School'.

Private Schools

Byne Villa — Miss Gleadah and her assistant Miss Mauchlin ran a girls' boarding school, which may have been the reason for the name 'School Hill'. The school moved to Sand Lodge in its latter years, nearer the village. Perhaps Miss Gleadah felt her young ladies were safer there and a poster shows that five guineas reward was offered in 1884 for information leading to the conviction of those who had '. . . by means of catapults, air guns or some other dangerous instruments, maliciously discharged, or thrown, leaden bullets, stones or missiles at and through certain Gas Lamps . . . at Miss Gleadah's . . .'. Miss Gleadah, a little old lady straight from the pages of a Jane Austen novel as remembered by Charles Mant, with ringlets on each side of her face and a little cap on her head, used to take her pupils for the traditional walks in 'crocodiles' whilst she drove a donkey trap alongside.

Talbot House — In 1907, Dr Lee's house on School Hill was taken by Mrs Edgell, and for a while it was a kindergarten for children up to the ages of 12-13 years. Mrs Edgell had two assistants, Miss Violet Edgell and Miss Dix, and their private school was held in high regard. Mrs Whitbourn (née Faithfull), a pupil there in 1908, remembers children coming from as far as Pulborough and said that 'what you learnt there, stuck'.

Mr Fowler ran Talbot House as a boys' school for a time, including among his pupils the late Duke of Norfolk. He was a priest who veered from Roman Catholic to Church of England in his outlook, and it was during a Roman Catholic phase that he ran the school. Miss Moon, who attended a girls' school in School Hill, remembers seeing the Duke of Norfolk who would raise his hat politely when he met any of the girls.

Talbot House was last used as a school when Miss Cooper ran it as a kindergarten for a few years before the Second World War. It is now a private house named Chilmark. About 1908-09, Mrs Edgell moved to a house next to the twitten in West Street, built at the turn of the century, and ran Roselands School from there. This school closed in the early part of the First World War.

Laura Cottage — Mr Manley ran a school for gentlemen's sons here in the 1860s. He built a schoolroom in his garden, reached by a gate in the rough cutting between School Hill and Mill Lane. He had been the Storrington schoolmaster for six years before starting private teaching, and taught for most of his life. His little school became too small and he moved to Byne Cottage where he died in 1898. The house is known today as 'Manley's' and is a restaurant.

Cootham Cottage — Miss Yeats established a school in Cootham Cottage with five pupils aged from four to 11 years, but later transferred it to the Village Hall, where she taught small children. Their day began with a hymn, which she accompanied on the piano with one finger. Miss Yeats was a very good teacher, who went to Canada during the First World War to teach farmers to read and write. The school continued until Miss Yeats reached a great age, and although her pupils were young, 'they didn't go there just to play'.

The College — The most widely-known local educational establishment, 'The College' as it came to be known, was founded in 1871 by Rev. George Faithfull, when examinations replaced the purchase of army commissions. It was actually an army 'crammer', the establishment extending from Forge House to Rosemary along Church Street — in those days it was just houses without shops. Pupils were boarded out all over the village with their horses, dogs and grooms. There were as many as 60 pupils at one time, increasing the village population considerably and adding to its prosperity. In 1888 Major Austin, who had worked with Rev. George Faithfull, took over the college and continued until 1899 and the outbreak of the Boer War, which claimed most of the students. The college became so empty that Major Austin went on active service, returning afterwards to Storrington.

In 1908 he was joined by Mr W. A. Fuller, a vocational teacher from a family of teachers, with a vast sympathy and love of his students. He had a gift with the duller ones and helped them a great deal. He had once been a special correspondent for the *Morning Post* and *Standard* in Berlin, Brussels, Rome and Paris and was a great linguist.

The college flourished once more until the 1914–18 war, when many pupils went on active service. Forty 'Collegians' gave their lives and Mr Fuller himself died in 1917 in a road accident. The college filled up once again, and Mrs Fuller continued to run it with the assistance of Mr Fuller's senior tutor, Mr Gerard Smith, another experienced teacher who enabled the college to continue successfully for another 10 years. Gradually, more and more students went on to University instead of the army, and took up professions all over the world. In 1918 a chapel was furnished and dedicated, the altar, furniture and roll of honour of which was accepted by the Dean and Chapter of Chichester Cathedral when the college closed down.

By 1927 Mr Gerard Smith was joined in partnership by Capt. Green, R. H. In January 1928 Mr Smith died suddenly. Mrs Fuller continued in partnership with Capt. Green but in 1930 the college closed down and Mrs Fuller went into retirement.

Two thousand pupils passed through the college from its foundation in 1871 until its closure in 1930, including Lord Montgomery of Alamein. There are many stories and memories of the boys: of their beagles; a four-in-hand; polo on the field where the council houses now stand; of sporting fixtures with Lancing, Hurstpierpoint, Brighton and Christ's Hospital; as well as less creditable incidents such as farmers' cows let out into the Square to mix together, stories of chairs being put through all the Church Street windows, of climbing lamp-posts and putting out the newly-lit gas lamps, of people's gates found floating on the village pond or the mill pond and of the tall telegraph pole outside the 'Dawes' being festooned with chamber-pots like a Christmas tree one Bonfire night. They made their presence felt in this quiet village, and 'Faithfull's Lambs' also made their mark in campaigns across the world, from Egypt and Afghanistan, Sudan, South Africa, Bechuanaland, Ashanti to the trenches of France. Their names appear in army lists of over 80 famous regiments many of them, like the college, now just names in the history books.

8. STORRINGTON AT WAR

World War One — World War Two — Preparations — A.R.P. — Home Guard
—Special Police — Women's Land Army — War Work — Ambulance —
Evacuees — Troops — Parham in Wartime — Air Training Corps

World War One

'THE WAR TO END ALL WARS' changed a way of life in Storrington that had ambled along through the farming year and church festivals. The first sign of war in the village was the disappearance of many men into the forces. Storrington's war memorial bears silent witness to those who left the village for ever, like young Billy Charman (plate 128). The Sussex Territorials were a strong and active unit before the war and many of them went straight into the army. There was usually a camp held at Sullington which was a festive occasion in peacetime, when the village was decorated with flags and Band concerts were given. Another great change was the disappearance of the lively young men from the army 'crammer' in Church Street (see page 73).

Lord Kitchener's appeal for another 100,000 men appeared in the local press and a rally was held in the Square. Over 300 volunteers came forward, and the village was dressed with flags as the Band gave them a rousing send-off.

Even Storrington's landscape changed dramatically. The plantation at Cootham and the woods at Sandgate and Roundabouts were all cut down early in the First World War to make pit-props for the trenches and the coal mines. Mrs Norgate (née Lidbetter) was 15 years old when her young brother joined Billy Charman and went off to France. Her father was a forester, and she joined him as a Land Army Girl in cutting down trees in the Plantation (plate 131). Her 'uniform' was her own clothing (which was quickly worn out with the rough work) and an official armband, to which was added a service stripe for every six months. She remembers the prisoners working there, always with their guard. Austrian prisoners were sent to Sandgate for 'agricultural purposes'— cutting down trees. Mr Ben Farhall claims that 'you could smell them coming' as they had come straight from the trenches and were filthy. There were one or two escapes. Sandgate Cottage was raided and food stolen, and on one occasion the lake was dragged for a missing prisoner, but nothing was found.

Army regulars guarded them, including Mr Black and Mr White, who lived with their families in Water Lane cottages. Miss Alice Trotter, daughter of George Trotter, went to Sandgate to give concerts to the guards. The delightful handbill (Fig. 16) shows that she organised many such entertainments: this one was in aid of the 'National Egg Collection'. Food was apparently just as scarce in the First World War as in the Second World War, and poultry keepers were asked to donate all spare eggs to hospitals.

Those left at home did their bit to help the war effort. A branch of the British Red Cross was formed in 1914 by Mrs A. Henderson of 'The Chantry'. Mr Charles Mant lent 'The Geddings' in Church Street for their HQ, and Mrs Greenfield was the Hon. Secretary. They did splendid work, providing articles for wounded soldiers and those fighting at the front. Everything that willing hands could make, was made. Skilled wood-workers among the members turned out trolleys, screens and bed-tables, and Mr Trotter made sticks and crutches. His Military Band did their bit by collecting funds. Mrs Emile Mond of Greyfriars, who had a son in the Royal Flying Corps, gave gifts of money and materials. The depot in Church Street was used for Red Cross business, and part of it sheltered Belgian refugees. Mrs Henderson organised an annual 'Our Day' fête at 'The Chantry' which resulted in the sum of £1,923 10s. 10d. being sent to Red Cross Funds.

Everybody helped. There was a gift auction and sale, when family treasures were put under the hammer by Mr Newland Tompkins, a noted auctioneer; a Chippendale sideboard, an antique grate, a Dresden china bowl, a Sheraton cabinet and other valuables joined the gifts of livestock and produce. People 'bought time' to keep the Red Cross going: £5 bought one minute; £2 10s. 0d. bought ½ minute; down to 10d. for one second. At another fête there was a parade of mannequins in historic costumes. The ladies then mounted an auction block and their costumes were auctioned.

An auction of war trophies brought the war right home to everyone. They had assembled a German helmet taken by Mrs Henderson's son, Lt. Gordon

STORRINGTON VILLAGE HALL.

GRAND

Entertainment

Will be held on

WEDNESDAY & THURSDAY,

SEPTEMBER 22nd & 23rd, 1915,

COMMENCING AT 8 p.m.

For two nights only, no Matinee.

In aid of The National Egg Collection for our sick and wounded Soldiers and Sailors, Storrington Depot.

Variety Performance,

Consisting of Violin Solo by Miss Goff,
Dance by Miss Trotter, etc., followed by

GRAND REVUE

Entitled :—" HOT STUFF,"

Written by Miss A. Trotter.

The Storrington Orchestra will attend.

The great success of the season, full of Bright Humour and Popular Music.

Book your seats early to avoid disappointment.

Tickets can be obtained from Mr. H. W J Peterson, Stationer, Storrington, where a plan of the Hall can be seen.

FRONT SEATS 2s.,   BACK SEATS 1s.,   GALLERY 6d.

Front and Back Seats are numbered and reserved.

Tickets for Back Seats can be obtained before the day of the performance for 6 eggs, Gallery 3 eggs.

H. W. J. Peterson, Stationer, Storrington.

Figure 16

Munro (later, Sir Gordon) during the Mons retreat; two gas helmets, one from Gallipoli and one from the Somme, still moist and smelling strongly of gas; and a sailor's towel riddled with shrapnel belonging to the stoker on the submarine E13, gunned by the Germans as it lay helpless on a Danish beach. There were items of jewellery made from wire from a shot-down Zeppelin. A bracelet made of this was purchased for five guineas (I wonder who owns it now?). Popular Aunt Sally targets were 'The Kaiser' and 'Little Willie'.

'The Geddings' headquarters closed in 1920. The Red Cross had dispatched 40,630 articles including shirts, socks, bandages, swabs, and wooden articles. The sum of £790 10s. 8d. had been collected to run the organisation and Dr Lee donated a motor car which raised another £200.

Children from the Sandgate Estate and elsewhere gathered masses of sphagnum moss which was used for dressing wounds. One First World War veteran said that he came home from France with a very nasty leg wound. This was dressed with sphagnum moss made into little pillows and put on hot twice a day. He said it was not a pretty sight when taken off, but a wonderful healer.

A Civil Guard was formed at Storrington with Mr W. A. Fuller as commandant and Mr H. M. Scott as drill instructor. He was an ex-policeman with army experience, and became a wartime policeman when the regular policeman, a reservist, was called up. Thirty men immediately offered their services and a drill was held the same night. The next one was held at Parham. The Civil Guard protected bridges and roads and their drills prepared the first 100,000 men to go to France. News of the retreat from Mons, where Lt. Gordon Munro was wounded, caused great dismay. 'The British Army could not possibly be driven back like that' was the general opinion. Charles Mant closed down his Animal Infirmary for the duration and joined the Army Veterinary Corps on active service.

Gradually Sussex newspapers began to carry reports of men killed and wounded in action and local names appeared — a gunner from Abbey Cottages, a 2nd Lieutenant, a private from Back Lane and many others to unite the village in grief. It was a war expensive in human life, and its cost was borne by every town, village and hamlet in the country.

When the Armistice was under discussion, the troops in France were forbidden to talk about it. Mr Peto, the Storrington carrier, wrote home on a dried leaf — there was no paper available — and signed himself 'A. Peace' instead of 'A. Peto', giving his family advance information that the Armistice had been signed. The great celebrations that followed are a matter of record. Many people in the village still have postcards and photographs of the great day.

The five Belgian refugee families brought the war to Storrington, and there are one or two 'Old Contemptibles' and other First World War veterans in the village, sadly growing fewer with the passing years. Mr Parsons is a veteran of Gallipoli and the Somme, where he won a D.C.M., and Mr Knight went to France straight from Regular army service in India. Another veteran of the Somme is Col. A. C. Wilkinson, whose distinguished service continued during the Second World War at Casino, and as head of the Military Government of Landes Steiermark, Austria. A representative of the Senior Service is Mr Cowdry, a Dardanelles campaign veteran.

One affectionate memory we have of Storrington's 'Old Contemptibles' goes back a few years to a time when some of them were a little more active and could enjoy regular constitutionals around the village. They always seemed to meet for a chat on the corner of the White Horse Yard, and it was not long before conversation became animated and walking sticks were raised to the shoulder and aimed like rifles at an invisible enemy. It was like watching a silent movie and we needed no captions to know that they were back in France.

On one occasion Mr Knight was invited to try out our newly-acquired air rifle. He scorned the telescopic sight and elbow rests, and raising the gun to his shoulder, scored a bull! He was in his seventies, and when we asked him how he could shoot so well, he said, 'It was worth an extra shilling a day to be a marksman!'

There are no doubt other 'old-timers' in Storrington with recollections of that terrible war. This tribute is to them all; we owe them so much.

World War Two

It was a mere 21 years later that Britain and Germany were 'at it again' in a war that would involve everyone, not only the men and women in the forces, but also those at home doing unfamiliar war work. For many women, it meant going out to work for the first time in their lives. War work often had to be done *in addition* to a normal day's work, and children were uprooted from their homes and families and sent to live with strangers.

Doors and windows disappeared behind a wartime cloak of sandbags. Thousands of tons of sand for this purpose came from the pits at Rock, and from Hall and Co. on the Worthing Road. The Basement of the Council Offices in Chanctonbury House, the Village Hall, the Telephone Exchange at the bottom of Manley's Hill and Den Mason's

Cycle Shop (the H.Q. of the Wartime Special Police) all had their sandbagged frontages. Iron railings were taken away as part of the Salvage Drive: every bit of usable scrap was valuable and helped save cargo space in hard-pressed Merchant Navy shipping: Georgian House, Turner's Dairy in the High Street and even some graves in the churchyard that had railings round them contributed their privacy to the war effort.

Among the preparations for the changing conditions of wartime was the blackout. Householders had to be sure that not so much as a thread of light showed between their curtains, and often heavy blackout material had to be hung inside windows or even wooden shutters fitted tightly into the window frame. The Parish Church was no exception to the rules but they managed to 'camouflage' the interior of their black-out which hid the stained-glass windows in a most suitable manner (plate 134).

Street lighting was extinguished for the duration of the war, and vehicles had headlights that were reduced to a top-shaded slit that barely showed a foot or two beyond the front tyres. Hand torches were very necessary, but they had to be similarly shaded and had painted reflectors, not polished chrome. Torch batteries soon disappeared 'under the counter', as harassed shopkeepers found themselves lucky if they obtained a box of twenty-four. (The old No. 8, a popular torch size, sold for 3½d.+¾d. P.T.).

The hazards of travelling at night brought a permanent change to our roads – the painting of white lines down the middle. Charles Mant recorded this event being photographed in the middle of West Street, beside the newly-painted white line. On some nights, as Mrs Mitchell said, 'It was so black you could almost *feel* it'.

Air-raids were anticipated from the beginning of the war and if one had looked towards the Corner Garage from the direction of the pond one would have seen, until recently, an iron ladder made by Harry Gray, which followed the roof angle to the ridge, installed together with an air-raid siren at the beginning of the war. Storrington's air-raid siren was, in fact, only sounded once when it brought forth such a complaint from a neighbour, who said that she would not put up with that horrible noise, that it was never used again. That, at any rate, is the local legend. The bell on the old fire station was used for a week, during which an inadvertent false alarm was given. Storrington C.P. School had a bell which was rung as usual by a monitor to announce afternoon school, without realising the confusion that would result. Mr Waller remembers that men of the volunteer fire brigade downed tools wherever they were at work and ran to the fire station, thinking it was the alert. After that, the rope on the school bell was shortened so that it could not be rung accidentally. Church bells, too, were silenced and handbells were used at the Parish church for services. Mr Farhall, bell-ringer for 50 years, remembered that the first peal of church bells was rung after the Battle of Alamein, and then the government ordered them to be rung for special occasions. Before Alamein, it had been decided that the ringing of church bells would be the signal that England had been invaded, but they were never to convey that message.

Eventually, the wailing siren was installed at the Council Offices to be set off by the Fire Brigade, who were notified of air raids by telephone.

Air-raid shelters were not officially provided for the school but after the fall of France, when 'tip and run' raids were an easy matter for the Luftwaffe from the coast of France, volunteers dug out some 5 feet zig-zag trenches on land behind the tennis courts. Children in the playground could shelter in them when they heard the guns of nearby planes. Children soon learned the different engine notes of 'one of theirs' from 'one of ours' and it was a matter of pride to be able to identify the type of aircraft.

In school, work carried on during raids, but the children were given regular 'desk-drill' and 'gas-mask drill'. The old-fashioned heavy desks provided some kind of protection, and the children sheltered under them when told. The school had heavy black-out curtains, and windows were painted with a sticky anti-splinter solution. All the electric light bulbs were painted with a special paint, leaving only a clear glass circle the size of a shilling shining directly downwards.

Mr Broadbridge's father at 1 Finlay Cottages dug an air-raid shelter in the garden, but found that his family were not keen on using it. After sitting up night after night during air-raids they were so tired that they decided to go to bed. That night there was a raid and they lost the tiles from the roof, but slept on without realising it. The Council supplied 'Anderson' shelters to those who wanted them, but few availed themselves of the offer, which would have needed an enormous hole dug in the garden to accommodate it.

A.R.P.

One of the first civilian defence organisations formed by the local Council was the A.R.P. (air-raid precautions). Mr Best was awarded a post-war M.B.E. for his work with this organisation. Volunteers signed on for duty at the offices and became Air Raid Wardens. While on duty they wore their own clothing with the addition of a black steel helmet with a white 'W' painted on the front. They each carried their cardboard gas-mask case across one shoulder and were equipped with one of the feeble wartime torches. Often, supplies of First Aid equipment were lodged in their homes. The A.R.P. wardens were responsible for issuing gas-masks and ensuring that people knew how to wear them. When adaptors were deemed necessary for various types of gas, the A.R.P. took these around and strapped them to the existing gas-masks with special adhesive tape. Another of their duties was to bang on doors if the householders were showing lights.

The first Air Raid Post was in the billiards room at the Village Hall. Mr D. Rapley was Head Warden there and Mr G. Cripps was a messenger boy. On Friday nights when the travelling cinema was showing the films there, they watched the film in reverse, standing behind the screen on the stage. They could not sit in the hall with the audience, because they were officially 'on call' and might have to cycle up to Greyfriars or Chantry if the alert came through, and call out other wardens.

Another post was in a semi-derelict cottage behind Ron Vine's radio shop. Bert Reeves, who drove cattle trucks to markets and abattoirs to supply the army, remembers meeting there from 8-12 p.m. The four wardens spent the time playing cards. If there was a red alert after midnight, a frequent occurrence with homegoing raiders, a boy cycled out to knock them up again. The old cottage has now been demolished but in 1954 there were still the tattered remains of posters pasted to the walls, showing anti-aircraft guns and gas drill charts, the remainder of a heap of coke which had fuelled the cottage's antique range and hundreds of water-purifying tablets scattered everywhere. They were forever being trodden underfoot.

Later in the war there was another post in a bungalow in the Worthing Road next to Sussexdown. It had been built by a retired admiral in the shape of a ship's prow and was commandeered during the war. It should be remembered that A.R.P. wardens did a normal day's work in addition to routine duties every fourth night, and turned out whenever they were needed. The telephones were manned all night at the Council Offices by volunteers. Miss Langhorne and Miss Maitland-Dougall were 'caller-uppers' in addition to the former's daytime job of driving Gingell & Taylor's butcher's van. When they were informed of a raid they dispatched messenger boys, Len Cheeseman, Den Anscombe and his brother, and Glynn Cripps before he was called up into the submarine service.

Storrington saw its share of aerial warfare. A Messerschmidt 109 actually landed at Parham airstrip in the early days of the war. The incident was hushed up and the pilot hastily whisked away, but Mr Cripps, then living in Cootham, remembered this particular incident well. He was walking his dog when he saw the M.E.-109 come down, closely pursued by two British fighters who made sure that it *did* land! He saw the pilot emerge and lean against the wing; there was no-one about but himself, and he walked all round looking at the plane, while the German watched him. Then he sat on the fence, '. . . and we just looked at each other for about 10 minutes, until the police and soldiers came and I was hustled away!'

There were several air crashes, but it is very difficult now to get accurate accounts. Many people remember a Heinkel that crashed at Greyfriars. Badly damaged by anti-aircraft fire, it could not clear the Downs and its nose ended up very close to the cottage where we now live. On another occasion, Miss Maitland-Dougall drove two Germans to hospital and recalled that 'they swore and carried on all the way there, and threatened to come back and see to everyone!'

One fighter pilot was arrested by a Hall & Co. driver who saw him crash and nipped out of his cab very smartly. The R.A.F. also went to great trouble to force down intact a yellow-nosed M.E., a new aeroplane that they wanted to study. The pilot baled out and the plane came down more or less in one piece. Ron Vine who was passing in his car saw what happened and went over to 'liberate' the M.E.'s radio, which he took home and proudly displayed in his shop window! Not unnaturally under the circumstances, the police paid him a visit, and he protested, 'They were cross about it, but it *was* mine. I took it out!' Nevertheless, he had to surrender his prize. A local serviceman on leave at the time remembers seeing the plane with guards all round it to protect it from the crowd of interested onlookers. He watched fascinated, as a little boy pushed to the front of the crowd, and calmly took off the ammunition carrier cover and walked off with it! That cover was used as the door of a hen-house for years. The serviceman later saw a picture of the Heinkel in the national papers. It had been on exhibition all round the country with its ammunition carrier cover missing. Souvenir hunting was a local sport. During the Battle of Britain planes were coming down all over the Downs and everyone tried to get something, even if it was only a piece of metal they could write the date on. One such souvenir, a fuel heater from a Heinkel, is now in the German section of the radio exhibition at the Chalk Pits Museum at Houghton, together with other items including a *West Sussex Gazette* firewatcher's helmet. Mrs Richardson remembers picking up a piece of perspex from a cockpit canopy, from which she tried to make a ring. This thick perspex was very popular for making jewellery. She also recalls seeing a 'dogfight' in progress overhead with planes diving all over the sky. One caught fire and crashed on the hill and it was only recently that she read about its recovery in the local press. Dick Cothard, familiar to Storrington folk for his peacetime job with Tom Smith's Fair, would cut up and take away crashed aircraft for the authorities.

At this point, I would like to refer to a strange letter sent to the editor of *The Times*, by Alfred J. Bethell of The Abbey, Storrington. The date is *1 July 1918*, towards the end of the *First* World War.

'Sir,

Yesterday, Sunday June 10th, about midday, I was speaking to a friend of mine, both of us being in the garden here about half a mile from the foot of the South Downs. The wind was south-east, sky clear, and a bright sun. Suddenly we both saw a great number of aeroplanes, apparently about one mile away south-west and perhaps 1,500 ft up, going through evolutions of an apparrently hostile character to each other. I should say there were anything between 25 and 40 of them, all of them over the top of the Downs, and spreading inland at first. My friend and I settled that they must be squadrons practising. We watched them for, I daresay, five minutes, and then, as they drew away over the Downs to the sea, we ran about 150 yds south-west from where we were able to get a better view. But we never saw another sign of them. We had seen, as we thought, certainly two and perhaps three, come down out of control from our first stand place. In the afternoon, I happened to call at a house which lay exactly inland of where we had seen the aeroplanes, and close to the Downs. The lady of the house casually mentioned that she had spent all morning on the Downs, exactly at the point where we had seen the aeroplanes. She had seen nothing save a single one passing at some distance. I then told her what we had seen, and she was amazed. I ought to add that neither my friend or I heard any noise, either of shots or of aeroplane engines, whilst we watched. Today I met a gentleman living between this place and the house I went to visit, and he told me he had watched the whole matter, and had seen one fall quite distinctly, and went to look for it on the Downs, but had found nothing.

There is, therefore, no doubt about three men, with good eyes, having seen the same thing at the same time. Was it an instance in England of atmospheric mirage reflected from the front? The planes, however, did not appear upside down, though they had a rather unsubstantial appearance, that made my friend observe twice that somehow they looked strange. I have often seen a mirage abroad, and so had my friend, but it never struck either of us that this might be an instance of it until after I had heard that someone had been sitting on the Downs right under the apparent battle and had neither seen nor heard anything of it.

Yours faithfully,

Alfred J. Bethell'

This letter was written 22 years before the Battle of Britain. I cannot help wondering whether these independent and obviously rational observers saw the ghosts of a battle still to come. Charles Mant wrote in his diary for 11 August 1940, 'Battle of Britain begun. Much bombing and aerial flights overhead during August and September, particularly around Sept. 4th onwards. Continual Fire Brigade duty Ethel on telephone duty every night — no rest.'

Storrington also had its share of bombs. One bomb with a delayed action fuse fell short of the Worthing Road end of Sullington Lane. More bombs fell across the village from Hurston Lane in 1941, the first one landing in Hurston Grove. The last one damaged a bungalow in Nightingale Lane so badly that Mrs Ryman who was there at the time, but was fortunately unhurt, had to move out into a caravan. It demolished the wooden building next door where the Colts Club used to meet. The real target was thought to be the sawmills which were missed altogether but a plane returned to machine-gun the workmen who had dived under a stack of wood and trees for shelter. Mrs Cripps, then Betty Price, an evacuee from London, was in Hamper's Lane when a plane came over and used its machine guns. She was the only one about at the time and instinctively dived for cover, before running to the nearest house after the attack to take shelter.

Cootham residents remembered watching a dogfight which resulted in a German plane being brought down and lots of incendiaries were dropped on that occasion. One of the frequent Red Cross dances was being held in the Village Hall when the air-raid warning sounded, and bombs were dropped all through the Plantation. The dance carried on because people had by then got used to such things; afterwards, Mr Cripps and his sister went home through the Plantation, through the bomb craters. A guard at the other end of the Plantation told them they could not get through that way and insisted that they return and use another route, so back they went through the craters to go home a 'safer' way!

One stick of bombs which fell on the village was blamed on a cowman at Fryern. He had been getting in the cows with the aid of a hurricane lamp, when a plane went over and was heard to turn and come back. One bomb dropped outside Dibble's bakery and burst the water main. Two more fell near the Comrade's hut and close to Mr Best's house in Rectory Lane. Another bomb fell at the front of Mr Waller's house but did not explode, and another landed in Hormare.

The deputy Head Warden for Sullington was Mr Huffer, foreman at the sawmills during the day. The main post was at Heather Way, where Mr Ashton the Head Warden lived. He bought, at his own expense, a hut which was installed at Mr Huffer's house in Warren Hill (later Warren Hamlet). This post was manned every night by a Warden who had the assistance of messenger boys before the telephone was installed.

Mr Huffer remembered the night when he heard a 'funny-sounding plane' come over and he went outside. There was a sound like a rush of wind — a full load of incendiaries had been dropped. He saw them flaring up everywhere as he ran through to Heather Way. People were beating the gorse and heather and seemed to have everything under control so he carried on towards Angel's sandpit and Water Lane, where two old ladies lived in a cottage. One incendiary had gone through their roof but had been put out. Leaving their cottage, he almost stepped on another, and drawing back realised he was on the very edge of the sandpit! Sandgate was full of soldiers, but the A.R.P. were responsible for checking and reporting on bombs, so that was his next call. He found the soldiers busy dealing with their share of the incendiaries.

Storrington's first V.1 was seen by Fred Scutt. The air-raid warning came through in the usual way and he went outside the Fire Station and looked up. The Barn's Farm searchlight battery had picked up a strange object in their beams, and Mr Scutt says he will never forget the sight of it exploding as the machine gunners got it. Another crashed on Greatham Common and many Storrington folk remember the Wiggonholt Farm V.1 and its sad consequences. The carter had just turned his horses out to graze for the weekend and was sitting on the gate watching them, when a V.1 landed, killing all the horses. They seemed to have been the only casualties of the bombing, which also appears to have done little damage to property.

The Home Guard

Storrington, in common with other towns and villages, had its own Home Guard platoon. Their headquarters were in the monastery vacated by the White Canons for the duration. The cloisters were used as a small-bore range, well protected by sandbags, by both the Home Guard and the new A.T.C. squadron (see pages 94–95). A full-bore range was built at Marley's sandpits by the Home Guard, the work done by Wicker's men, and used for bombing, grenade practice, and assault training by the Canadians. The Home Guard were sometimes allowed to use Kithurst Ranges by the kind intervention of the Canadians. Mr Ben Farhall remembered the early issue of Winchester rifles and said that 'they weighed a ton! The magazine held five rounds of .300 ammunition, a bastard size and very awkward'. Towards the end of the war, they had short Lee Enfields 'very roughly made, the barrel often stuck out of the stock by a couple of inches, but they worked'. Another Home Guard weapon was a discharger cup for throwing the 36 hand grenades, which were used at the Marley range. They had three or five second fuses. 'You soon found out just how long those few seconds were', said Mr Farhall. 'The theory was, if you could throw a cricket ball, you could throw a grenade'. If this was the case, Storrington should have produced some good grenadiers! Practices were held on Sunday mornings either at Washington or Steyning.

Col. Thynne from Muntham Court was an old horse artilleryman and early in the war established the *Horse Patrol*. The Gatleys were members and Mr Tom Gatley bought a horse called 'Pride' for Harvey Sadler, an employee, so that he too could ride with the patrol. Men from as far away as Worthing, Steyning and all along the Downs were involved and the secrecy which surrounded their activities gave rise to several theories. One was that they were mounted messengers watching for possible invasion. The Downs were to be the second line of defence if the coastal areas were overrun. Col. Thynne carried binoculars and a lead-tipped riding crop, but otherwise they were not armed. Another theory was that they would have stayed behind enemy lines and 'gone underground' as part of a resistance group if the feared invasion swept over the Downs. They never talked about their activities and their wives did not know what they were doing — it was a very security-conscious organisation.

Home Guard duties included manning various strategic points. Orders were to make access to towns and villages impossible or extremely difficult in the event of invasion.

Storrington Home Guard had two places ready, one on the old Bostal and another between Rock and Steyning, which were mined and the detonators hidden in massive drainpipes. With both of these roads unusable, Storrington would have been cut off from Worthing by road. There were also coils of barbed wire kept in readiness to block all roads to villages. 'Dad's Army' may raise a smile today, but there is no doubt that they would have been a force to be reckoned with and a great nuisance to the enemy.

Prior to D-Day, the Home Guard really came into its own when their military training enabled regular servicemen to be released from local duties. There was a build-up of supplies coming to the South Coast, ready for the invasion of Europe. Every night two heavily-laden ammunition trains travelled to the coast via Amberley. The long isolated tunnel at Stoke was felt to be vulnerable to sabotage, and the Storrington Home Guard mounted a guard of three, one at each end and one in the middle. They were changed every two hours until morning. A memorable moment in this lonely guard duty came when the trains thundered through the tunnel.

The other special duty was the *Coastal Patrol*. There were regular army defence units along the South Coast, which had to be checked nightly and reports sent back. The Home Guard had to ring every night to get their starting time (which would be any time between 8.30 and midnight) and the night's password; the units must never know what time the check would be made on them. The inspecting contingent consisted of an officer, an N.C.O. and a driver. Storrington's posts for inspection stretched from Littlehampton to Pagham.

At Bognor a section of the pier had been removed to stop invaders using it and this had to be crossed on a plank to check the coastguard station at the end. A rough sea combined with the blackout made this journey a hair-raising experience. Lights, of course, were forbidden. The coastguards had a powerful telescope, and the invasion boats gathering in the Solent could be seen very clearly. Security was tight regarding D-Day, but the night that the boats began to move the Home Guard knew that the invasion was under way.

There was another sentry station at the end of the shingle at Aldwick. The beaches were heavily mined, and the only marking of the safe path was white-painted beach stones, which had to be identified without the aid of lights. The Home Guard were always relieved to recall the password here when challenged. The last post was a searchlight and A.A. post near Pagham churchyard, which was very eerie indeed, but after that the Coastal Patrol could return home, arriving at any time between 1.30 a.m. and 5 a.m. As Mr Waller said, it was then 'a rest, a wash, change and shave, and off to work'.

The Special Police

Mr Waller, headmaster of the Village School, wore several hats with distinction during the war. In the early days, one of our own planes was in trouble and the crew baled out over the Downs. Knowing only that parachutists had been reported, Major Cook, peacetime Master of the Storrington Beagles, paraded through the village blowing his hunting horn to warn residents. Mr Waller in his office as Sergeant of Special Police, with Mr Ron Mitchell, Special Constable, armed themselves with improvised truncheons and approached the Downs from the Springhead direction with far more heroism than confidence. Mr Waller admitted 'The Good Lord only knows what we would have done had we met any invaders — I'm sure I don't!'

It may seem a little Gilbertian that two spare-time policemen should try to tackle what, for all they knew, was the beginning of the invasion, but it reflects the spirit of the times. Ill-equipped, untrained and uninformed, they were prepared to keep the enemy out of England personally with whatever lay to hand. One baled-out German even found himself facing farm labourers armed with pitchforks, totally disregarding the gun which he wore in his holster, but prudently left where it was.

The Special Police in Storrington had two sergeants — Mr Waller and 'Wag' Stocker, the local garage owner. There were about twenty constables who were tradesmen, farmers, bus drivers and professional men when not in police uniform.

Beside School Hill Garage was an office which was the H.Q. of the Special Wartime Reserve Policemen, who were mainly retired constables recalled for the duration to relieve men of fighting age for other duties. They brought to this special service their valuable lifetime's experience and training. Mr Stenning and Mr Jeffries were two such men.

Women's Land Army

A vital civilian job taken over by women was agriculture. The Women's Land Army was formed in June 1939 and had 1,000 women trained and ready at the outbreak of war. The Hon. Director was Lady Denman, D.B.E., sister of the Hon. Clive Pearson of Parham.

Mrs Alice Batchelor, daughter of 'Punch' Edwards joined the W.L.A. aged 17½ and went to work for John Turner. There were five local girls working there, all living at home. Mrs Batchelor does not remember any formal organisation, but they did have the standard uniform which indicated that they were not available for call-up into the forces. The day began at 5.30 a.m. when the girls caught the horse and harnessed him to the cart. This, of course, except in mid-summer, was still during the black-out. They then loaded the cart and went out on the milk round. Back at the dairy they washed bottles and filled them with milk ready for the next round. The girls could turn their hands to anything that needed to be done, and Mrs Batchelor enjoyed her work with the W.L.A.

Another land girl was Mrs Connell, daughter of Mr Eliot, the head keeper, who worked in Parham gardens under George Whitehead. All Parham's pre-war gardeners had joined the forces except Ned Lidbetter and Amos Daughtrey. Mrs Connell had been working at Rackham Rectory, and in 1942 had the choice of going either into the forces or the W.L.A. She, too, says that the girls could turn their hands to any job, and did all the work in the gardens. One of today's guides, Philippa Forwood, was another Parham Land Girl. Her father was Mr Cook, Master of the Storrington Beagles.

Ena Whitehead, now Mrs Richardson, joined the Parham Land Girls after working in a Horsham shoe shop and in a munitions factory at Ifield. The girls grew vegetables for the Good Housekeeping Institute Canteen in London. Twice a week they cut truckfuls of cabbages and weighed out carrots, packing them in hampers to take to Pulborough station. They also took orders for vegetables from the cook from the officers' mess and at times supplied the soldiers' mess as well.

Other Land Girls remembered from those days were Iris Smith from Amberley and Jean Blunden (Daughtrey). Mrs Tritton recalls that in the early days of the war the farm had two very beautiful girls working there who had joined the Land Army after peace-time careers as models. These two were always being whisked away to pose for recruiting and propaganda pictures, much to the annoyance of the farm manager. Mrs Tritton furnished Rod Cottage in Clay Lane for them. The cottage next to *Fighting Cocks* was also a hostel for town girls under the charge of Mr Whitehead.

Land Girls were entitled to travel warrants so that they could go home and local girls already living at home used their warrants to visit other places. Ena Richardson had fond memories of her wartime travels. She often went to London, staying at the W.L.A. Hostel, queueing with a friend to get tickets for the ballet to watch Margot Fonteyn dance. She and Jean Blunden went to South Wales and stayed with Fred Nutbeam, head gardener at St Donats castle, who later became head gardener at Buckingham Palace.

Whilst there, they visited Mrs Jones, who had been a teacher at Rackham School. Ena Richardson's longest trip was to Edinburgh. Membership facilities of the Y.M.C.A. were available to Land Girls, so accommodation was no problem.

At Houghton and at Parham near the Douglas Lodge were Y.M.C.A. canteens where the girls went to concerts given by Entertainments National Service Association (ENSA), film shows and Forces' Talent Shows. The W.L.A. also had their own meetings organised by Mrs Scarisbrick, which might be about anything from lectures about abortion in cows, to concerts or singsongs. They were entertained by such well-known people as Joyce Grenfell, Celia Lipton and Michael Tippett.

War Work

Many industries had to abandon, or at least to reduce, production of their normal range and use their machinery and manpower for war work. Mr Eustace, an office furniture manufacturer from Battersea, took over an old workshop in Spinney Lane and turned his machinery over to making ammunition boxes and trays. A dozen local people worked for him under George Moore, doing work of a high standard. This factory shed is now someone's garage.

Miss Rogers began the war at Parham, but was asked by Bob Cripps to work on the buses — depleted by the departure of men into the forces. Miss Rogers went for her test at the Southdown in Worthing, and was measured for a uniform whilst being interviewed. She became a conductress straight away, working with Mr Bexfield and was 'on the buses' for five years, when she went into the Southdown office. Another 'clippie' was Mrs Dot Barratt who later ran the dairy in the High Street.

Storrington had its NAAFI next to Dibble & Curtis in the Colonnade (now a hair-dresser). Mrs Francis remembered the Canadian troops coming in there and asking for 'A peanut butter sandwich please, without butter'. The premises were shared with the Welfare Office, whose West Sussex Officer was Mrs Pledger. Welfare Food, orange juice, dried milk and cod liver oil was distributed at the Girl Guides' Hut on Thursdays for many years, although Mrs Mitchell remembers collecting it from Mulberry House 'Up the stairs and first left'.

The W.V.S. started the Meals-on-Wheels service for the elderly during the difficult days of food rationing. Meat, of course, was in short supply, but was eked out with rabbits, and tinned meat from American Red Cross parcels sent to the W,V.S. Twice a week, Mrs Francis cooked 100 meals in the old Market Room of the *White Horse* Hotel, and these were supplied to people in Arundel, Pulborough, Ashington, Washington and Storrington.

The Ambulance

The Storrington and District Ambulance Association was formed after a meeting on 22 July 1940, at which Dr W. R. E. Harrison, Messrs J. C. Allwork, J. H. Ashton, C. H. Campbell, R. H. Fleming, D. H. Rapley, and E. Snell discussed Storrington's need of an ambulance and opened a subscription list. Harwoods of Pulborough had a dark green Dodge ambulance, which was secured for a deposit of £50, and CXH 915 was garaged at Stocker's Garage.

Run by volunteers, the ambulance was available to the public 'for the duration' under control of the A.R.P. It was insured for £9 9s. 0d. plus £2 8s. 0d. for eight passengers and a driver. Mr Fleming, the chemist, donated dressings and others gave a first aid haversack, blankets and Red Cross articles. Petrol was rationed and could not be used wantonly. Mr Rapley filled the tank from the A.R.P. allocation and other users had to fill up from their own rations. The garage and maintenance costs were 15s. per week (75p), then considered expensive.

By September 1940 house to house collections raised £160 10s. 9d. from 129 subscribers. The sum of 2s. 0d. entitled a family to convey one free stretcher case to hospital per year within a 20-mile radius. Outside this area 4s. 2d. covered man, wife and children for a year. Fourteen journeys had been made by September and it was decided to buy two new tyres before Purchase Tax was imposed. Mrs Barnard, who ran a hand laundry in Finlay Cottages, did the ambulance laundry, and an emergency service outside the subscription area was run for 1s. 6d. per mile.

During the first year Miss Maitland-Dougall and Miss Langhorne drove the ambulance 28 times. Finances were so healthy that £200 was put into Defence Bonds and another £50 added during 'Warship Week'. By 1942 all journeys were free to subscribers. Another 250 National Savings Certificates were purchased.

The Association bought Miss Joyes' shed in Mill Lane and the adjoining property for £500 in 1943 to provide their own garage. The old A.R.P. calling-out centre, Storrington 319, was being closed down, so the N.F.S. took calls and, later, Mr Hues at Saggers' Garage did this service. The war had lasted four years, and great demands had been made on people's time and efforts: staffing had become difficult. It was thought that the post-war ambulance should be professionally run and by the end of 1945 the Association was paying for journeys with trained assistants up to 20 miles. They had invested £110 in three per cent Defence Bonds and held the limit of National Savings Certificates.

A new Austin 'Wayfarer' ambulance was offered by Mrs Saggers in May 1947, the last available for allocation that year owing to post-war shortages. It was the year of the National Health Service Act, and after 31 March the W.S.C.C. ran the ambulance and paid an agreed mileage rate. The Council was offered the new ambulance, and the old Dodge was sold to the St John Ambulance Brigade, their equipment going to the District Nurses.

When the accounts were made up, there was a credit balance of £10 14s. 9d. and investments of £1,000. The Charity Commissioners approved reconstitution of the Association as The Storrington Ambulance Trust, whose funds today are invested and applied '. . . for the benefit of sick poor persons resident in the six parishes'.

Evacuees

When war started, the government decided to evacuate children from vulnerable areas of London to the country. For several years Storrington was destined to be the home of many East End children.

Mr Waller was a billeting officer for evacuees. During a cricket match at Hove (even the war paused for cricket!), the Sussex Martlets v. Kent Yellow-hammers — a team which boasted the inclusion of Alan Knott's father — he received a telephone call to say that the first batch of evacuees were in transit. Hastily abandoning the game, Mr Waller arrived in Storrington to find that the evacuees were pregnant women in a very distressed state after an uncomfortable journey. He housed the first coachload in the Horsecroft, opposite the church.

Thereafter, Mr Waller's headaches really began. His village school suddenly acquired more than double its pre-war number of pupils and went from 300 to 700. Mr Waller was well known in many local activities and was able to '. . . commandeer empty premises, but in a nice way', as he put it. He used the Cootham parish room, the music room at the Abbey and the Comrade's Hut and the Sullington Parish Hall as overflow schoolrooms. A meticulous timetable had to be drawn up and applied. All written work was done in the village school, and other work in the out-rooms which had no desks, pens, ink or books. The pupils took mornings and afternoons at the school on alternate weeks. Everything worked smoothly.

Mrs Connor, wife of the policeman, was one of the warm-hearted people who made room in their homes for evacuees. She took in four girls. Most of these children had never been away from home before and now they were in a different world. One autumn day the evacuees had been helping to pick blackberries, obviously wondering what they were for. Mrs Connor, ekeing out wartime rations and thinking she would provide the children with a special treat, made a blackberry and apple pudding. The horror on their faces as it was served was almost comical, and they flatly refused to eat it. Mrs Connor's eldest daughter tucked into her helping with great relish, asking for more. The evacuees, realising that they were missing something good, cautiously tasted some, and were won over; blackberry and apple pudding was in demand every day for weeks, with the evacuees eagerly bringing in the blackberries.

Mrs Gatley had evacuees on the farm. One little girl, while looking fearfully out of the window at acres of fields and hills without a street or building in sight, said, 'Please Miss, does all this belong to England?'. Another girl wrote home to her parents saying that the pigs smelled so bad they needed their gas-masks! The pigs must have become tolerable, because her whole family made their home here!

Sometimes evacuation was privately arranged between London families with country cousins, but this area was a restricted one and people could not come and go without official permission. One lady had a sister and small niece living in London. When the Blitz became intolerable, she asked if she could come down to get away from the bombing. Permission was sought from the local policeman who, following orders, regretfully refused. The sister, weary of air-raids, simply got on a train and turned up on the doorstep. Her sister in Storrington naturally gave them a home, but it was an extremely difficult situation; they could not use their ration books as they were here unofficially. The first time they all visited the village, they met the policeman who spoke to the resident in the normal way, studiously avoiding 'seeing' her illegal guests!

Troops

Wartime Storrington was an island in the middle of military camps, with more khaki than 'civvies' to be seen in the village. Barns Farm Camp was built during 1939–40, and Canadian soldiers were camped at Water Lane, Sandgate, Monkmead Woods, Fryern Hall, Heath Common and Parham. Officers were billeted in Southdown House and Greyfriars, and the author's own cottage was commandeered as a wireless station.

At Monkmead, the Canadians draped loudspeakers from the trees and played loud dance music far into the night. There were stacks of petrol cans on the little road leading to the golf course from Roundabouts and local people were terrified about the fire risk, not daring to smoke out of doors. The army made the sandy track into a permanent road with concrete stands for the tanks and large vehicles, which used to drive through Storrington. Steel-tracked tanks on the road often chipped the kerbstones, sending sharp fragments flying like shrapnel. At the Heath Common camp, there was a fire which devastated the area, beginning in the stores and causing so much damage that the camp had to be abandoned.

In 1941 the Welsh Fusiliers in Sandgate had a church parade before leaving, complete with their regimental mascot — a goat. They were succeeded by Lancers and then by Canadians. There was a guarded ammunition dump in a patch of trees opposite Hall's sandpit, and another under the cedar trees in the park. The whole area was restricted and the bus from Horsham was stopped above Rock crossroads, where passengers had to

TO STORRINGTON

BARNS FARM CAMP

TO WASHINGTON

32   Gunnery Staff Offices
33   Lecture Rooms
34   Lecture Rooms
35   Cinema and Demonstration Room
36   Sports store

BARNES FARM LANE

Electrical
stores and
workshops

Lecture
Room

Control
Room

Office
and
Stores

Guard
House

Cold
store

Dining and Cook
Room   House

REME
workshop

Garage

Fuel
store

32

33

34

35

36

Men NCOs

Men NCOs

Men NCOs

Stores

Instruction hut

Pavilion

LIVING QUARTERS

Q.M. offices
and stores

W.O.s and
Sgts living
quarters

PARADE
GROUND

Sgts
Mess

Carpenter
and
Barber's shop

Fire Engine House

Officers
stores

Regimental
Institute

Regimental
Offices

OFFICERS MESS
AND QUARTERS

PLAYING
FIELD

IRRIGATION AREA

Sewage

Disposal

BARNS
FARM
HOUSE

show their identity cards. Miss Lois Puttick went to post a letter at Crescent Rise and found the Canadians were there, checking people. Miss Puttick had left her identity card at home and a small boy passing by was asked if he knew her. 'Oh yes, of course', he said, 'It's the lady who goes to church'. (So shines a good deed in a naughty world!).

The Sandgate Canadians used to hold parties for local children and would save up 3d. pieces to give them as they left the parties. Many children tasted their first ice-cream at these parties, which the soldiers used to make for them. It was almost unobtainable in the shops.

The Canadians had a Gas and Flame-thrower school at Sandgate, and the Downs were used for practice. There was a tremendous explosion in the crude mixing plant one day and lorries and oil drums caught fire and blew up. The Fire Brigade soon had its three engines there and managed to put out the fire, but several men were burnt.

It must have been very strange for a quiet village to see large military vehicles and tanks rumbling through its streets. On one occasion there was a near tragedy at the narrow bottom of Manley's Hill. Mrs Bourn, who was living in Virginia Cottage during the war, was getting ready to take the children — her own and a neighbour's — for a walk. The children were waiting in the tiny front garden for her, when the eldest child ran in to say that a tank had hit the wall and knocked it into the pram. Mrs Bourn rushed out to find a young Canadian tank driver standing there, '. . . looking as sick as I was feeling!' she said. The bricks landed in one end of the pram, wrecking it, although by some miracle the baby was not even scratched.

The Canadians provided a glamorous social life for the young ladies. The Red Cross organised dances with very good bands at the Girl Guides' hut and the Village Hall. Wartime romances led to quite a few weddings between Canadians and local girls, including Connie Martin, Barbara Hunt, Joyce Parsons and one of the Gilbert girls.

Mr F. Sutherland, landlord of the *Anchor* Inn, married a Findon girl after the war. He joined the Queen's Own Cameron Highlanders of Canada from Winnipeg, and in 1941 he and his colleagues were on their way to the South Coast. During the early months of the war there were still fears of an invasion, and he remembers being issued with five live rounds of ammunition (which had to be handed in again shortly afterwards) 'Though what good that would have done, I'm sure I don't know', he said. Mr Sutherland saw much of Sussex — Newhaven; Seaford; Horsham; a few months on the Isle of Wight training for the Dieppe raid; Fittleworth and Petworth. Then came Dieppe and 550 men of his unit passed through Storrington to the coast. Seventy-two returned from that bloodbath. Then he was at the Canadian Battle School in Wyndlesham House School. He saw quite a bit of Storrington as instructor for battle drill and bren gun carriers.

The Canadians did assault courses at the Marley sandpits where the terrain lends itself to this kind of exercise, involving climbing 30 ft quarry fences, crossing the river on ropes, and crawling through culverts. Other popular places for training with the carriers were the steep lanes around Warminghurst church, where 'Germans' (Canadians dressed in German uniforms) could ambush them, dropping down from the high banks. They used to link some of their training with that of the Home Guard, by dropping German-uniformed Canadians at remote points with instructions to return to base. They would inform the Home Guard to watch for the 'Germans' and every attempt would be made to catch them. The reward for getting back was a weekend pass, so the soldiers devised tricks such as turning their German uniforms inside out and simply walking down the road!

One vivid memory was of several carriers on exercise, one being filled with 'German' troops when the unit stopped for lunch. As the 'Germans' got out of the carrier, a British officer drove past on a motorcycle. Having verified that the unbelievable sight was not his imagination, he returned to deal with the situation though, '. . . what he thought he could do about it all on his own . . .'. Sgt Sutherland said, seeing the funny side of it.

Mr Sutherland returned to England within three months of his demob to play ice hockey, and of post-war Storrington he said, 'Storrington is a lovely place and so is all of Sussex. People should pay just to live here'.

But our lovely Downs were out of bounds during the war, and people were not allowed to go beyond a certain place at Barns Farm, Sullington Lane and Greyfriars. Once when the Misses Puttick went up via Sullington Lane to gather elderberries, they met the Rector talking to a soldier as they came back down. The were asked where they had been, and informed that it was not allowed. The next day was Sunday and as they went to church they saw a large notice just beyond the church, forbidding further access!

Chanctonbury Ring was used as an ammunition dump and was surrounded by barbed wire. Large areas of the Downs were training areas: Cobden and Lee Farms locally were used for target practice. A walk on the Downs today after a field has been ploughed inevitably reveals bomb fins, bullet cases, shrapnel in thick jagged lumps and even live mortar bombs buried since the war which have worked their way to the surface. These are still dangerous and should always be left untouched and reported to the police. The author found a live phosphorous bomb leaning against a fence, with a bent firing pin, which was still highly dangerous. The Bomb Disposal Squad exploded it, scattering phosphorous over a wide area. The author and her husband reported seeing what was believed to be a mortar bomb on another occasion. The police, on investigation, found several more in the same spot.

Many Storrington men saw little of the war at home, because they were in the services. A Cootham resident, Trooper Ronald H. Greenfield, Royal Tank Regiment, put his hamlet in the news by becoming 'one of the heroes of an episode in a battle in Italy' (*Worthing Herald*). 'Daring rescue of trapped tank men' proclaimed the headline over Tpr. Greenfield's picture, 'Eleven men pulled to safety under shell fire'. He had been abroad on active service for six months in Egypt and Sicily, when he joined the battle of Gerbini. He was ordered to drive his scout car out and rescue the men from six Sherman tanks silenced by German gunfire.

'It was my first time in action, and it looked just impossible to me. But I though to myself, "This is a queer job, but I suppose it's the sort of thing that happens". So we drove in amongst those shells and picked up four wounded tank men. We got them back and Lt. Waddel thought we should go out again. Three times we went out and got 11 men out of the crews!'

That was Tpr. Greenfield's account of the action to a military observer, but his family first heard of it from the *Herald* reporter; there was no word of it in his letters home. From driving horses for Mr Gatley, to scout cars among 'shot and shell' is a very long way.

Mr Greenfield's neighbour, Mr Bernard Dibble, also saw action early in the war. Evacuated from Dunkirk, his family received the standard printed postcard, 'I have arrived safely in England' and signed with his name, which was all the evacuees were allowed to send. Mr Dibble's war continued in North Africa, where he carried his family photographs in a leather pocket-frame made for him by his saddler. and harnessmaker father, Percy Dibble.

Mr G. Cripps joined the Submarine service on reaching call-up age in February 1943. Based in Scotland, he saw most of his service in the Norwegian Patrols, serving on *Surf*, *Safari* and *Spirit*. Asked about the dangers of that particular service, Mr Cripps said, 'They had to find me first!' His nearest brush with death was not on active service, but on exercise!

Back at home, Mr Taylor, the butcher in Church Street, used to run a social evening. When the Cootham men returned from the war, each of them was given £5 of the money he had raised.

The war, which seemed to go on for so long, ended at last. Storrington celebrated V.E. Day (and night!) with many festivities, joining the national sense of euphoria. The lights went on again and the black disturbed nights of air-raids receded into history. The Canadians dug out a large V-shaped trench on the hillside and filled it with their lethal flame-thrower mixture and set light to it. They, too, could look forward to going home.

Parham in World War Two

Mrs Pearson was asked by the billeting officer what accommodation she could offer children. They were already housing several private evacuees: Susan Ertz, the novelist (Mrs McCrindle); Sir Brian and Lady Godfrey-Fawcett, an equerry to King George V who lived in the Ranger's Lodge in Hyde Park which had been bombed, and the Siamese cat; an elderly aunt of Clive Pearson's: and Mrs Pearson's old governess and her sister. Mrs Pearson agreed to take 30 small boys in addition. There were rooms over the estate office where the indoor staff lived — they were moved into cubicles made in the long gallery in the house and the Peckham children used their rooms.

Some of the boys came with their elder sisters from a senior girls' school. They arrived at Pulborough station one day and as the girls went off one way with their leaders, the boys aged 4-10 were packed into a bus by the billeting officer with two of the senior teachers. The little boys had soon taken off their coats, to which were attached labels with their names on. The bus arrived in the courtyard at Parham, the gates were closed on each side so that the children could not run off and get lost and the driver disembarked his passengers and their packed luncheons and drove away.

All the cottages around the district housed the boys' sisters who had no idea where the bus load of pale and bewildered children had been taken. After two weeks some of the boys exchanged placed with the sisters of the other boys. The girls and problems arrived together. They were older and burdened with their mother's advice such as not to eat any vegetables that had not come out of a tin! This caused difficulties: at first, they were told that the vegetables served were from tins but after a while Clive Pearson solved the problem by setting aside part of the garden and dividing it into small allotments where pairs of children were given tools and seeds and help to cultivate them. The allotments may have only produced a few brussels sprouts, but the children happily accepted a large dish of them on the dining-table as the result of their own efforts!

Clive Pearson built them a summerhouse in the park which became their base. One thing which these London children craved was fish and chips and eventually the cook managed to give them this great treat. The appetising smell met the children before they reached the dining-room and anticipation on both sides of the serving table was great, but doomed to disappointment. The fish was not what they expected as it was coated in breadcrumbs, not batter!

Mrs Pearson gave the children an enormous Christmas tree in the Great Hall. It was the first one many of them had ever seen. During the snowy winter, they were taught to toboggan on tin trays down the hill behind the church.

Another of Mrs Pearson's great kindnesses to these uprooted children was to invite any of their parents who were able to get away, to visit and stay for Sunday lunch. The children waited at the end of the drive for this weekly reunion and the parents, who were not at all well-off, would arrive with large toys. The bombing of London eased for a while and many parents wanted their children back home. Mrs Pearson was not sure it was at all safe and pleaded with them to leave their children 'Just a few more days — a week or two'. Those persuaded by this kind lady were grateful for her concern when the bombing resumed. Others, understandably, wanted their children back at once.

The evacuees were a complete little school with three teachers, but later when they were needed elsewhere, the school was disbanded and they returned to London. In 1942 the children were re-located in homes all around the district and went to local schools. As the cars came to take them away, the Parham ladies watched them go with tears streaming down their faces. They were not to miss them for long, because in the afternoon the children returned with their new 'foster parents' to show them Parham. One family of three children was later joined by two more sisters. Their father was a barber who came to Parham regularly to cut all the children's hair. Today, one of the boys is a policeman, and he and his son regularly renew their fishing permit at Parham. The feelings of the evacuees are perhaps summed up best by a heartfelt poem, written at the time by Georgina Stevens, of which there is a framed copy in Parham's annexe.

Parham Park

It stands alone, that grand old place
Amid the beautiful Sussex Downs,
There's no other place that's quite so grand
For miles and miles around.

It stands alone, that grand old home,
Of a lady sweet and kind,
A lady whose graciousness and love
Is felt by people of every kind.

It could tell you some tales, that grand old place,
If only tales were told
Tales of beautiful morning hunts,
Of lords and ladies bold.

A lovely sight as the morning sun
Shone on the riders colours so gay
With their beautiful horses and hundreds of hounds
All eager to be on their way.

It could tell you tales of masquerade balls,
Of light and love and laughter,
Of happy couples joined together
In its little church way yonder.

But today it tells a different tale,
For Britain is at war!
And Germany has dared to try
To land upon our shore.

He has dared to bomb our capital,
And truly he will pay,
But our first thoughts are for our children,
They must be sent away.

Away from the bombs of the murderous Huns
To the country sweet and green
Away from the sound of our mighty guns
To where all is quiet and clean.

And so the doors of Parham Park
Are opened far and wide,
As she takes the kiddies to her heart
And makes them welcome inside.

Nothing is too good for them,
They play in the fields all day,
And our hearts are filled with thankfulness
To know they are looked after that way.

You see them on Sunday mornings
Happy and proud as can be
As they wait at the end of Parham drive
Their Mummy and Daddy to see.

That grand old place surveys the scene
As parents greet children dear,
As she stands and watches the kisses and smiles
She cannot suppress a tear.

So may God bless dear Parham Park
And her beautiful mistress too,
And keep all safe within her walls
Till this cruel war is thro'.

Mrs Tritton remembers everyone sitting in the evening in the Great Hall early in the war, knitting woollen garments for the men at the searchlight station at the top of the hill. Some knitted better than others, and consequently some fairly odd-shaped sweaters and garments were constructed. Mrs Pearson said, '. . . there are several men up there, and there must be someone who this will fit — or nearly, anyway'.

The residents at Parham also had their own war work. Mrs Pearson was D.P.K. (domestic poultry keeper) of the fowls kept on the lawn in front of the house. They were safe from depredations by the troops, because the Canadians themselves guarded them.

Major John Gillington of the 20th Field Company made a gate to the chicken run known as 'Gillington's Gate'. There were definite benefits in having engineers on the premises. Mrs Tritton was D.V.F.O. (deputy voluntary food officer) and a sheet of invasion instructions shows how Parham prepared for invasion in the early years.

RACKHAM RECTORY

INVASION

1. If Germans actually reach this area, we are to 'stay put' and not to go out into the roads which will be used by the *Military alone*.

2. If you have urgent reason for going out for anything, only paths and fields may be used.

3. It is important that each household should make sure of having in hand some seven days' supply of food. Always keep a stock of flour especially (and Baking Powder), for Bread will be difficult to obtain. DO THIS NOW.

4. When the Home Guard are ordered to their Stations which means actual invasion, you should go to your Food Centre (Parham House) and take with you,
   (a) The outer cover at least of your Ration Book.
   (b) Bags and baskets for carrying the tins, etc.
   (c) Money.
   The food allotted for each person costs 6/-. It consists of—

3¾ lbs biscuit	)	
1 tin corned beef	)	
1 tin soup	)	
1 tin condensed milk;	)	= 6s. 0d.;
1 lb sugar	)	
4 ozs margarine	)	
2 ozs tea	)	

5. Although this supply is to be fetched by you as soon as invasion really occurs, it is not to be used until your other food has been finished. You *may not* need it at all in which case you should keep it most carefully and return it to the Food Officer.

6. There ought to be plenty of milk, but you may have to fetch it yourself.

7. Apply to the Rectory at Rackham if you are uncertain what to do.

H. W. Weatherhead, *Voluntary Food Officer*
Veronica Rueff,   Veronica Rueff, *Deputy Voluntary Food Officer*

One German pilot shot down on the Parham Estate demanded to be taken to the German authorities! One wonders just what they were told about the progress of the war.

The house was requisitioned in 1942. The authorities had issued orders saying that any house of historic interest must be vetted before the requisition order was applied so that protective work could be assessed and carried out. Mr Scotcher, an army clerk of works, went all over the house to see what was needed and continued to look after the house during the 'occupation'.

At first there was a camp in the Park and the Gloucester Hussars kept their tanks on a hill, until one rolled down under its own steam. Then the Canadians arrived. Guards were posted at the gates and passes had to be shown by civilians. Fortunately, the Division allotted to Parham were engineers and any damage was speedily put right. The Canadians were impressed by the historic importance of the house and treated it with respect.

There were three camps in the park West Lodge camp, East Park Wall camp and Strawberry Grove camp. The H.Q. was at Pulborough Golf Club. In 1942 the 1st Canadian Division was in Storrington, with officers at Greyfriars and the mess at Gerston. The 3rd

Canadian Infantry Division built the camps in the park and Headquarters Company were in the west half of the house. They had the endearing habit of nick-naming officials, so that the padre was 'Jo Bible', the dentist 'Jo Teeth', the M.O. 'Jo Pills' and the pay-master 'Jo Money'.

The years 1943–44 saw the arrival of the Mine School with various companies coming and going, and it was one of their number, Sapper George Horse, an American Indian, who repaired Parham's basketwork chairs. From December 1944 to September 1946 there were three wings: one at Sandgate; one at Storrington; and one at Wiston with the H.Q.

After the engineers, the Canadian Battle School arrived at Parham with a more or less permanent staff. The garage became the mess and NAAFI for the troops. When the troops left, General Anders' Polish soldiers camped by Douglas Lodge.

The Canadians liked parties, and on one occasion they invited the Parham ladies to inspect their decorations in the Great Hall. They had draped it with camouflage netting and into this had stuck rhododendrons and bracken, which they solemnly assured the ladies had not been cut in the park. The soldiers asked permission to borrow a load of building stone, delivered just before the war and not used. It was used to construct a goldfish pond by the screens. A compressor outside pumped water into the pond and two goldfish hired from Worthing for the occasion were fighting for their lives against the strong current. At Mrs Pearson's anxious suggestion, two sappers built the fish a quieter backwater where they spent the rest of their time at Parham.

The Canadian engineers held some exercises which left a vivid impression. One of their jobs was underwater repairs to bridges, and the Parham swimming-pool provided an ideal place to practise. Mrs. Tritton recalled the experimental diving kit which she was invited to try out. They had devised a pair of weighted army boots, an ammunition belt, also weighted, and a gas-mask with a snorkel attachment made of Hoover hose. This Heath-Robinson equipment was surprisingly efficient and she enjoyed walking along the bottom of the pool in her bizarre kit, especially as one boot was weighted with 11 lbs and the other with 10 lbs and it was impossible to walk in a straight line! The gas-mask was supplied with air by a compressor.

One relic of the 3rd Canadian Engineers was the grain dryer on Charity Farm. A new crane truck had arrived and they were looking for some work for it. The grain-dryer, of pre-cast concrete sections, had never been assembled and it proved an ideal task for the Engineers' new toy. Clive Pearson, with his great interest in building, recorded everything and put up a notice with the names of all the engineers who had built it.

The Battle School was still in residence on V.E. Day. They celebrated the end of hostilities in Europe in their own unique manner. A party was held on top of the Downs where a large V for victory had been cut into the turf. All spare ammunition was taken up there and set off. Mrs Tritton sat on Parham's roof ridge to watch the fun, and houses that had survived the war unscathed lost various bits and pieces as the celebrations exploded joyfully. One house even parted with its verandah.

After the war Mr Scotcher, the army clerk of works, applied for a job at Parham and was employed with alacrity. His first job was to supervise the removal of protective measures taken during the war. He lived on the estate in his retirement, having finished his working life at Parham.

The house, shorn of its temporary residents, suddenly looked and smelt dirty. As the estate staff filtered back from their war service, a director of Southern Railway, of which Mr Pearson was also a director, asked him if he could employ some painters returned from war service and temporarily with nothing to occupy them. They were set to work scrubbing and cleaning and painting things 'railway yellow', and Parham emerged from its war work fresh and clean, although Mrs Tritton remembers seeing a soldier hosing down the stairs from the annexe, with another man brushing the water out of the door!

The airstrip now used by the Southern Gliding Club was covered in bomb damage rubble to stop German landings during the invasion scare, and old cars from Gray and Rowsell were parked as further obstructions. There were dummy aircraft on the site which were towed to different positions daily by tractor. A searchlight battery of seven lights was stationed at Bog Common and one night they picked up a bomber. He dived down the beam, dropping nine bombs in the Park. One, an oil bomb, scorched some trees, but otherwise did little damage. Others did not explode and on Sunday morning Mr Pearson and Mr Mitchell went to examine the crater of one unexploded bomb, which went up at 2 p.m. leaving an enormous hole. It had been fitted with a delayed action fuse.

Air Training Corps

At the outbreak of war some of the older schoolchildren were already helping local defence organisations as messenger boys and, as in the First World War, when boys reached the age of 17¼ years they were called up into the Forces. The cadet forces provided a group of youngsters familiar with service discipline and basic training in some necessary skills.

Mr C. R. Waller, who attended a selection board at the Air Ministry in 1942, was given a serving commission in the training branch of the Royal Air Force Volunteer Reserve. Although applying for active service he was considered to be doing valuable work already and was sent back to Storrington.

In 1941 'C' Flight, 1140 (Chanctonbury) squadron of the Air Training Corps was formed and paraded regularly in the Village Hall. Mr Waller prepared and called the first roll call in July 1941, and became F/O C. R. Waller. The other officers were Col. Tyndall and Mr. A. N. Francis, both of whom left in 1942 for active service. 'C' Flight was disbanded in 1945, when the demand for aircrew lessened. During that time 59 cadets received instruction and 47 went into the services; 18 in to the Royal Air Force, seven of whom gained their wings.

The cadets were a credit to their instructors: 23 out of 24 passed their first class exams and the nine who took the Final Air Crew Proficiency Exam all passed. The instructors, Capt. Hodges, Mr R. H. Saggers, Mr E. Davies, Mr L. Holdrup and F.-O. Waller were all unpaid volunteers, who gave 1,101 hours of instruction between them, of which F.-O. Waller gave 910 hours. They covered aircraft recognition, aircrew calculations, arithmetic, English, mechanics, morse and radio, musketry and shooting, navigation, physical training, drill and principles of flight. They attended 14 Church Parades and every local ceremony and celebration.

'C' Flight closed down because of post-war circumstances but it was not to be the end of Storrington's Air Training Corps. In the 1960s a new unit was formed, 2464 (Storrington) Squadron. They have their own headquarters building at R.A.F.A. Sussexdown, and parade every Monday and Friday evening. Boys aged between 13 years 9 months and 18 years are taught to fly gliders and powered aircraft, to shoot with .22 and .303 rifles and SLRs, to operate radio transmitters and receivers on their own network, as well as studying spaceflight. They attend summer camps at R.A.F. bases in this country and abroad, where they have further opportunities to fly in modern aircraft, and they can take part in a variety of local activities. The proximity of the Downs gives unlimited scope for exercises to test their physical training, map-reading, leadership and general resourcefulness. Cadets who show real leadership qualities and abilities may achieve N.C.O. rank and attend courses at R.A.F. bases.

Volunteer staff give time and expertise to the training of these cadets. Their recent commanding officer was Flight-Lieut. John Keegan, employed by Link Miles, whose tour of duty in America encouraged three Civil Air Patrol members to visit the Squadron. He was assisted by W/O. David Longdon, an ex-R.A.F. regular and more familiar to most Storrington people as the assistant postmaster, as well as civilian instructors. Ron Ham taught the cadets radio, radar, parts of their space training course and shooting, and Pilot Officer Douglas Golds was the training officer who taught map-reading and engines. He took over as Commanding Officer when John Keegan's work took him to live permanently in America.

9. NEIGHBOURS

Estates and Large Houses – Parham – Fryern Hall – Sandgate – Sullington
Rectory – Sussexdown – The Chantry – Greyfriars House –
Gerston/St Joseph's Hall – The Abbey – Heath Common – Farms

Estates and Large Houses

STORRINGTON USED TO BE surrounded by imposing houses and large estates. Most of the estates have been broken up and many houses have gone, but there are still old inhabitants of Storrington who began their working lives in those gracious surroundings.

Parham

D. G. C. Elwes, in his *History of the Castles, Mansions and Manors of Western Sussex* (1876), describes Parham as 'one of the most important mansions of western Sussex'. It holds the distinction today of being the only estate left in the Storrington area. Parham, mentioned in the Domesday Book, has existed throughout 1,000 years of history, the house itself a few years less. Robert Curzon, 15th Lord Zouche, inherited the estate from his father in 1873. He served in the Boer War with the 78th Company Imperial Yeomanry and his return was marked by triumphal arches of flags and foliage across the drive, with the estate cottages flying more flags. Crowds welcomed him home, and the band of 'L' Company 2nd Volunteer Battalion Royal Sussex Regiment added to the excitement. His arrival was preceded by cheering, and the carriage was drawn 'by eager hands' into the courtyard. Lord Zouche, who had been away for 14 months, was welcomed home with an address signed by 'the tenantry and residents on the Parham Estate'. The hospitality of Parham was extended to those present and 'the company were allowed to walk at will over the grounds'.

The staff were all expected to go to church in those days and women had to wear bonnets. The men were not paid if they missed Divine Service on Good Friday. One of the staff in plate 153 was the lamp-man. His full-time job was filling and maintaining the household lamps. The Greenfields' day book notes:

'At a Garden party at Parham, 5 August /03 (Wednesday) catered for 100 coachmen, Band etc. Mr and Mrs Lucas and J. Curtis left here at 1 o'clock with van and all goods washed crockery there both before and after use. Had use of laundry (2 rooms) and copper and firing free. Percy biked, all home 8.45, £3.17.6 incl. pd Mr and Mrs Lucas 5/-, Curtis 2/-, Percy 1/-, use of horse and van 2/6d. They put up table and forms on turf under Mulberry tree. No table cloth used. (N.B. They are not a hungry class of people)'.

The coachmen's and chauffeurs' garden party was a regular event.

Lord Zouche also seems to have financed the Parham School treats. The daybook itemised:

1899	£19.17s.6d.		1906	£15.3s.4d.
Xmas 1902	£13.6s.7½d		1908	£10.5s.5d.
1903	£15.4s.8½d	Xmas 1909	£8.16s.10d
1904	£15.5s.0½d.			

Robert Curzon, Lord Zouche, died in 1914 without an heir and the title and estate passed to his unmarried sister, Darea, 16th Baroness Zouche, who survived him by only three years.

She took an active interest in the Sussex branch of the Red Cross and the West Sussex Benefit Nursing Association. She died in 1917 and her coffin was brought home from London so that she could be buried in Parham churchyard. The path from the church to the graveside was edged with Storrington Boy Scouts and her grave was lined with ivy, violets and moss. The title passed to the daughter of her cousin, Mary Cecil, 17th Baroness Zouche who married Sir Frederick Frankland Bart. of Thirkelby. Lady Zouche sold the estate to Viscount Cowdray's younger son and in 1922 the Hon Clive Pearson brought his wife and young family to Parham. The change of ownership was fortunate for the preservation of the old house. Mrs Tritton remembers that when they moved in, there were just five 25 watt bulbs to illuminate the whole of the long gallery, making it very dark and gloomy. In addition, there were estate-made bookcases jutting out from the walls, making it very creepy and spooky and full of dark corners.

One of the first essentials was to instal proper sewage works. The house had three bathrooms, one for family and guests, one for maids and one for men, all draining into the Pleasure Pond! The children were forbidden to play there at that time. Mr Pearson then partitioned off the end of the Long Gallery where the priest's room and chapel were situated. These rooms were converted into day and night nurseries, with a bathroom for the children, who were installed here with their nanny. Three bathrooms were installed in the guest rooms, although at that time it was against the law to do so! The water came to the house in an old pipe from Springhead and had to be hand-pumped. For the big Goodwood house-parties, men were needed all night to pump water.

Four large reservoirs were dug out on top of Windmill Hill, to the left of the deergate. These were to provide against fires, as there was no adequate water supply for firefighting. A 4 inch cast iron water-pipe was laid from Springhead to Windmill Hill with a filter and softening plant to treat water from the reservoir for the house. It was not until about 1975 that mains water was laid on.

The first electricity was generated by a private plant, a baby Austin of First World War vintage which charged cells. It was run late in the evenings to supply electricity for parties as the cells did not hold a charge for very long. A Hornsby engine and dynamo took over and then a National Gas engine which ran off diesel. The first installation was done by Trollope & Colls from Dorking, in surface wiring with cleats and was finished in time for the first Goodwood house-party. The public electricity supply was laid on in the 1930s.

Heat was provided by coal boilers and wood was used when this ran out. Coal came from Pulborough station by the trainload and was fetched by horse and cart.

The 1930s were years of intense activity and a great deal of work was carried out. The architect, Mr Victor Heal, was left in charge while Clive Pearson was often away on business for long periods. He took a keen and active interest in every detail of the restoration and insisted that no original evidence be destroyed, so every time a workman discovered dressed stone Mr Pearson had to be contacted by Mr Heal so that it could be assessed and further procedure discussed. Parham contains much beautiful old panelling which had been repaired with oddments of wood and heavily painted when this was the fashion, causing problems during restoration. Every piece of panelling was removed in turn to be stripped and cleaned and most of it was found to be solid oak, quarter sawn to show the grain — much of it was Jacobean. Work was not allowed to be hurried. Clive Pearson's care that no original evidence should be altered or destroyed is revealed in the South Library. A section of panelling between the windows can be moved to one side to show the stone of an original window and when the panelling is in position it is not apparent that it is hinged and movable. On the second floor in a bedroom in the private quarters, two bricked-up windows were discovered overlooking the Great Hall from above the screens. These, with the results of other loving and patient work, can be seen by today's visitors to Parham.

The ground beneath the Great Hall and Saloon was quite solid. Mr Pearson dug into the sandy ground in two places to make wine and storage cellars. Today the shop occupies the original cellar.

Mr Pearson enjoyed every tiny detail of the restoration of Parham, which was interrupted by World War Two, and Mrs Tritton thought that he would probably have been quite disappointed to see the work finished. She herself supervised this according to the original plans, discussed in the family for many years. Lord Cowdray, visiting Parham in the 1950s, expressed surprise at seeing scaffolding still in place. He knew that work had been started in the 1920s in his grandfather's time.

Parts of the house are very old, notably the great kitchen believed to be the original building of the Abbot of Westminster dating from 1350. The foundation of the present house was laid in 1577. The earliest drawing of the house is by S. H. Grimm, 1734-94. (This artist also drew Storrington Church.) The Grimm drawing shows a remarkable difference in the arrangement and number of windows and gables. Later hands drew suggestions for an entrance gate, including a towered gatehouse and drawbridge, before the present happy arrangement was built. Another artist who drew the house in 1934 was Edward Lear. These drawings are to be seen in the annexe. A feature of local interest is the arch between the Great Hall and West Library, built of free chalk from the White Pit at the Houghton Chalk Pits (now part of the museum). This had to be sealed with milk to prevent it rubbing off the surface.

The present house and its treasures are lovingly described with a wealth of photographs by Mrs P. A. Tritton in *Parham Park, Sussex*, the guide book obtainable at the house.

The present garden flats, once the hayloft, still have stables underneath. In 1921-22 the hunters and Mr Pearson's polo ponies were stabled there. West of the stable yard were the cow stalls. Milk was carried to the house in pails on a yoke. The garden flats were also once the bothy where single grooms, chauffeurs and gardeners lived. With the advent of the motor car, Mr Pearson drove a yellow Rolls-Royce or a Bentley, but Parham still used horses for work and to bring up wood for the fires and boilers.

The Parham airstrip, laid out in Mr Pearson's time when he was chairman of British Airways, was sown with 'airfield mixture' grass seed. Brooklands flying club used it for training and in the 1930s a biplane piloted by a doctor's son, Michael Foot, crashed while stunting over the field. The pilot was unhurt, although his plane was wrecked, and was made to go up again in another plane at once so that he would not lose his nerve.

Fryern Hall

East of Parham was Fryern, stretching from West Chiltington to Storrington and including parts of Thakeham and Sullington, with the Stor winding through it. Elwes recorded in 1876 that the 'present owner' of Fryern or Fryersland, was Frederick King Esq., who inherited a repaired and enlarged house from his mother, Charlotte, Baroness King.

In 1921, 680 acres of agricultural and outlying portions of the estate were auctioned including eight small farms, a water corn-mill, two private residences, a baker's shop and wheelwright's premises, and seven cottages. Among this property was Champion's Farm, Threal's Farm, West Wantley, East Wantley, Windmill Copse with its 'valuable crop of clean oak trees', Bine Farm and its water-mill, Holly Lodge, Horse Croft Farm with over 42 acres of grass and arable land, the Manor House and Smuggler's Croft.

In 1928 two members of the King family died, and the 'Fryern Estates' were put up for sale, fetching £9,250. These were probably more outlying portions. In 1946, Fryern Home Farm and 176 acres of Hormare Farm were sold for £17,820. One year later, Fryern Mansion was on the market together with two lodges and the chauffeur's cottage with 40 acres. This raised £14,000, and for a while, Fryern became a Country Club. In 1953, it was again sold with a cottage, small farmery and 23 acres (Fig. 18) to Linfields as a hostel for their employees.

Mrs A. E. Cripps lived at Peacock Tree in Mrs King's time. Her grandfather worked for the Estate foreman, Mr Upton, and she went to school with their daughter, walking across the fields to the village school and back. After school she collected the free milk from the East Lodge. They were also entitled to receive 100 faggots. Mrs King would visit the tenants with a round tin of pink and white sugarplums, and, if the children were good and polite and curtsied prettily, they would be given two or three. Another tenant of the Lodge was Mr Mitchell, Mrs King's coachman. Plate 159 shows him in full livery waiting outside the Manor House Hotel.

Mr Francis, in charge of Linfield's 80–100 mushroom pickers, had very different memories of Fryern Hall. The firm expanded rapidly and in 1954 an executive of Linfields visited Malta to recruit more workers. Mr Francis and a colleague met the girls at Heathrow in an old coach. They were lodged at Fryern Hall, where Mr Francis and his wife went to take charge of them. Italian girls came over, then Irish, Scots and even English! They lived in dormitories with a bathroom to every two rooms and had a communal dining-hall, two lounges, one with television and the other left for general recreation. Coaches took them to work and back, and boyfriends could escort them as far as the bridge. (Plate 157). They had to be indoors by 11 p.m. and Mr Francis had little trouble with them. Italian men worked on the roses at Linfields and romance blossomed for quite a few of the girls. Mr Francis represented their fathers and gave several brides away: the first one was Nora, an Irish girl who married Luigi Ruggieri. They now run Gerston Farm. Mr Francis can never visit Worthing without an effusive welcome from ex-Linfields workers he happens to meet. The numbers at the Hall gradually diminished until there were only 20, and the Hall was closed down. It was sold to Mr Williams in the early 1960s.

The place became derelict and vandalised, and permission was given for the demolition of this old Georgian mansion. It was a sad end for the beautiful gardens, the rhododendron walks, the lake stocked with trout and the days when Mr Francis' father, coachman for Rev. Goring of Wiston, drove a four-in-hand over the little bridge to deliver his passenger to a party.

Sandgate

In 1876, Sandgate House in Sullington was the property of George Carew C. Gibson, by which time it had been converted to 'an Elizabethan mansion of considerable size and beauty' (plate 161), with an estate covering 4,000 acres. Mr Carew-Gibson owned the well-known Sandgate Thoroughbred Stud. The great stallion 'Rosecrution' was stabled in Hampers Barn in the early 1890s. Abbot's Leigh on the Washington Road was always known as The Stud. Carriage horses had stables off Water Lane, the field opposite Barns Farm Lane was known as Twenty Boxes, and on the other side of the road was Stable Field. In its heyday, the Sandgate Stud held an annual sale of yearlings on the Saturday after Goodwood Races. Mr Carew-Gibson married Miss Tattersall, a name synonymous

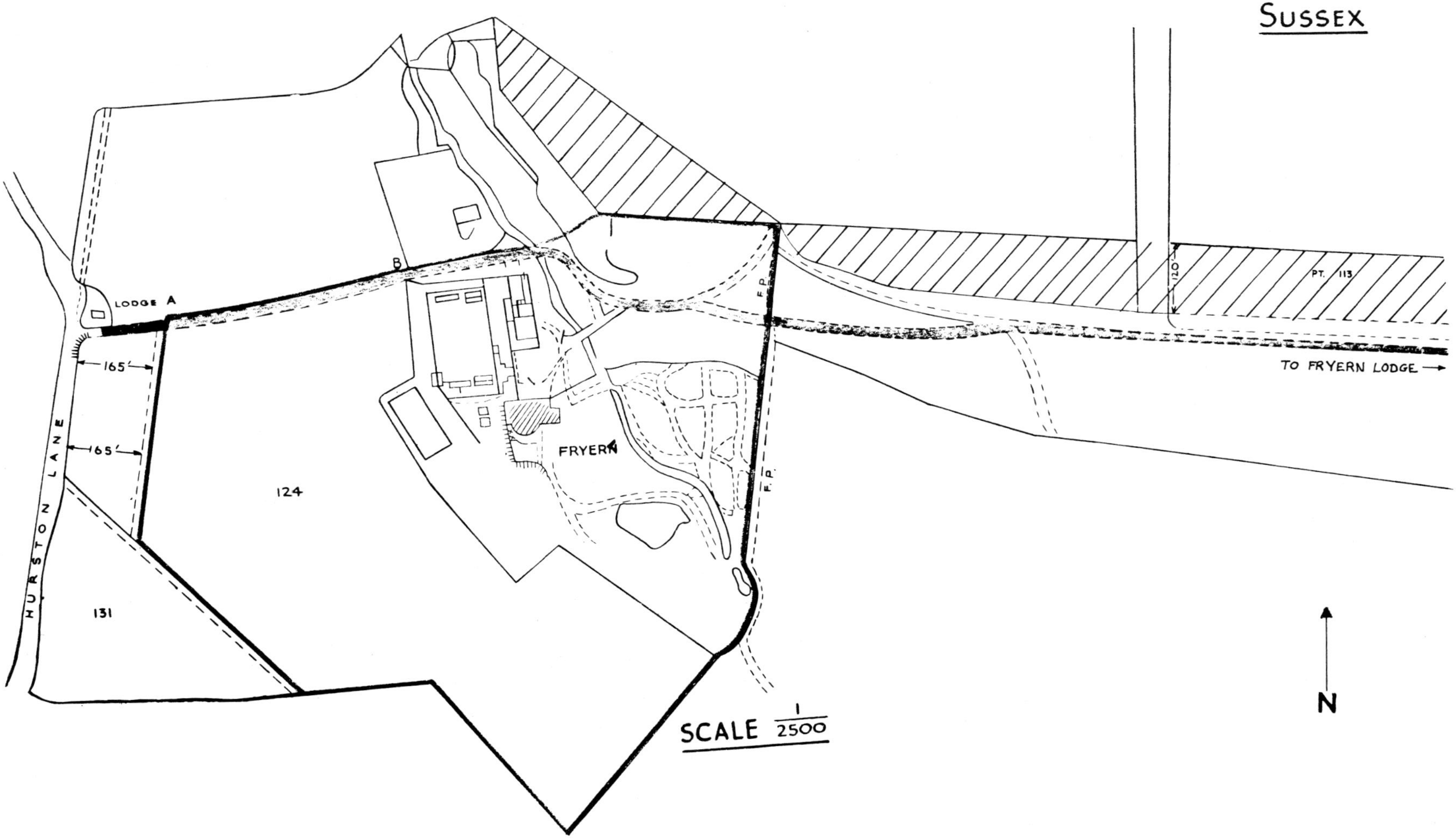

SUSSEX

N

PT. 113

TO FRYERN LODGE →

120'

SCALE 1/2500

FP

FP

FRYERN

B

124

LODGE A

165'

65'

131

HURSTON LANE

Fig. 18. Fryern Estate sale map.

with thoroughbred auctions. Two letters mentioning his horses were written to Mr Carew-Gibson by the Chief Constable at Petworth, which tell their own story.

Chief Constable's Office,
Petworth.
30th December 1881

Dear Carew-Gibson

I have to acknowledge your letter of 28th inst. received this morning. I received a letter from a private individual some days back informing me that a disease had broken out in your stables at Sandgate, 5 mares having died, and that it was expected more would die. I directed (in my capacity as Chief Inspector under the Contagious Diseases (Animals) Act) Superintendent Parnell to make the usual inquiry as is customary on receipt of such reports. He has reported to me that he has made inquiry and finds your mares were attacked with influenza.

I regret exceedingly if there were any circumstances connected with Mr Parnell's visit that could be taken objection to. I will inquire from him the particulars.

It is probable that Mr Parnell did not like to trouble you personally for the information he was required to obtain, but had he not been satisfied that there was nothing to be feared as far as the public were concerned from the malady which visited your stud farm, he would certainly have communicated with yourself.

Trusting that this explanation will be deemed satisfactory,

I remain, Dear Carew-Gibson, Yours truly . . . .

Dear Mr Carew-Gibson,   1st January 1882

In reply to your letter of 31st December, I am very sorry to be unable to comply with your request to give you the name of the gentleman who wrote to me. I feel sure you will understand that in saying this I do so with no wish to disoblige you, but when communications are made to me as Chief-Constable I am in duty bound to consider those confidential. In the present instance, the writer with whom I am acquainted wrote to me on another subject, and the latter part of his letter referred to your horses. I may say positively that no mention was made with malicious intention, but regret expressed at the occurrence.

I feel sorry I did not in the first instance write you a note to say I had directed inquiry to be made as it appears you would have preferred this, but I have never done so on similar occasions.

I am very glad to think that the result of this inquiry is that no contagious disease existed.

In 1887 the Estate was sold to Mr Felton, as a result of the crippling financial blow suffered by Mr Carew-Gibson when illness struck the stables.   Mrs Felton is pictured in the group in plate 162 just a year before she died. Mr Felton remarried in 1915, but died one year later.

Mr Puttick the Estate carpenter came in 1903, and his daughters have many memories of growing up on the Estate, such as of their father looking at a tree and telling them how many pales he could cleft from it. He was never wrong.

A walled garden adjoining Abbott's Leigh, which was the kitchen-garden, and a little path through a shrubbery led to the tennis courts and lawns. A hard path emerged at Sandgate Lodge behind Abbott's Leigh and up to the front of the house. This was the old road to Washington. Sullington schoolchildren were sometimes given the afternoon off to field balls from the shrubbery for tennis parties. This was always on a Friday afternoon, and if they missed any they would go back on Saturday morning to find the missed balls. The Puttick children also collected fir cones (pineys) for the house fires and were paid 1d. or 2d. per bushel. Dry cones were easy to carry, but wet ones were very heavy and unpleasant. They had a box-cart, sacks and two trugs for this task. On Sunday afternoons they often went with their father along a favourite rhododendron walk to the lake.

The two cottages, school and strip of land on the west side of Water Lane were given from the Estate to the Rector and Church-wardens in 1920. The Puttick family lived in one end and Miss Alder, one time nanny to the Feltons, lived in the other. The cottages had their own bakehouses where they made bread, the ovens being heated by gorse. They had earth closets, and a rainwater cistern for domestic water. Drinking water was carried to the cottages from the house. The Sanctuary was a thatched cottage known as Piglands, where Mr Raglass lived. He grew beautiful strawberries for sale in the village, and he could often be seen taking the footpath across a field where the sandpit has since been dug out, carrying a basket lined with cabbage leaves and full of strawberries.

On the death of Mr Felton, the Estate was sold in 1917. The Plantation, 250 acres of Scots pine where Heath Common is now, was sold to Mr Longbottom for timber to be used for pit-props and matches. German P.O.W.s did most of the tree-felling and the timber was taken by waggon to Pulborough, en route for Mansfield and Sheffield. It was at that time that Water Lane was made up to take the weight of the big Foden engines. Wood from Sandgate was also transported via Chantry and Chantry Post to make Littlehampton Pier.

Sandgate was later turned into a 'Christian Guest House' by Miss Gaunt-Woefl and from 1923 until the outbreak of the Second World War many East-enders stayed in the cubicles which had been made in the mansion's big rooms.

In the 1920s Vera Pragnell bought part of Heath Common from Mr Stacey and allotted one acre to a couple and half an acre to a single person as part of a back-to-the-land experiment. They built little houses, often of wood, where they squatted. Many people from this country and abroad visited the project. Major James from Worthing sent Mr Sayers, a master carpenter, plans and drawings of a Swiss chalet which was copied to the last detail in the Sanctuary, as the area came to be known. It was also said to be a refuge from the police but perhaps such an experiment, attracting as it must have done some unconventional and eccentric people, would naturally give rise to such allegations and wild tales. Strangers trying to find their way around there today, even though it is now more developed, with its tiny rough lanes that twist and turn through woodland around old boundaries, impassable under certain weather conditions, would rapidly be lost. Mr Ham always asks *exactly* where customers live before making house-calls!

Three Gates sandpit started operations in 1924, in a field that grew oats, rape and turnips for sheep-feed. Houses along the Worthing Road boundary of the old Estate started being built by Mr Frank Knight about 1922–23, soon after he started the sandpit by the Chantry Mill pond,where he made sand and cement blocks. The pits were later taken over by Marley.

Sullington Rectory

This house was the home of the Palmers, Rectors of Sullington. By 1924 father and son had served in that capacity between them for 100 years and Rev. Henry Palmer, M.A. was to remain until 1928. He became Prebendary of Bury in 1909 after 50 years as Rector and marked his half-century with the gift of a porch to Sullington church.

The date of the earliest rectory believed to have stood on the site is uncertain. Prebendary Palmer laid the foundation stone of the present Rectory in 1845 as a boy, but like other large rectories built to be run by servants it gradually became too expensive. In 1938 Rev. Sydney le Mesurier sold it and bought the present rectory on the Washington Road.

Dr A. J. Cronin bought the house, and alterations were carried out by J. Dillistone of Worthing. Mr Alfred Ham remembered working there with the firm and playing cricket on the lawn during the dinner hour. The men ensured that the last man in to bat was the foreman, as this meant an extended dinner-hour whilst he finished his innings!

The house had a succession of distinguished owners; Dr Cronin was followed by Lady Cynthia and the Hon. Herbert Asquith; and following the declaration of U.D.I. in Rhodesia, Sir Gordon and Lady Munro. Sir Gordon was High Commissioner for Rhodesia and no stranger to this district. At one time his mother had owned the Chantry, where he grew up, enjoying the countryside and especially the company of the shepherds up on the Downs. Rev. G. Mackenzie, an old friend of Sir Gordon, remembers the time when the church council were considering what to do about the church bell at Sullington. It was badly cracked and needed rehanging, but they were doubtful about spending money on it in view of the state of the bell itself. Sir Gordon Munro, a church council member, said that he had heard and loved the old bell all his life, cracked or not, and he would personally pay for its rehanging.

Sussexdown

In 1925 Mr A. Hecks sold some land between the Worthing Road and Chantry to Mr Gellatly, a shipbuilder. Mr Redgrave Cripps designed a Georgian-styled house which was called 'Candia' where Mr Gellatly lived until after World War Two. During the war, Canadian soldiers were quartered there and the lodge at the end of the drive was used as a mortuary.

In 1946 Mr John Wolstenholme, a Lancastrian, bought the house and renamed it 'Sussexdown'. He was chairman of Walmsley's (Bury) Ltd. an engineering firm building paper-making machines and chairman of other public companies. He was a man of great natural talents, which ranged from playing first division football, playing the violin and singing tenor solo in *The Messiah* with the Hallé. His war service was in the Ministry of Supply with Lord Beaverbrook, and his other interests were Masonic, in which capacity he became Grand Treasurer of England.

John Wolstenholme lived in quiet retirement at Sussexdown for 15 years, looked after by Miss Jones, the cook/housekeeper; Beatrice Anderson, housemaid; Mr Rushton his chauffeur who lived at the Lodge; and Mr Davidson and Mr Sturt, who kept the 6¾-acre garden in trim. The top floor of Sussexdown was a flat where his secretary Miss L. Pritchard lived. Mr Wolstenholme presented a handsome silver challenge cup to the Storrington and District Horticultural and Handicrafts Society. He died in 1960 and in 1964 the house was sold. Despite a good offer from the Marley Tile Works, who wanted to demolish the house and exploit the sand on which it stood, Mr Wolstenholme's family accepted a lower price from R.A.F.A. so that they could turn the house into a convalescent home.

The post-war branch of R.A.F.A. in Storrington had folded by 1949, but in 1965 the London branch wrote to Mrs W. Carn, and ex-W.R.A.F. radar operator, asking if it was possible to reform now that the Association had a permanent home in Storrington. Mrs Carn, who had spent two spells of convalescence in the home, called an immediate meeting of local ex-R.A.F. personnel and was gratified when 55 members attended that inaugural meeting, one of the largest branch figures in the country. Membership is now over 170. Mrs Carn was chairman for eight years until her health deteriorated and she was forced to resign, although she still has a great interest in R.A.F.A. and its activities.

Sussexdown opened as a convalescent home, but it was soon obvious that accommodation and care was needed for permanent residents. In the 1960s extensions were started, and the first permanent resident soon moved in, whilst building continued. In 1968, the Association's 25th year, the Duke of Edinburgh, staying at Arundel with the Queen, piloted a helicopter of the Queen's Flight to Mr Hecks' field and visited Sussexdown as President of R.A.F.A., touring the home with its new wing and meeting 23 residents. He spoke of the need for more rooms.

In 1972 Sussexdown welcomed H.R.H. the Duchess of Gloucester who opened the Lord Tedder and Dame Helen Gwynne-Vaughan wings. The home enjoys great support from the world of show business, as well as royal patronage; the Bernard Delfont rooms — the physiotherapy, occupational therapy and workshop department were built and equipped with £44,500 raised during Battle of Britain Week in Mr Delfont's cinemas.

Sadly, the need for care and sheltered accommodation does not diminish with the passing years, and many still pay a heavy price for our victories of 1939–45.

Building to the north of the house and out to the Worthing Road has continued. These flats provide sheltered accommodation for 60 people with financial help for the project coming from the Council, who have the allocation of six of the flats.

The Chantry

Westwards from Sullington Lane is the Chantry. This stone-built farmhouse is named after the tiny chapel at the foot of the terraced lawns, where an owner had a bell installed. It is said that he escaped trouble one foggy night on the Downs by hearing a church bell and had the building consecrated as a thanksgiving, but it is no longer used for religious purposes.

The Chantry was built in the 1890s by Mr Hainsworth on the site of the Shepherd's Hut, an old single-storied house and farm buildings. Mr Hainsworth added another wing to his house on the south side and laid out fine gardens. He made two lovely ponds at the head of the Stor where it emerged from the hillside, divided by a turfed bridge and footpath, a delight in the spring with their close-cut grass and daffodils, swans, ducks and coots. The spring keeps the bonds beautifully clear. The lower pond has a tumbling bay which retains water in the ponds and allows the stream to flow to the waterfall. There used to be a sheepwash, made by bricking along the banks of the stream and damming across with a tumbling bay. A trap was put in to raise the water level and make a wash of about four feet deep. Sheep were flung in and drenched with the running water. The methodists in their early years held their first public baptism here, the pastor standing in the water and ducking the people who presented themselves for baptism.

In 1903 Mr Henderson bought the Chantry. Mrs Henderson was Commandant of the Storrington branch of the British Red Cross Society and threw open the gardens of the Chantry for big fêtes in aid of their funds.

After the Hendersons, Capt. and Mrs. Scarisbrick and their three children lived there. Capt. Scarisbrick owned large areas of Lancashire, where many roads are named after him. The household had a big staff consisting of a butler, two footmen, a parlourmaid, pantrymaid, head housemaid, four maids, cook, kitchenmaid, scullery-maid and between-maid, boots, six gardeners and three or four grooms. One of the grooms was Mrs Kirker-Head's father, Arthur Charman, who later ran his own riding stables from the Half-Moon stables. His daughter still takes children up on the Downs for riding lessons. The Chantry was always full of guests and house-parties, so the staff were kept busy. Capt. Scarisbrick and his son joined the Home Guard when war started (plate 135).

Mr and Mrs Henderson next owned the Chantry, and sold it later to Mr Alan Pockett, who farms the land between Chantry and Greyfriars, and up the hillside to the top, with a large dairy herd, sheep and arable land. The Storrington Minibus is garaged at the Chantry at Mr Pockett's invitation, and the squash court there is used by many people.

Greyfriars House

This attractive house of honey-coloured stone, a landmark from the top of Kithurst Hill (see cover illustration) was built by Mr Hainsworth about 1890. An early owner was Sir James Erskine, M.P. for Westminster and a founder-director of the Sussex Motor Road

Car Co., the 1904 forerunner of our No. 1 bus service. He was one of the intrepid passengers in the inaugural run of the new Clarkson Steam Bus to Warnes' Hotel, Worthing.

The next owner was Mr Emile Mond, related to Lord Melchett and connected with the Mond Nickel Co. Capt. Francis Mond, whose fine memorial tablet is in the church, was killed at the age of 22 over Bouzencourt-sur-Somme, in 1918, after surviving a plane crash on Kithurst Hill.

Next came Major J. R. Abbey. Mrs Margaret Greenfield was one of the staff and came to Storrington with the Abbeys, working in the kitchen at a salary of £28 per year under the cook, Mrs Wonup. There was a nanny, a German governess, butler, footman and groom and the gardeners. Mr Bolland's wife had Greyfriars Farm, then the Home Farm, while other staff lived in cottages at the end of the drive—one of them, Mrs Lamden, lived there until the beginning of 1982. Her husband worked in the gardens until the Abbeys left.

Major Abbey was internationally known as a collector of fine bindings and his library at Greyfriars was lined with glass-fronted bookcases. In 1967 Major Abbey's books were auctioned at Sotheby's. They published four hardbound catalogues, in themselves collector's items because of the descriptions and illustrations of beautiful books, which contained details of 2,532 separate items, many of which were exhibited in a Madison Avenue gallery in New York for overseas buyers to view before the sale. The library contained vellum books, incunabula, limited private press bindings, royal library bindings and fine colour-plate books, and took 10 days to auction.

Greyfriars was next sold to Mr Horne, who lived there until his children grew up and left home and the house became too large. He retained the old walled garden and a plot of land to the east of it to build a fine south-facing bungalow, and later the coach-house became 'Orchard House'. This, with the cottages at the end of the drive, is now privately owned.

The house, grounds and paddocks were sold to Mr John Rose, who made it a fine family home with ponies in the paddocks, the girls frequently taking part in Pony Club events. By now the indoor staff and team of gardeners had been reduced to a married couple. Mr and Mrs Don Buss, who lived in the bungalow to the east of the house. Mr Buss single-handedly maintained the gardens in the front, the vegetable gardens, greenhouse, lawns, hedges and driveway as well as his own piece of garden. His personal successes at the Flower Show testify to his horticultural skills. The gardens were always productive and immaculate.

The house was sold again early in 1979, for development. A stream of contractor's lorries rattled up and down the drive during the year and the house has now been converted into several flats. The 'gentleman's estate' that was Greyfriars is now a thing of the past, as with so many others.

Gerston/St Joseph's Hall

A steep drive from Greyfriars Lane bordered by high grass banks and chestnut trees leads to another large house built in 1913 by Mr George Trotter, then living at the Abbey. Gerston is a lovely house, where local materials are used to display their intrinsic beauty, and it enjoys the sun and magnificent views to the south to the full. The outer walls are of flints in white mortar, knapped at ground level with round flints above, and with chalk dressings. The roof of old Horsham stone has the well pulled-down appearance of a comfortable hat. Mr Trotter, who ranged far afield to obtain old materials for his house, bought some old barns with Horsham stone roofs and had the slabs taken off and loaded with great care into straw-padded waggons to preserve the lichen. The Horsham stone was used on his new house without disturbing the weathering and lichen.

Inside the house, chalk blocks and Sussex marble form a splendid entrance hall with a large fireplace. Chalk blocks are used freely in the house, making three well-proportioned arches to divide the sitting-room from the corridor, and framing the staircase. The dining-room has another huge fireplace, topped with an enormous wooden beam from the demolished *Bear* inn at Horsham. The domestic offices were planned to provide every amenity: kitchen; scullery; larder; dairy; pantry; 'ice-making room'; sitting room; stores; wine-cellars; laundry; and staff quarters. A walled yard conceals outside stores and facilities. Mr Virgo Snr. worked on the building of Gerston.

The gardens, too, were well planned and equipped, with a walled kitchen-garden, a second large kitchen-garden, potting shed, fruit store, cottage, cow stable, garage, engine house to provide electricity for the house and a complete range of three large modern glass-houses. The estate also had 38 acres of meadow. The usual staff ran the house. Laura Charman (plate 172), now a lively lady in her 80s, worked there as a young house-maid. Her brother was a butcher's boy, and her father (plate 173) worked in the gardens.

The Trotters were hospitable people and entertained many guests. One of these, Paul Hardy, who drew the delightful picture (plate 171) in the visitor's book also painted the memorial tablets for the Storrington men of the First World War, which once hung outside the Market Room of the *White Horse* (plate 133). Mr Hardy, possibly related to Thomas Hardy, is remembered in Storrington for designing the church weathervane, and the organ screen made by himself and Mr Crowhurst at the Forges, West Street. George Trotter sold Gerston in 1919 for £16,500. It was bought by Mr Philip Henderson, who later sold it to the Monastery.

In 1956 Gerston became a hostel for Hungarian refugees fleeing from the Russians. During World Refugee Year (1959) 210 Yugoslavs who had escaped to Italy were admitted to Britain and 50 came to Gerston. When they had been found jobs and homes in Worthing, another 31 'arrived. A Devonshire couple, one of whom had taught in Belgrade and whose wife was herself Yugoslav, taught them English. Wing-Commander V. G. Byrne leased Gerston for this work and Mrs Marika Cleugh was in charge of the house. The W.V.S. provided furniture, and over 700 displaced persons found temporary refuge there. During this time, John Kush on behalf of the Central Office of Information, made a documentary film called *Escape to Life*, telling the story of a typical refugee family. Some of the scenes in the film were shot at Gerston and residents took part in crowd scenes.

In 1965 the Roman Catholic diocese of Southwark was divided and a new Bishop was appointed to the new see of Arundel and Brighton. The first incumbent, Rt Rev. David Cashman from Arundel, made his home at Gerston, renaming it St Joseph's Hall. The house underwent many repairs and was completely rewired before this, and the author and her husband came to know it very well, as Ham & Knight Ltd designed and carried out the new electrical installation. No expense was spared and a first-class job was installed.

Overseeing the work and running and cleaning the house as various contractors came and went were four sisters from the Franciscan Missionaries of the Divine Motherhood, at Ladywell, Godalming. The domestic area, a self-contained wing, made a separate convent for these hard-working nuns, with bedrooms on the first floor of this wing as their enclosure. They lived their quiet religious lives amidst near-impossible chaos, at one stage with only one room in the whole house clear of workmen and their debris. A bedroom was converted into a beautiful chapel for their private use and, as the house settled into a proper routine and Bishop Cashman took up residence, they managed his household, catering for his guests and parties of invalids who came from a Home for a day's outing to this beautiful spot. Sister Mary Gabriella did the Bishop's secretarial work and Rev. Mother Mary Immaculate Heart was in charge of the household and convent. She was passionately fond of gardening, and the large gardens and greenhouses showed the results of her care and attention. The author persuaded her to join the committee of the Storrington Horticultural and Handicraft Society, where she was an active and enthusiastic member. We exchanged many slips and cuttings, and on one occasion she produced Victoria plums the size of apples, which won a well deserved R.H.S. medal. The tree had never produced much fruit, and she threatened it that if it did no better it would go — the result was enormous and delicious plums!

Rev. Mother and her sisters were highly talented and entered beautiful handicraft work, mouthwatering cookery and superb flowers and vegetables in the Show, as well as spending hours making welcome Christmas presents for friends and the needy in the parish.

Bishop Cashman died prematurely in 1973, and Bishop Michael Bowen was appointed. The nuns were recalled to Ladywell and a new order took their place. When Bishop Bowen became Archbishop, Bishop Murphy-O'Connor, the third Bishop of Arundel and Brighton, came to live at St Joseph's Hall. Bishop Murphy-O'Connor had the honour, in 1982, of welcoming Pope John Paul II to Gatwick, in company with Rt. Rev. Fr. Joye from the Priory.

The Abbey

On the corner of Greyfriars Lane stands the Abbey, dating from 1870. When the Rev. George Faithfull came to Storrington, the existing rectory to the south was very dilapidated, so the rector used the stone to build a new rectory — the central and northerly part of the present building as far as the timbered section. After 20 years, Rev. George Faithfull moved down Church Street into Chanctonbury House, retaining the Abbey as a private house.

The Abbey, so-called by Mr Faithfull's pupils, was let and later taken by Mr and Mrs George Trotter of Philadelphia. He came of Quaker stock and his wife was a New Yorker of Dutch origins, a Westervelt, whose family had arrived in America in 1678.

George and Florence Trotter had two daughters, Alice and Mary. Alice Trotter had a talent for writing (Fig. 16). A revue which she wrote was performed at the Village Hall (*see also* page 74). George Trotter started the Band, an account of which appears on page 65. He left Storrington for the Isle of Wight in 1919.

In 1911 Mr Bethell, an antique collector, bought the Abbey and made several additions; one in particular — the reproduction Burmese teak doors set in the corner of the garden wall in Brown's lane — has become something of a landmark and intrigues passers-by with its incongruity (plate 176).

Col. Ravenscroft came to the Abbey in the 1920s. He added a ball-room and music room to it, and during the next 10 years donated the wooden pulpit and choirstalls, and presented the weathervane made by Paul Hardy and Alfred Crowhurst to the church. In the village his benevolent influence was felt in the formation of the Comrades' Club and the Bowling Club, for which he gave the land where the greens were laid out as well as other amenities. When Pat Ravenscroft married in 1938, a carpet was laid from the Abbey to the church and the whole village turned out to see their 'fairy godfather' escort his daughter to the parish church for her wedding to Sir Walter de S. Bartelott of the Coldstream Guards.

The 'Colonel's Cricket Match' was one of the events of the year, immortalised by Hugh de Selincourt in *The Cricket Match*. Eric Hues, a promising young footballer and cricketer at an early age, recalls the teas done by the ladies and the ice-cream made by Mrs Goring. The boys who helped her cleared up the remains!

The Abbey was almost a self-supporting community, even growing its own wheat. Col. Ravenscroft's name is perpetuated in the Council Estate south of Meadowside. After his death in 1952, the Abbey was purchased by the Dominicans and turned into a convent and school (page 70).

Farms

Storrington's other large neighbours are the farms, which at one time not only surrounded the village, but were an integral part of it.

Right in the centre of the village, actually bounded on the south side by the High Street, was Bine Farm run by the Terry family. Unlike today, there was no Colonnade in the 1920s, just the saddler's on the corner. The field came right down to the road and well past the present Colonnade site. A little way up School Hill were the rick-yards and barns. Along the course of the Stor was the Bine Mill and pond and some pigstyes. The two Miss Terrys farmed there. They lived at the top of School Hill, and one of them taught in the village school. Their orchard was where Mr Gatley's corn and seed chandler's now is, bordered by a wall topped with cement, broken glass and barbed wire to keep the children from temptation — which it failed to do! Many people still remember Miss Terry in the long black dress which she always wore, taking her one old cow (which the sisters thought the world of) through the village on a halter.

In 1921 Bine Farm, part of the Fryern Estate, was bought by Mr Tom Gatley. Mr Reg Gatley acquired it in 1928 and in 1957 the land was sold for development, which was to include a bus shelter. Its potential had been seen by the auctioneers of 1921, who listed the farm in their catalogue as possessing '. . . POSSIBILITIES FOR PROFITABLE DEVELOPMENT'.

Mr Elliott told the author that his grandfather came up from Devon in the late 1890s and rented Hurston Street, then part of the Petworth Estate. Hurston Place at that time was owned by Mr Emery and it had been in his family for generations. After a waggon accident, he had to have his leg amputated and he sold the farm to Petworth. Thomas Elliott rented both Hurston Place and Hurston Street from the Estate.

An old mill at the end of Hurston Place·drive was turned into a cart shed. Thomas Elliott died in 1907, and Hurston Place was taken over by Thomas W. Elliott, who later bought it. The mill was then intact but derelict, and collapsed one winter's night. After 1911 the landlord supplied a Petter horizontal oil engine and a set of barn machinery which did the work of the old mill. The farm was pretty well self-supporting with its own brick-lined sawpit, blacksmith's shop, cyder press, malthouse, deer pound, cowstalls, lambing pens and shepherd's hut. In 1929 the land was sold to a consortium including Col. Ravenscroft and the Hon. Clive Pearson and they built the West Sussex Golf Course.

It had been a mixed farm, with corn, sugar beet for Essex refineries and cows whose milk was sent to Pulborough Station en route to London. They were hand milked twice a day. Farm work was done by horses and two carters were employed. The first tractor was bought about 1918–19 and was a rather rare International Mogul. Mr George Elliott remembered his father ploughing the mill field with this four and a half ton giant. Its last job on Hurston Street farm was to thrash 232 sacks of oats in a day.

A 1917 Fordson replaced the Mogul. This saved the horses much hard work *once* it was started, but this was so difficult in cold weather before car batteries were available that farmers lit a fire under the engine! On one occasion Mr Elliott's father was ploughing with the Fordson and at the headland turn where there was a sunken road the front wheel hit a tree stump, causing the tractor to change direction rapidly, and plunge towards the road. Thinking quickly, he dropped the plough into work, and the tractor stopped vertically on its radiator in the road. Mr Elliott was unhurt, thanks to his timely 'anchor'.

In 1925 Mr Kitto sold his West Country Farm, buying Hurston Street Farm and some West Chiltington common land. It was part of the 1920s 'invasion' from the west, when farmers bought cheap land in this area. Several came to Storrington from an area of less than 20 miles square in Cornwall.

Mr Tom Gatley bought the farm in 1928, although some land was sold for building. West Chiltington Common was all heather with footpaths, like Sullington Warren. The farm was still mixed, mainly dairy cows with sugar beet and corn grown, but Reg Gatley added Southdown sheep to the farm, later changed for a crossbreed. Potatoes were grown and seed potatoes sold as, 'Scotch seed once grown'. The farm stretched from Fryern Road, took in West Chiltington Common and the Golf Course where sheep grazed during the war, and down Hurston Lane to New Barn; in all about 248 acres. Six acres were taken over by the Water Board to build the Hurston Treatment works. Mr Gatley also had Bine Farm at the time.

Lower Hurston was farmed for Lady Bartelott by one man who had cattle there. Lady Bartelott asked Reg Gatley to farm these 140 acres at the beginning of the war.

In 1925 Mr Herbert Knight came to the farm at first as a carter. He lived in part of the farmhouse until a cottage became available, working a seven-day week for about £2. They began at 4.30 a.m. by milking the cows, which were kept in sheds overnight because of the early start. They went home to breakfast between 7.00-8.00 a.m. and worked on until dinner at 12.00-1.00 p.m., finishing work at 4.30 p.m. Casual labour was employed in summer, and there were three permanent cowmen, a lad and a labourer who did the thatching and hedging. Milk was cooled by mains water installed during the war by Canadian soldiers. Before the Second World War, four shires and a cob did the farm work. Mr Knight remembered that they used to run away and were never where they were wanted in the mornings. A contractor was hired with a tractor after harvest every autumn to plough deep and clean the ground. When Britain needed to grow more food during the war, extra ground had to be ploughed and tractors arrived on the farm. They had no tyres, but 50 lugs on each wheel, fixed with nuts. As well as farm work, the tractor was put on a dynamo twice a week to charge the cells that produced 60 volt lighting for the farmhouse. While this was being done, another drive was taken from the tractor to the animal food cutter installed above.

The farm was a little community, 'a life apart'. Mrs Knight used to keep poultry and sell eggs, but this enterprise had started accidentally, when Mr Knight bought three old hens at Steyning market intending them for the pot. They started to lay and were reprieved. Eventually Mrs Knight had a flock of about 60 hens. Farm workers had cheaper milk, it was 3d. per pint, and sometimes got a swede or pea and bean sticks and manure for their gardens.

There were other farms in the area, often parts of larger estates. Springhead Farm was rented from Lord Zouche by Thomas Gatley, another Cornishman. He had horses and cows and sheep on the Downs. Odd men were employed to pick up flints on the hills which were sold to the Council. 'Pincher' and his wife lived in an old shed on the hill and did this work.

Mr Wills farmed Springhead and Chancton. He had three horses and two Sussex waggons (Fig. 6) which took feed from one farm to the other, returning before lighting-up time. The last horse plough in the district was seen working at Springhead.

Lee Farm was on the Downs. The farmhands in this remote farm had two yearly holidays — a day for the Storrington Flower Show and another for Christmas Eve. The men would walk over the hill to the village, visit the pubs and then walk home again.

Steam ploughs were used on the difficult land on the hills. A great engine would be situated at one end of the field and another at the other end. They were fitted with circular drums underneath, and ploughs with four or five ploughshares were dragged back and forth across the field by steel cables, using alternate engines to wind it in. One of these big engines was being driven through the village towing its equipment, ploughs, living van and coal truck, when it fell through the road into the steam by the gasworks. A man walked in front of the entourage with a red flag to warn oncoming traffic; horses were terrified by the engines.

Ormare Farm (Hormare) was owned by Mr Clements, the editor of *Sporting Life*, and in 1928 by Mr John Turner, who ran the first dairy in the Square.

Spierbridge was all farm land before the Council Estate was built just after the war.

South of the village was Fairfield's Farm owned by Mr and Mrs Keen. In 1962 Mr John Mills ran it as a pig farm with the barns next to Abbey Cottage (where four houses now stand) for the farrowing sows. The sound of a lawn mower in any of the gardens brought a rush of pigs to the fence for the succulent grass cuttings, and the birds had no chance with any of the bread one put out! The great boar was a particular favourite. He would lie against the fence with a big grin on his face to have his back scratched with the bass broom. The author's lovely old black and white cat would sit and 'talk' to the pigs for hours, obviously aware that intelligent communication was to be had there.

Behind Gerston was another small farm which once supplied the house. In the Rev. A. F. Faithfull's time the fields were glebe land which he farmed. Now they are a part of Gerston Farm run by the Monastery. In between they formed John Turner's dairy farm.

Kithurst Farm under the Downs was Blackmore's sheep and fatstock farm. This is now part of the Parham Estate, run at one time by a tenant farmer. Greyfriars Farm further east is now managed in conjunction with Chantry Farm and has a very large dairy herd and modern milking parlour, run by Mr Pockett.

Sullington Manor Farm is identified by tradition as the site of the manor of the De Coverts, 13th-century Lords of the Manor of Sullington. In 1785 it became part of the Leconfield Estate, and Cordelia Shelley willed it to her two nephews, the Dalbiacs, in 1864. Another West Country farmer Mr Albert Hecks, came here in 1907, bringing his entire farms of cows, sheep, horses, pigs, and farm machinery in 37 trucks with three engines from Bridport to London and from London to Pulborough. Bernard Hecks, his son, generated electricity from the Chantry watermill and had electric milking machinery installed (plate 36). In 1920, Albert Hecks bought the farm from Lord Leconfield. He died in 1951, his son tragically meeting with a fatal farm accident in the same year.

The present farmer is Mr J. I. Kittle. Sullington Farmhouse is a fine old manor house near the church, dating back to Norman times. 'Sullington Cheddar Cheese', made there by Miss Queenie Hecks, was stored in the attics and was well known in the village, one cheese always being presented as a Flower Show prize. This farm has a great tithe barn, 115 feet in length, with the date 1685 cut into a beam, and accommodating 3,000 sacks of wheat (2¼ cwts each) with ease.

Bread Farm or Charity Farm at Cootham was run by the carrier, Mr J. Reeves, who also farmed the present Parham airstrip in the 1920s. May Coates endowed a charity in 1779 for 'bread for the poor not receiving parish relief', and the wheat for the loaves was grown here. Storrington parish church has many deeds, conveyances, mortgages and leases telling the history of this little farm back to 1620. It must be one of the best-documented areas in the parish, right from the reign of James I to the present day. Old leases refer to it as 'Glovers Farm'. In 1894 a lease had a plan attached (Fig. 19, facing page) which shows it as the corner at Parham's main gate, surrounded by the land of Lord Zouche and Lord Leconfield.

LORD LECONFIELD

Lord Leconfield

Lord Leconfield

THE LAGGS

P.O.

PRIVATE

LORD ZOUCHE

To Storrington

Occupation Road

Yard

ROUGH LAND

LORD ZOUCHE

To Pulborough

From Parham

PLAN OF GLOVERS FARM, 1894 (inside dotted line)

10. GATHERING PLACES – SACRED AND SECULAR

Village Hall – Library – Cootham Mission Hall – Cootham Village Hall
– The Chapel – Trinity Methodist Church –
The Roman Catholic Church and Priory

Village Hall, Reading Room and Public Library

IN 1922 THE *Worthing Gazette* published an article with a picture of the Village Hall:

> Those who live in villages know that for pure social amenity there are few places in the world
> to compare with a village club. Without exaggeration we may say that no more wholesome and
> socially hygienic institution exists. The village club offers to men who spend their working hours
> in comparatively solitary pursuits opportunity for the circulation of that goodwill which is the
> life and soul of a village. It keeps lads from lounging about the streets: it makes bearable the life
> of the lonely bachelor living in lodgings: it tames the egotistical 'master of the house' and thus
> benefits everybody.

The *Gazette* continued to extol the virtues of a village club, stating that in 1894 the
villagers of Storrington had built their Village Hall, started a library and formed a 'first-
rate Social Society'. The money had come from the extinct Eighth Sussex Rifle
Volunteers, whose members authorised their trustees to hand over their funds, and a
subscription list was opened. 'Everybody' subscribed, and fund-raising events such as
bazaars, jumble sales and 'even shares in the concern (on none too advantageous terms)'
resulted in the Hall being built on land given by the Rector, Rev. G. Faithfull. Two
years later rooms were added behind the stage and a billiard room was built above them.

The library began life in the lobby and soon moved to one of the rooms behind the
stage. Local families donated books until in 1898 Mr James Constable endowed the
library with a gift of £500. Miss Georgina Mant was honorary librarian, helped and
later succeeded by her niece, Miss Daisy Mant, who gave her services both as librarian
and book repairer for over 25 years. She was later joined by another honorary librarian
with a 'wide acquaintance with literature', Mr H. J. Tumman. The library opened on
two evenings every week, issuing about 5,000 books per year.

By 1922 the limits of the Village Hall and reading room were apparent. Firstly, there
was no reading room and the Village Hall, serving the interests of the village, left the club
without a real home. The library room, overcrowded with books, often did duty as a
dressing room. The hall itself was hired for all kinds of entertainment and was used by a
travelling cinema and for concerts; and the Social Club, using the hall only when it was
available, found it too large for a comfortable clubroom. The First World War caused
plans to be shelved, but soon afterwards ideas for a reading room and caretaker's flat
above were put forward. Mr A. C. Allen drew up plans of the hall and proposed
extension work to the west. Also included was a small 'serving room' where refreshments
(non-alcoholic in accordance with the Trust Deed) could be obtained. A new library at
the back of the extension was envisaged. It was estimated that all this would cost about
£1,200, £800 for the club room and flat, or £325 for the club room alone.

A public meeting on 9 January 1922 published the plans and invited donations. The
club room and flat were built, although the new library was delayed until 1929. Mr
Joe Page became the first resident caretaker from 1923-57. Described as 'the finest

bowler outside county cricket', Joe Page was a good all-rounder in the Storrington Cricket Club. Hugh de Selincourt immortalised him in *The Cricket Match* as 'Sid Smith', and Storrington as 'Tillingfold'.

An annual subscription of 7s. 6d. for men and 5s. 0d. for women allowed use of the library books, newspapers and magazines, and of the Billiards Room where there was a small charge for playing. That subscription (although voluntary donations increased as the years went by) continued unchanged for many years, bringing in an average of £30 per year.

The hall was hired out to a travelling cinema once a week. The Dramatic Society and other organisations, including the Benefit Clubs, Oddfellows, the Band, the Territorials, political organisations, the W.I., the Football Club, the School Clinic, and the Parish Council hired its rooms, and in 1937 came the ominous preparations for war – air raid lectures.

Keep Fit classes, the Red Cross and the Horticultural Society used the hall in the early part of the war, and by 1941 the change that war had brought to village life showed in the hirings of the Village Hall – army concerts, school accommodation (because of evacuees), a W.V.S. clothing centre, A.R.P. lectures, the Home Guard, Greenfields Stores accommodation for staff meals plus the usual activities. The running expenses included blackout and War Damage Contribution. In 1942 the newly formed Air Training Corps met in the hall, and police lectures also took place; the County Library Service came into operation from 1 January, replacing the private library.

A school canteen was started and the children were fed in two sittings. They would walk across the church meadow from the village school to the hall. This continued until the new County Primary School was built in Spierbridge in the 1960s. In 1945 the Ministry of Works distributed ration cards at the library and Worthing Hospital carried out physiotherapy there. A Welcome Home Fund was started, and S.S.A.F.A. held meetings in the hall.

After the war, Miss Yeats started a little school which used the old billiards room and new hirers were the Cricket Club and Tennis Club, V.P.A., R.A.F.A. and W.E.A. A dancing school was started in 1950, and in 1972 the Horticultural Society held the first of its Spring Flower Shows in the Village Hall and has continued to do so to the present day.

Mrs Pat Pickworth, the part-time librarian in 1949, recalls that it was not very busy: 'On Monday afternoons we spent most of the time painting posters'. By 1954 there were 800 borrowers. The Library occupied the front half of the 'new room' with the bay window. There was an old-fashioned high wooden desk-counter for the librarian to work and issue books, and shelves all round the walls with a free-standing shelf unit in the middle. Being used to Worthing Public library from a very early age, the author collected her first consignment of books wondering how many weeks it would be before she ran out of reading material – her very lifeblood!

By 1972 the old library was very much bursting at the seams and it closed its doors for the last time at 5 p.m. on Saturday 17 June. The newly-built County Library in North Street opened at 10.00 a.m. on Wednesday 21 June. It opened every day after that, and had 2,681 borrowers. The numbers using the library have trebled in the past eight years and it has grown with demand. In 1978 an extension was built, giving more space for a reference section and a specially-designed corner with small stools and low shelves for children's books. Tables and chairs were added to make the library comfortable and the area above the bookshelves is used to display the work of art groups and schools. The light glass foyer is ideal for exhibitions displaying the work and interests of local groups, or for the library to stage a display on current events or specific subjects. The library, with the many facilities it offers today, is much more than a place to borrow books.

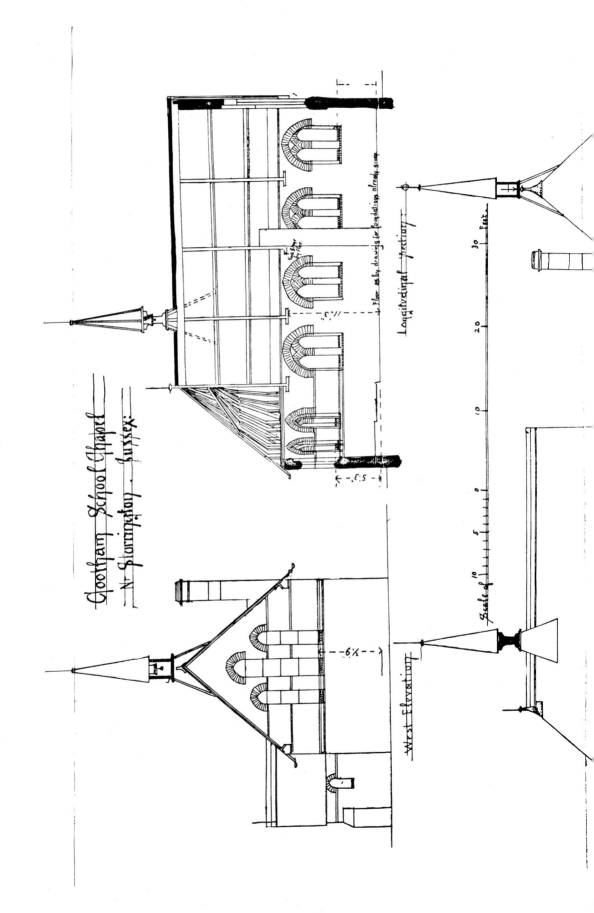

Cootham School Chapel
Nr Storrington. Sussex:

Longitudinal Section

Floor as by drawing for foundation already given

West Elevation

Scale of 10 5 0 10 20 30 Feet

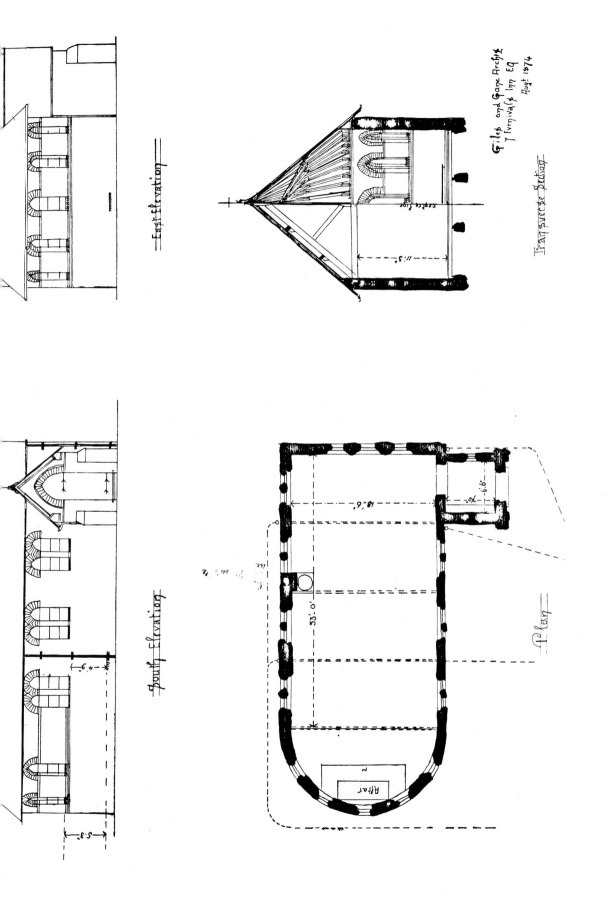

East Elevation

South Elevation

Giles and Gane Archts
1 Furnivals Inn EC
Augt 1874

Transverse Section

Plan

Altar

Cootham Hall

The story of Cootham Hall begins in the 1870s with 'dissenting practices on the Parham Estate'. Lord Zouche wrote to the Rector, Rev. George Faithfull:

May 13, 1872   Parham

My Dear Sir,
    One of my maids Jane Smart, daughter of the Bailiff here has left my service, and her father's protection on account of some confusion of ideas about the Millenium which Mr Stamford has put into her head, and her father, a very good man I believe, is much grieved about it.
    He has just told me that Ned Wright is coming to preach in the barn at Cootham on Tuesday.
    I much disapprove of these expositions on serious subjects by ignorant self conceited men, and should be glad to know whether you think that any steps should be taken on this subject as it is in your parish. Mr Stamford being a parishioner of Mr Beck's would you confer with him. I am sorry to be obliged to go to London tomorrow at ¼ to 12.
                                    Yours very truly
                                        Zouche
    I do not know the law but I doubt whether Mr Stamford has any right to lend my barn to itinerant preachers, neither do I suppose that the Almighty has given any particular revelation to him, about the Millenium, which has not been accorded to the most learned and best educated divines of any Christian Church.

The subsequent story is concisely summed up in a letter from Rev. A. F. Faithfull to his churchwardens in 1908:

                                                                        28th September 1908

    Dear Sirs, I am sorry you cannot meet me at present to discuss the Cootham difficulty, so am writing you a few particulars which may be unknown to you.
    1872. In this year my father received a letter from the late Lord Zouche complaining of dissenting practices on the Parham Estate, and Binstead, tenant at Springhead Farm forbade the shepherd to use Cootham Barn for meetings —
    1873. My father erects a building (at his sole cost) on Lord Zouche's property and holds some sort of service (reading *Pilgrim's Progress*). The shepherd holds services in his own cottage. Those attending are informed by Binstead that such practices are objectionable to his Lordship. —
    1874. Mrs Vallance gets up a petition signed by over a hundred people begging Lord Zouche to allow the shepherd's services to continue. —
    1875. My father obtains the Bishop's licence to hold C of E services in his building at Cootham.
    1883. The present Lord Zouche conveys to the Rev. George Faithfull, James Greenfield and George French Mant, a piece of land, to be applied as a site for a place of Worship, and for a burial place, *and for no other purpose whatsoever*. The Revd. George Faithfull fences the site at his own expence —
    1892. My father repairs the building he had erected, inside and out, at his own expence, and continues to pay all expences, fire insurance, caretaker, expences of services and to provide a minister, which he did until his death in 1900 — Twenty seven years —
    1905. The wardens report to the Archdeacon that the services have been discontinued for some little time. —
    1908. The Archdeacon holds a visitation, and requests an explanation why they have been discontinued.
    I greatly regret that I cannot see my way to continue my father's unlimited generosity but shall be pleased to co-operate with the wardens and arrange Church of England services under an adequate endowment scheme, or on the other hand if the wardens desire to take the sole responsibility and open the building for unauthorized meetings will they kindly obtain the Archdeacon's instructions and I shall be pleased to hand them the key.
                                    Believe me
                                    Very Truly yours
To the Churchwardens   A. F. Faithfull, Rect[r]

The architects, Giles and Gave, prepared a drawing (Fig. 20) and by 24 August 1874, an agreement was drawn up between Rev. G. Faithfull and Mr H. Terry to build a chapel at Cootham from this design, to be completed before 1 December. There was a penalty clause of £2 per week after this date 'except in the case of strikes of workmen', and the price for the building was £390, to be paid in three stages. The final cost, completely borne by Rev. G. Faithfull, including altar, stove pipes etc., and installation, oak plinth for a reading desk and various other extras, was £550.

Services were held in the new chapel until 1904, by which time many Cootham people were attending the Parish Church instead. Cootham Chapel fell into disuse and dilapidation and gradually became a real eyesore, continually vandalised by children, until in 1920 Rev. A. Faithfull thought it would be better demolished. The land conveyance was void because the chapel was not used for worship, and it was suggested this should revert to the Estate.

The Parochial Church Council wanted to revive services there and approached the Estate with their suggestions. Baroness Zouche repossessed the land and handed the building to the trustees for conversion to a Village Hall for the use of Cootham inhabitants.

Mr Fox, a lay reader from Brook House, came to Cootham daily to read to a blind man and he started giving talks in the little hall. Storrington rectors or their curates were again holding services there on Sunday afternoons, and Miss Lilly played Moody and Sankey hymns on the harmonium. By the 1930s the hall was really showing signs of age and there was a hole in the roof. The people of Cootham put on various events to collect money for repairs. The Hon. Clive Pearson, a trustee, helped them by guaranteeing the necessary £300 at the bank for roof repairs. Concert parties from Storrington came to the hall and Whist Drives and other events took place there. Miss Rankin ran a weekly library with books loaned by Mrs Sinclair until the County Library supplied them. They built a green room, kitchen and lavatory.

In the 1950s a W.I. was formed which did home-made teas in the hall when Parham was opened to the public, prepared and run by Miss MacDonald, Mrs Pledger, Mrs Greenfield, Miss Swindells and Miss Rankin. The annual Cootham Flower Show is held there and it has become very much the centre of social life.

One little mystery about Cootham Hall has always been, 'what happened to the bell?' It disappeared one night and one old lady positively told the author that the gypsies had stolen it for scrap metal. The gypsies were much maligned in this, and its fate and approximate whereabouts may now be revealed.

The Hon. Barbara Frankland, daughter of the 17th Baroness Zouche described how her elder brother and some of his friends took the pony trap and ladder and stole the bell. This was carried back to Parham and buried under a big tree along the West Drive and the boys held a big 'funeral service' for it. Barbara, the young sister, was delegated to keep watch and although some distance away from the proceedings she heard some of the 'obsequies'. The poor girl was terrified and never forgot her midnight adventure. Her brother, ringleader of the exploit, died during the war and the precise tree under which the bell was buried is no longer known. Some of the trees are no longer there. Mr Scotcher searched the area with a metal detector but since the 'army occupation' during the war there appears to be a great deal of buried metal among the big tree roots, and the Cootham bell remains hidden in its secret grave at Parham Park.

Cootham Mission

Before the turn of the century most Cootham people went to Mr Mustow's Mission Hall (now Cootham Cottage) where non-conformist services were conducted. There was a Sunday School for children, especially popular in autumn because of the apple trees in the garden! Such social life as there was revolved around the Mission Hall. Mr Mustow lived there with his family of nine children. In the 1920s the chapel was stripped and converted into extra rooms and a kitchen. The old panelling is still visible in the kitchen of Cootham Cottage, and the big girders are also still there, making it easy to trace the outlines of the original Mission Hall throughout the house.

Pastor Mustow's influence spread to Storrington, and in 1909 a corrugated iron building was erected opposite the Gas Works. The permanent Chapel was built in North Street in 1932, and Mr Charles Greenfield bought the old Chapel which was consecrated by the Bishop of Chichester as a Chapel of Rest. At the back was their upholstery workshop and garage. In 1970 this building was demolished and its site is now a grass plot beside the stream, bringing a sweep of greensward right into the village centre.

Trinity Methodist Church

Storrington had no Methodist Church at all until 1960, when some interested people met in a private house. In 1961, 15 residents formed themselves into a Methodist Society and held regular services, first in the Village Hall and then in Sullington Community Hall, conducted by Rev. M. Bold. They bought the Thakeham Road site in 1962 and started fund-raising, aided by grants and gifts. The Trinity Methodist Church opened in 1967, and at the first Sunday service their sermon was preached by Rt Rev. David Cashman, the Roman Catholic Bishop of Arundel and Brighton, whose home was in the village. Sadly, Mr Bold did not live to see this happy day. Trinity Methodist Church now has a Junior Church and pleasant airy rooms which form the Trinity Centre, where special events can take place. The attractive gardens around the church are a memorial to Mr Bold.

The Roman Catholic Church

In 1882 some French refugees landed at Newhaven. They were Canons Regular of Premontré, evicted from their home in Frigolet by the French Government. The Duke of Norfolk, recently reinstated as Lord of the Manor of Storrington, gave them some land and they were temporarily housed in Sand Lodge, School Hill.

The Priory Church in Storrington grew with the new century under the pioneers, Fr. Xavier and Fr. Francis, until the outbreak of the First World War. The Canons were allowed back to France, and Storrington just had a parish priest, Fr. Philip Beasley-Suffolk. He was the last of the old community to live here and he died in 1940. A different group of White Canons looked after the parish for the next 12 years. During the Second World War the Monastery was 'occupied' by troops, and the cloisters were used for Home Guard and A.T.C. training.

On 21 August 1952 the Priory was officially re-opened and Fr. Phelim Colwell was installed as Prior. Bishop Cowderoy sang the Mass in the presence of Abbot Stalmans of Tongerlo Abbey in Belgium. In 1954 an outdoor shrine was built in the sandpit opposite the church, and five years later on 19 June the Priory Church was consecrated, followed the next day by the Crowning of the Statue in the shrine by Bishop Cowderoy. Thousands of people attended the event, which was preceded by a joyous procession through the village, with convent children presenting tableaux and the Statue being carried in a flower-covered open car.

Fr. Kevin Cassidy, ordained 10 years before his appointment here, has been parish priest since 1952. He was completing his studies in Tongerlo in 1940 when the Germans invaded Belgium, but he was able to escape. He first came to Storrington in 1947 to help the parish priest of the day, Fr. Ryan.

Fr. Cassidy is a popular and well-known figure with many friends (by no means confined to his Roman Catholic parishioners). He has a great fondness for his adopted home and its history, and was only too willing to lend books and supply information during research for this book. Fr. Cassidy cannot walk far from the Priory without meeting someone who wants to stop and chat to him, and he is never to busy to talk to people. In 1977 he marked his Silver Jubilee as parish priest in Storrington with a special Mass, after which he was presented with a portable television set and a cheque for £400.

Since the arrival of the Canons Regular of Premontré in Storrington, there have been 12 Priors:

Fr. Louis de Gonzague Daras	1882–87
Fr. Joseph Ibos	1887–90
Fr. Justin Guyomard	1890–94
Fr. Norbert Philibert	1894–00
Fr. Godefroid B. Guigue	1900–03
Fr. Xavier Rieux	1903–12
Fr. Francis Laborde	1912–29
Fr. Philip Beasley-Suffolk	1929–40
Fr. Phelim Colwell	1951–54
Fr. Hubert Mathee	1954–60
Fr. Joseph Gerebern Neill	1960–70
Rt Rev. Fr. George Joye	1970–

*   *   *